100 MATHS LESSONS

YEAR 3

Published by Scholastic Ltd,
Villiers House,
Clarendon Avenue,
Leamington Spa,
Warwickshire CV32 5PR

© **2000 Scholastic Ltd**
Text © Sue Gardner and
Ian Gardner 2000
1 2 3 4 5 6 7 8 9   0 1 2 3 4 5 6 7 8 9

SERIES CONSULTANT
Ann Montague-Smith

AUTHORS
Ian Gardner and Sue Gardner

EDITOR
Joel Lane

ASSISTANT EDITOR
David Sandford

SERIES DESIGNER
Joy White

COVER PHOTOGRAPH
Kim Oliver

ILLUSTRATIONS
Ray and Corrine Burrows

British Library Cataloguing-in-Publication Data
A catalogue record for this book is available from the British Library.

ISBN 0-439-01687-8

ACKNOWLEDGEMENTS

The publishers wish to thank:
The Controller of HMSO and the DfEE for the use of extracts from *The National Numeracy
Strategy: Framework for Teaching Mathematics* © March 1999, Crown Copyright (1999, DfEE,
Her Majesty's Stationery Office).
Galt Educational and NES Arnold Educational Supplies for kindly loaning the equipment
used on the front cover.

CONTENTS

INTRODUCTION

100 Maths Lessons is a series of year-specific teachers' resource books, for Reception to Year 6, that provide a core of support material for the teaching of mathematics within the National Numeracy Strategy *Framework for Teaching Mathematics* (March 1999) and within the structure of the 'dedicated mathematics lesson'. Each book offers three terms of medium-term planning grids, teaching objectives and lesson plans. At least 100 maths lessons are given in detail, with outlines for all the others needed to provide support for teachers through a whole year of maths teaching. Photocopiable activity pages and resources are included to support the learning. Regular assessment is built into the structure of the book, with assessment activity pages which can be kept as evidence of attainment.

The activities in this book are designed to encourage pupils to develop mental strategies, to use paper and pencil methods appropriately, and to use and apply their mathematics in realistic tasks. There is a strong emphasis upon encouraging pupils to explain to each other the mathematics that they have used and the strategies that they employed, and to compare these with each other to determine efficiency of method.

Each *100 Maths Lessons* book provides support across all the mathematics topics and learning objectives specified for a particular year group. However, the pages of the books have been hole-punched and perforated so that they can be removed and placed in teachers' own resource files, where they can be interleaved with complementary materials from the school's existing schemes. This makes it easy to integrate favourite material into work based on this series.

These books are intended to support the dedicated mathematics lesson for the school mathematics co-ordinator, teachers and trainee teachers. The series of books can be used as the basis of planning, teaching and assessment for the whole school, from Reception to Year 6. These resources can be adapted for use by the whole school for single-aged classes, mixed-age classes, single- and mixed-ability groups, and team planning across a year or a key stage. There is sufficient detail in the differentiated group activities to offer guidance to classroom assistants working with a group.

The content of these activities is appropriate for and adaptable to the requirements of Primary 3–4 in Scottish schools. In schools which decide not to adopt the National Numeracy Strategy, choose activities to match your planning.

USING THIS BOOK

THE MATERIALS

This book provides at least 100 maths lesson plans for Year 3, and further activity ideas to support all other dedicated maths lessons required during the year. Each maths lesson plan contains ideas for developing pupils' oral and mental maths, a detailed explanation of the main part of the lesson, ideas for differentiated activities and suggestions for the plenary session. The book follows the Year 3 planning grid given in the National Numeracy Strategy *Framework for Teaching Mathematics*; and so for each teaching section (whether one, two or three units of work), there are some detailed lesson plans and some outlines for the other lessons. These materials should be regarded as a core for developing your own personalised folder for the year. More detail on planning and managing all aspects of the National Numeracy Strategy can be found in the *Framework for Teaching Mathematics*.

ADAPTING AND PERSONALISING THE MATERIALS

The materials are based on the 'Teaching programme and planning grid' for Year 3 from the *Framework for Teaching Mathematics*. What follows is a suggested method of using this book to its full potential; however, bear in mind that you may need to adjust these materials in order to meet the learning needs of the pupils in your class.

Separate the pages of the book and place them in an A4 ring binder. Check that the activities are of a suitable level for your pupils, and agree with colleagues who teach higher and lower years that the entry level is a good match. If not, you can use materials from the *100 Maths Lessons* book for the previous or subsequent year as appropriate.

Add your own favourite materials in the relevant places. If your school uses a published scheme, insert suitable teacher and pupil resources from that into your file.

PREPARING A SCHEME OF WORK

All schools are required to write detailed schemes of work, and this series has been designed to facilitate this process. The termly 'Planning grids' given in each book (see page 18 for example) are provided at the beginning of the work for each term and list all the learning objectives covered.

ORGANISATION

The **Organisation chart** outlines the key activities for each part of each maths lesson in a unit, and can be used as a weekly plan:

LEARNING OUTCOMES	ORAL AND MENTAL STARTER	MAIN TEACHING ACTIVITY	PLENARY
LESSON 1 • Order whole numbers to at least 100 and position them on a 100 square (Year 2 revision). • **Know what each digit represents,** and partition three-digit numbers into a multiple of 100, a multiple of ten and ones. • Read and begin to write the vocabulary of comparing and ordering numbers, including ordinal numbers to at least 100.	HTU CHART: Read out and combine numbers on a place value chart.	MIX, MATCH AND ORDER: Make and order two-digit numbers.	Discuss place value; record numbers on a 100 square.
LESSON 2 • **Read and write whole numbers to at least 1000** in figures and words.	SPIDER SUMS: Find ways to make target numbers (to 10).	MAKE IT: Use place value cards to create numbers given in words.	Rehearse number bonds within 10.
LESSON 3 • Round any two-digit number to the nearest 10.	CROSS THE BRIDGE: Add by bridging through 10.	ROUNDING GAME: Round two-digit numbers to the nearest 10.	Round flashcard numbers to the nearest 10.

ORAL AND MENTAL SKILLS   Read whole numbers in figures and (say them) in words. Understand the operations of addition and subtraction; use the related vocabulary. Add a pair of numbers mentally by bridging through 10.

LESSON PLANS

After the **Organisation chart** comes a short passage detailing which lessons are shown as full lesson plans and which are extensions of what has already been taught in a previous lesson. Some of the latter will be shown in outline (grid) form.

DETAILED LESSON PLANS

Each detailed lesson plan is written to the following headings:

Resources
Provides a list of what you need for that lesson.

Preparation
Outlines any advance preparation needed before the lesson begins, such as making resources or photocopying worksheets.

Learning outcomes
These are based on the objectives in the 'Teaching programme: Year 3' from the *Framework for Teaching Mathematics*. All of the objectives are covered at least once in this book, and key objectives for Year 3 are highlighted in bold (as they are in the *Framework for Teaching Mathematics*). If a lesson does not cover an objective in its entirety, then only the portion which is intended to be covered is listed in the Learning outcomes (or in the grids provided).

The specific objectives for the **Oral and mental starter** and the **Main teaching activity** are listed separately. All learning objectives are explicitly taught in **Main teaching activities**, and may be revisited in **Oral and mental starters**. There are some minor exceptions to this pattern: where aspects of calculation or other number skills are slight extensions of Year 2 work (for example, knowledge of multiplication facts), the new content may be covered through progressive use of **Oral and mental starters**.

Vocabulary

The National Numeracy Strategy *Mathematical Vocabulary* booklet has been used to provide the vocabulary lists. New or specific vocabulary to be used during the lesson is listed. Use this vocabulary with the whole class, so that all the children have a chance to hear it and begin to understand it. Encourage pupils to use the vocabulary orally when asking or answering questions, so that they develop an understanding of its mathematical meaning. Where flashcards are suggested, these can be made by printing out onto card the appropriate sections from the CD-ROM which should have accompanied your school's copy of the *Framework for Teaching Mathematics*.

Oral and mental starter

This section contains activity suggestions to develop oral and mental work to be used with the whole class, based on what has already been taught. This work is designed to occupy the first 5–10 minutes of the lesson, but its duration is likely to be more variable than that. Some suggestions for differentiated questioning are included to show how all children can benefit. The detail provided will help you to provide a variety of sequentially planned oral and mental activities throughout the week, use a good range of open and closed questions, encourage all the children to take part and target differentiated questions to individuals, pairs or small groups. Although a brisk pace is important, it is also vital that thinking time is given in some sessions where the answer is not immediate, or when questions are open to interpretation.

Main teaching activity

This sets out what to do in the whole-class teaching session, and typically occupies about 30 minutes. Each of these sessions combines some whole-class, interactive teaching with some activities for groups, pairs or individuals following. The relative amounts of time given to these two aspects is variable. The detailed lesson plans provided will help you to organise this session appropriately.

Differentiation

This section suggests activities for differentiated group, paired or individual work, aimed at the more able and less able children within the class. These activities take the form of reinforcement, enrichment or extension, and many provide challenges to encourage pupils to use and apply their mathematics.

Plenary

This session is a chance to bring the children together again for typically a ten-minute whole-class session. This offers opportunities to assess pupils' progress, summarise the key facts learned, formulate general statements, compare strategies used, make links to other topics and plan for the next topic.

EXTENSION LESSON PLANS

These provide activities which extend those already covered. They are less detailed, as they are based on one of the previous lessons for that week. (For an example, see page 35.)

OUTLINE LESSON PLANS

These contain brief descriptions, as grids, of further lessons. They extend the scope of the book to give sufficient material for a year's work. (for an example, see page 27.)

USING THE LESSON PLANS

The plans are designed so that you can work through them in order if you so wish. However, you may prefer to choose the lessons that are most appropriate for your pupils and combine these with your favourite activities from other sources. By placing the pages of this book into a ring binder, you can easily incorporate your own supplementary materials.

In principle, the transition from Y2 to Y3 offers no greater obstacle than any other movement across year groups. However, for some children a change of school represents a further challenge, particularly when there are significant shifts in the 'classroom culture'. It is thus important to pursue liaison between schools in order to avoid unnecessary problems. In some cases, you may need to make allowances in the short term – a point which is supported in this book by the use of Y2 revision and consolidation in some of the Term 1 activities.

You will need to consider whether the range of levels presented in the activities (especially as defined by the **Differentiation** suggestions) provides adequate scope for the capabilities of your teaching group. In a particularly able group, you may need to refer to learning objectives for Years 4, 5 or 6, especially those which complement or extend the Year 1, 2 or 3 objectives. Please bear in mind that it is often preferable (for the vast majority of children) to broaden curriculum experience rather than to begin with 'new' content.

WEEKLY PLANNING

If you wish to use the ready-prepared plans, follow the **Organisation chart** which appears at the beginning of each unit (or block of units) of work.

If you prefer to plan your week using some of the lesson plans in the book and some activities that you have chosen yourself, then make some photocopies of the blank 'Weekly planning chart' on page 11 of this book. These can then be completed with details of all the activities which you intend to use: those chosen from this book and those which you have taken from other sources.

MIXED-AGE CLASSES

If you have a mixed-age class, you will probably need to use the materials from more than one book in this series. You will find the blank 'Weekly planning chart' (page 11) a useful planning tool for this purpose, as you can combine planning from two books on this chart.

BLANK WEEKLY PLANNING CHART

Make photocopies of this chart; complete a copy on a weekly basis, and keep it in your planning file. You may prefer to enlarge the chart to A3 size.

Week beginning: *6/9/00*

Learning objectives for oral and mental skills	● Read whole numbers in figures and (say them) in words. ● Understand the operations of addition and subtraction and use the related vocabulary. ● Add a pair of numbers mentally by bridging through 10.			
Oral and mental starter	Main teaching activity	Differentiation	Plenary	Resources
Monday HTU chart: Whole class around poster to rehearse reading numbers aloud, starting with regular sounds.	Mix, match and order: Whole class work on making 2-digit numbers from 3 numerals. Put in order. Try with different set of numbers. Organise group work on same type of activity.	Less able: Provide set of prepared 2-digit numbers for ordering. More able: Record _all_ possible combinations on 100 grid and look for any _general_ patterns.	Prepared flashcards (for whole class to see). Questions involving adding on, place value and partitioning (HTU). Provide all with number grid to colour. Any pattern?	Photocopiable pages 21 and 16, pointer stick, coloured pencils.

CLASSROOM ORGANISATION

WHOLE-CLASS TEACHING

During a whole-class session it is important that all the children can see you, the board or flip chart and their table top. In many classrooms space is at a premium, so it is worth spending time considering how the furniture can best be arranged. If you have a carpeted area for whole-class work, think about whether the lesson you are planning to teach would work well with the children seated on the carpet, or whether they would be better placed at their tables – especially if they need to manipulate apparatus such as interlocking cubes, or to spread out numeral cards in front of them.

GROUP WORK

Again, it is important that the pupils sit so that they can see you, and the board or flip chart if necessary. While they are working in groups, you may wish to ask whole-class questions, or remind pupils of how much time is left to complete their task, so eye contact will help to ensure that everyone is listening.

WORKING WITH OTHER ADULTS

If you have classroom helpers, brief them before the lesson starts on which groups you would like them to work with, the purpose of the task, the vocabulary they should be helping to develop and some examples of the type of questions they should be asking. Check that all the resources needed are available, or if not, that the helper knows where to find them. You may want to ask a classroom helper to work with just one or two pupils who are finding the work difficult, or who have been absent and are catching up on missed work. Whatever the helper's involvement, always make sure that he or she is well briefed before the lesson starts, and allow a few minutes after the lesson has finished to discuss any specific observations that he or she would like to make.

CHILDREN WITH SPECIAL EDUCATIONAL NEEDS

Include children with special educational needs in the whole-class work. If you have a classroom helper or support assistant, ask him or her to sit beside the pupils with special needs in order to provide support. This might include repeating the questions quietly, or encouraging the children to use individual resources (such as counting apparatus, a number line or number cards) to find the answer. During differentiated questioning, make sure that some questions are specifically focused for these pupils, and encourage them to answer appropriately.

To assist all pupils in reading new vocabulary, and particularly to help those with reading difficulties, make flashcards for the specific mathematic vocabulary which will be used in a series of lessons and encourage the children to read these.

Pupils who are partially-sighted or deaf will need to sit close to you, so take this into account when considering the layout of the classroom for maths lessons. Those with emotional or behavioural difficulties will benefit from the structure and routines of the daily maths lesson, and where possible, from the support of a helper who can encourage on-task working. For children who are learning English as an additional language, speak more slowly, repeat instructions, and provide visual clues on worksheets or puzzle cards. For pupils who have an Individual Education Plan (IEP) which includes mathematics as an area of learning difficulty, use other books from this series to find activities at an appropriate level which can be linked to the work of the rest of the class.

HOMEWORK

For Year 3 pupils, it is recommended that homework is given regularly on a weekly basis. These activities might be designed to be shared with a parent or carer, or could include skills practise or simple puzzles that could be done more or less independently by the child. A homework diary, which is completed at home and in school, is a useful tool for logging what homework has been set and how the pupil responded. Use a range of different types of tasks for homework.

Choose favourite shared homework activities, and send these home regularly. Suitable material may be found in *IMPACT Maths Homework* titles for Key Stages 1 and 2 and *Mental Maths Homework for 8 year olds*, all written by the IMPACT Project (published by Scholastic). Suggest some games, books and/or audio tapes that parents or carers can use to practise multiplication facts with their children in a fun and relaxed way – for example, *Let's Learn At Home: Ten Steps to Improve Your Child's Times Tables for ages 7–8* (Scholastic). Suggest some practical activities that children can discuss while out on a car journey or going round the supermarket. Provide advice to parents and carers through a newsletter or by hosting a curriculum evening.

RESOURCES

PHOTOCOPIABLE SHEETS

These support the work, and can be resource pages or activity sheets. They are marked with the photocopiable symbol (see left). Some sheets have broad application and can be used throughout the year: these appear at the end of this Introduction on pages 13–16. Other sheets can be found at the end of the relevant units (or blocks of units).

Resource sheets

These include numeral cards, symbol cards and a 1–100 square, and are provided on pages 13–16. It is a good idea to have a plentiful stock of copies of these pages at the start of the year. Photocopy the pages onto card, then cut out and laminate as required. You may wish to ask parents and friends of the school to help you make these resources.

For the numeral cards, consider whether to use different-coloured cards so that the children can sort them more easily, using the colour of each set as an aid. These cards can be stored in small polythene bags or tins, so that the pupils can keep them in their own desks or trays. Alternatively, store them with a rubber band around each set and give them out at the beginning of the lesson.

Activity sheets

These are located at the end of the relevant units (or blocks of units) and relate to specific activities. They may offer practical activities, more traditional worksheets or games. Photocopy the pages onto A4 paper for the pupils. Some activities may require an extra A3, or OHT enlargement for whole-class use. Some sheets may be better enlarged for pupil use, especially when provided as paired tasks.

CLASSROOM EQUIPMENT

All the equipment used in this book can normally be found in any primary school. The following list shows what will be needed on a regular basis, but alternatives are suggested where they would be equally appropriate. It is important that you create a mathematically stimulating environment for the children in which they regularly encounter numbers. It is therefore assumed that all classrooms will have a long class number line and a large 100 square. Ideally, the children should be able to read all the numbers on these resources easily from their seats. A chalkboard and chalk, or flip chart and marker pens, are essential for interactive whole-class sessions. Although it is not essential, an overhead projector lends itself well to enlarging photocopiable sheets for whole-class use. You will also need:

- a 'washing line' for stringing across the room (particularly useful for arranging multiples and other number sequences printed on cards)
- counting apparatus, eg counters, wooden cubes, beads and laces
- a counting stick: a metre length of wood or foam lagging, divided into ten alternately-coloured sections (some metre rulers are marked in this way)
- calculators
- Cuisenaire rods or rods made of interlocking cubes, one colour for each numeral
- measuring apparatus (including 'junk' materials)
- shape apparatus (eg shape tiles, 3-D shapes, a feely bag, tessellating shapes, attribute blocks, art straws)
- 9-pin, 16-pin and 25-pin geoboards with elastic bands and safety mirrors
- Base 10 apparatus (ones, tens and hundreds)
- construction kits (eg Polydron, Plasticine)
- coins (preferably real) and simple drawings of banknotes
- dice (both standard 1–6 dice and giant blank dice)
- a programmable floor vehicle (eg Roamer or PIP)
- dominoes (standard, nine-spot and random spot)
- lots of interlocking cubes (eg Multilink)
- squared and isometric paper
- timers, stopclocks, geared clocks and clock stamps
- a wall calendar or 'year at a glance' poster
- shopping catalogues (for Term 3)
- mathematical dictionaries.

USING INFORMATION AND COMMUNICATION TECHNOLOGY

Make use of your favourite mathematical games software for paired or small-group activities Some of the activities in this book offer potential for the use of a programmable floor vehicle such as Roamer or PIP. Pupils can use data-handling software to prepare simple graphs.

PUBLICATIONS

Use your favourite mathematical stories, poems and rhymes, as well as the published materials available in school. The following Scholastic publications contain some useful ideas:

Oral and mental starter
Developing Mental Maths with 7–9 year olds
by Jon Kurta

Homework
IMPACT Maths Homework (Key Stages 1 and 2)
Various authors
Mental Maths Homework for 8 year olds
by Ceri Morgan and Kath Morgan
Quick Mental Maths for 8 year olds
by William Hartley

Main teaching activity
Maths Focus Kit 3
Various authors
Practising Mental Maths with 8 year olds
by Jon Kurta
Quick Mental Maths for 8 year olds
by William Hartley

Assessment
Maths Focus Kit 3
Various authors
Scholastic Portfolio Assessment: Maths KS1
by Jean Edwards and Ian Gardner
Scholastic Portfolio Assessment: Maths KS2
by Ian Gardner and Jean Edwards

ASSESSMENT

In advance of the assessment units for Year 3, you have the benefit of 'end of KS1' assessment information. This will comprise both teacher assessment and results from statutory tasks and tests. This data can be particularly helpful in judging whether particular individuals are likely to encounter any difficulties in accessing the KS2 content and expectations of the NNS.

At the end of each half-term, an assessment period of two lessons is built into the planning. This gives you the opportunity to make medium-term assessments of the key objectives for Year 3 as listed in the *Framework*. The aim of these assessments is to:
● Find out what progress each pupil has made; what he or she knows, understands and can do; whether he or she can apply and use their mathematics in context; and whether he or she has any weaknesses.
● Give you information on which to base feedback to pupils and their parents or carers. It will also help you to plan work for the next few weeks.

ASSESSMENT ADVICE
This appears before each pair of photocopiable assessment sheets. Here you will find a summary of the aspects of mathematics which will be assessed; some assessment activities which can be used for oral and mental starters with the whole class; and others which can be used with groups, pairs or individuals.

ASSESSMENT ACTIVITIES
These activities have been designed so that you can observe pupils at work and ask questions. Explain the purpose of the activity to them before they begin, as this will help them to show you the things that you need to observe, such as clear recording, discussion of which strategy they used and why they used it, and so on. Target a small group with a specific activity for a set period of time and work with them, observing how individuals respond to the activity. You may find it useful to take informal notes on observations and discussions.

If you have a classroom helper, he or she can also be involved in this process. Explain the purpose of the assessment, what to do and what to look for. After the lesson, take time to discuss observations and keep notes on individual pupils' achievements and weaknesses.

ASSESSMENT PHOTOCOPIABLE SHEETS
There are two photocopiable sheets for each half-term assessment period. Each sheet has specific assessment criteria printed at the bottom. Photocopy the pages for individual pupils to complete while you observe others undertaking the group assessment activities.

Mark the completed sheets, then give pupils feedback on their strengths and set targets for improvement in their areas of weakness. The sheets can be included in an ongoing portfolio of evidence of the children's achievement.

CLASS ASSESSMENT RECORDING SHEET
This is provided on page 12. It lists the key objectives for Year 3 from the National Numeracy Strategy *Framework for Teaching Mathematics*. Photocopy this sheet, enlarge it to A3, and record individuals' progress on it. By the end of the year, after six assessment sessions, you will have a wealth of assessment evidence to pass on to the children's next teacher.

Each half-term assessment offers opportunities to assess all the key objectives that have been taught. Some key objectives recur in later assessments, so it may not be necessary to assess every child on every key objective each time. Use your assessment records to decide whether it is appropriate to leave out a specific assessment objective which has already been learnt, or to reassess the child on it.

Please note that the key objectives for Year 3 do not cover knowledge of shape or of measures (apart from time). Therefore, you should make sure that your formative assessment includes adequate attention to these important elements of the year's work.

Weekly planning chart

(Photo-enlarge to A3.)

Week beginning:				
Learning objectives for oral and mental skills:				
Oral and mental starter	Main teaching activity	Differentiation	Plenary	Resources
Monday				
Tuesday				
Wednesday				
Thursday				
Friday				

Year 3: Class assessment record sheet

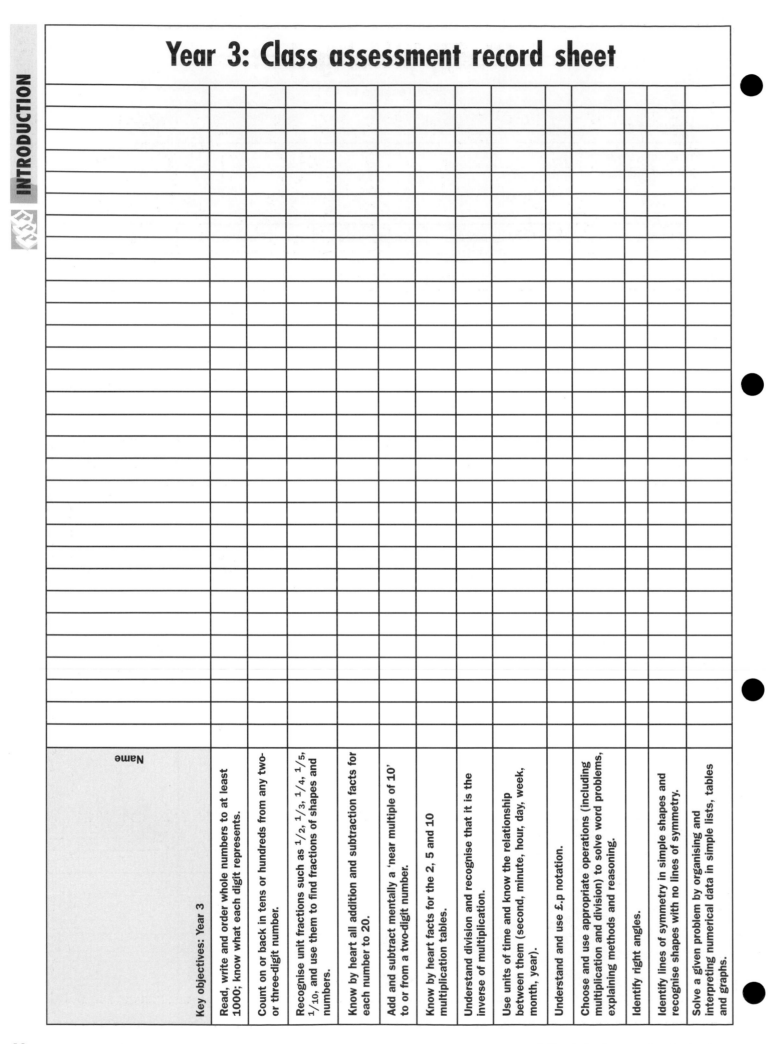

Name												
Key objectives: Year 3												
Read, write and order whole numbers to at least 1000; know what each digit represents.												
Count on or back in tens or hundreds from any two- or three-digit number.												
Recognise unit fractions such as $\frac{1}{2}$, $\frac{1}{3}$, $\frac{1}{4}$, $\frac{1}{5}$, $\frac{1}{10}$, and use them to find fractions of shapes and numbers.												
Know by heart all addition and subtraction facts for each number to 20.												
Add and subtract mentally a 'near multiple of 10' to or from a two-digit number.												
Know by heart facts for the 2, 5 and 10 multiplication tables.												
Understand division and recognise that it is the inverse of multiplication.												
Use units of time and know the relationship between them (second, minute, hour, day, week, month, year).												
Understand and use £.p notation.												
Choose and use appropriate operations (including multiplication and division) to solve word problems, explaining methods and reasoning.												
Identify right angles.												
Identify lines of symmetry in simple shapes and recognise shapes with no lines of symmetry.												
Solve a given problem by organising and interpreting numerical data in simple lists, tables and graphs.												

Symbol cards

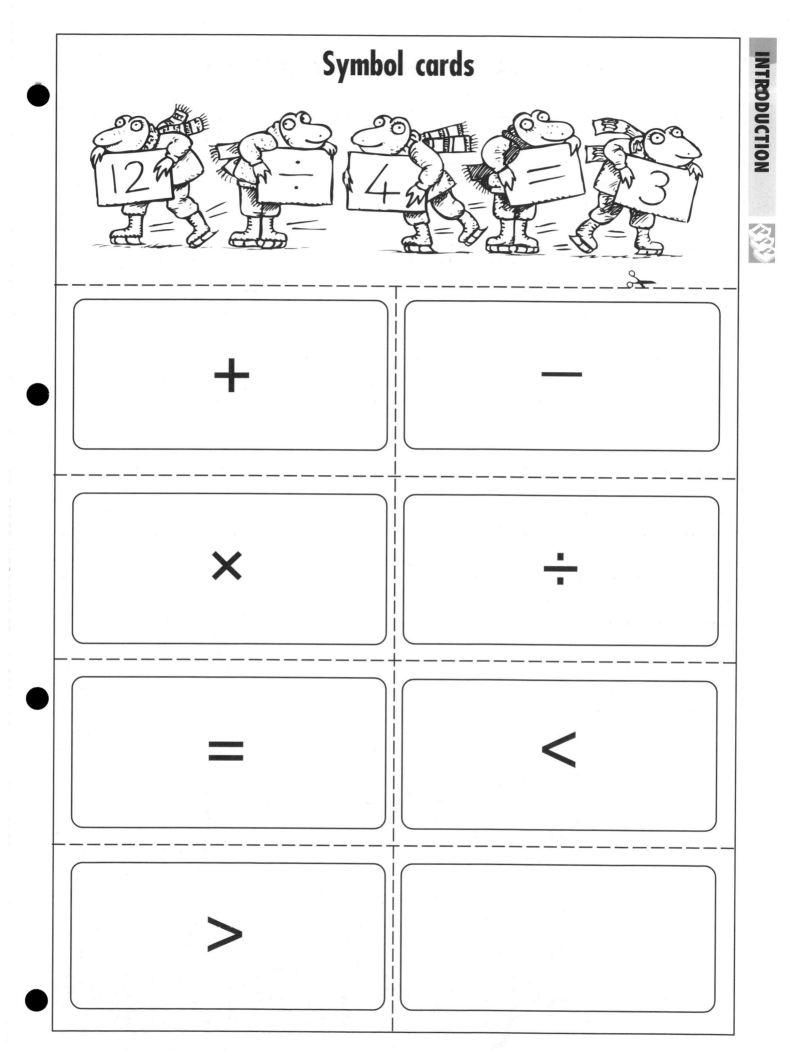

+	−
×	÷
=	<
>	

1–100 square

1	2	3	4	5	6	7	8	9	10
11	12	13	14	15	16	17	18	19	20
21	22	23	24	25	26	27	28	29	30
31	32	33	34	35	36	37	38	39	40
41	42	43	44	45	46	47	48	49	50
51	52	53	54	55	56	57	58	59	60
61	62	63	64	65	66	67	68	69	70
71	72	73	74	75	76	77	78	79	80
81	82	83	84	85	86	87	88	89	90
91	92	93	94	95	96	97	98	99	100

TERM 1

This term begins with work on place value and ordering to 100. Addition and subtraction continue as ongoing themes. There is a focus on recall of number bonds and techniques for deriving answers. The wider range of numbers and topics begins to make pencil and paper methods an important skill. Multiplication and division are explored, arising from repeated addition and subtraction. There is a growing use of recognised conventions of recording. Pupils will become familiar with the multiplication tables for 2, 5 and 10, and develop the confidence to derive and extend sequences from known facts. Problem solving features as an integral aspect. Work on measures develops understanding of length and mass, including reading from scales. The properties of 2-D shapes are examined as a basis for sorting and classifying. Carroll and Venn diagrams are introduced and compared, using both shape and number.

ENLARGE THIS SHEET TO A3 AND USE IT AS YOUR MEDIUM-TERM PLANNING GRID.

ORAL AND MENTAL SKILLS   Read whole numbers in figures and (say them) in words. Understand the operations of addition and subtraction; use the related vocabulary. Add a pair of numbers mentally by bridging through 10. Understand that addition can be done in any order, and that more than two numbers can be added together. **Know by heart all addition facts for each number to 20.** Find a small difference by counting up. Derive quickly doubles of all whole numbers to at least 20 and corresponding halves. Extend understanding that subtraction is the inverse of addition. Check subtraction with addition. Use known number facts and place value to add/subtract mentally. Solve word problems involving money, and explain how they were solved. Recognise all coins.

Unit	Topic	Objectives: children will be taught to...
1	Place value, ordering, estimating, rounding. Reading numbers from scales.	● **Order whole numbers to at least 100 and position them on a 100 square** (Y2 revision). ● **Know what each digit represents,** and partition three-digit numbers into a multiple of 100, a multiple of ten and ones (HTU). ● Read and begin to write the vocabulary of comparing and ordering numbers, including ordinal numbers to at least 100. ● Read and write whole numbers to at least 1000 **in figures and words.** ● Round any two-digit number to the nearest 10.
2–3	Understanding + and –. Money and 'real life' problems. Making decisions and checking results.	● Use patterns of similar calculations. ● Use knowledge that addition can be done in any order to do mental calculations more efficiently. For example, put the larger number first and count on. ● **Know by heart all addition and subtraction facts for each number to 20.** ● Extend understanding that subtraction is the inverse of addition. ● Use known number facts and place value to add/subtract mentally. ● Recognise all coins (to 50p). ● Solve problems involving money, including finding totals and working out which coins to pay. ● Check subtraction with addition. ● Derive quickly doubles of all whole numbers to at least 20 (eg 17 + 17 or 17 × 2). ● Understand that more than two numbers can be added (Y2 revision). ● **Choose and use appropriate operations** and ways of calculating **to solve word problems.** ● Extend understanding of the operation of subtraction and use the related vocabulary. ● Extend understanding that more than two numbers can be added.
4–6	Measures, including problems. Shape and space. Reasoning about shapes.	● Classify and describe 2-D shapes (triangles), referring to properties (number and relative length of sides). ● Make and describe shapes and patterns. ● **Identify** and sketch **lines of symmetry in simple shapes and recognise shapes with no lines of symmetry.** ● Classify and describe 3-D shapes, including the hemisphere and prism, referring to their properties (number of faces, edges and vertices). ● Relate solid shapes to pictures of them. ● Know the relationship between kilograms and grams. ● Suggest suitable units and measuring equipment to estimate or measure mass. ● Read scales to the nearest division (labelled or unlabelled). ● Begin to use decimal notation for metres and centimetres. ● Measure and compare using standard units (m, cm). ● Record estimates and measurements to the nearest whole or half unit, or in mixed units. ● Solve mathematical problems or puzzles, recognise simple patterns and relationships, generalise and predict. Suggest extensions by asking 'What if...?'
7	Assess and review.	

ORAL AND MENTAL SKILLS   Use patterns of similar calculations. Investigate a general statement about familiar numbers by finding examples that satisfy it. Check subtraction with addition. Extend understanding that subtraction is the inverse of addition. Recognise all coins. Use known number facts and place value to add/subtract mentally. **Know by heart the 2, 5 and 10 times tables.** Begin to know the 3 and 4 times tables. Solve mathematical problems or puzzles, recognise simple patterns and relationships, generalise and predict. Count on in steps of 3, 4 or 5 from any small number to at least 50, then back again. Recognise two-digit multiples of 2, 5 or 10. Say or write a subtraction statement corresponding to a given addition statement, and vice versa. Use doubling or halving to multiply or divide, starting from known facts. Derive quickly: doubles of multiples of 5 to 100; doubles of all whole numbers to at least 20 (eg 17 + 17 or 17 × 2). Check halving with doubling. Identify near doubles, using doubles already known. Understand multiplication as repeated addition, and use the related vocabulary. Extend understanding that multiplication can be carried out in any order.

Unit	Topic	Objectives: children will be taught to...
8	Counting and properties of numbers. Reasoning about numbers.	● Count larger collections by grouping them: for example, in tens, then other numbers. ● Give a sensible estimate of up to about 100 objects. ● Describe and extend number sequences: **count on or back in tens or hundreds, starting from any two- or three-digit number.** ● Solve mathematical problems or puzzles, recognise simple patterns and relationships, generalise and predict. Suggest extensions by asking 'What if...?'
9–10	Understanding × and ÷. Mental calculation strategies (× and ÷). Money and 'real life' problems. Making decisions and checking results.	● Understand multiplication as repeated addition. Read and begin to write the associated vocabulary. ● Extend understanding that multiplication can be carried out in any order. ● Understand division **as grouping (repeated subtraction). Read and begin to write the associated vocabulary.** ● Check division with multiplication. ● Solve word problems involving numbers in 'real life'. Explain how the problem was solved. ● Use known number facts and place value to multiply and divide mentally. ● Recognise all coins and notes.
11	Fractions.	● Recognise unit fractions such as $\frac{1}{2}$ and $\frac{1}{4}$ and use them to find fractions of shapes. ● Begin to recognise simple equivalent fractions. ● Use doubling to multiply, starting from known facts. ● Begin to recognise simple fractions that are several parts of a whole, eg $\frac{3}{4}$. ● Use halving to divide, starting from known facts.
12	Understanding + and –. Mental calculation strategies (+ and –). Time, including problems. Making decisions and checking results.	● Use informal pencil and paper methods to support, record or explain addition. ● Count on in steps of 3, 4 or 5 from any small number to at least 50, then back again. ● Bridge through a multiple of 10, then adjust. ● Use the +, – and = signs. ● Understand and use the vocabulary related to time. ● **Use units of time and know the relationships between them.** ● Read the time to 5 minutes on an analogue clock and a 12-hour digital clock.
13	Handling data.	● **Solve a given problem by organising and interpreting numerical data in simple lists, tables and graphs,** eg Venn diagrams (one criterion), Carroll diagrams, simple frequency tables, block graph.
14	Assess and review.	

UNIT 1

ORGANISATION (3 LESSONS)

LEARNING OUTCOMES		ORAL AND MENTAL STARTER	MAIN TEACHING ACTIVITY	PLENARY
LESSON 1	● Order whole numbers to at least 100 and position them on a 100 square (Year 2 revision). ● **Know what each digit represents,** and partition three-digit numbers into a multiple of 100, a multiple of ten and ones. ● Read and begin to write the vocabulary of comparing and ordering numbers, including ordinal numbers to at least 100.	HTU CHART: Read out and combine numbers on a place value chart.	MIX, MATCH AND ORDER: Make and order two-digit numbers.	Discuss place value; record numbers on a 100 square.
LESSON 2	● **Read and write whole numbers to at least 1000** in figures and words.	SPIDER SUMS: Find ways to make target numbers up to 10.	MAKE IT: Use place value cards to create numbers given in words.	Rehearse number bonds within 10.
LESSON 3	● Round any two-digit number to the nearest 10.	CROSS THE BRIDGE: Add by bridging through 10.	ROUNDING GAME: Round two-digit numbers to nearest 10.	Round flashcard numbers to nearest 10.
ORAL AND MENTAL SKILLS Read whole numbers in figures and (say them) in words. Understand the operations of addition and subtraction; use the related vocabulary. Add a pair of numbers mentally by bridging through 10.				

All the lessons in this unit are shown in full.

RESOURCES

Photocopiable page 22; copies of page 16; pointer; colouring pencils; number flashcards.

PREPARATION

Enlarge photocopiable page 22 to make an A3 (or larger) place value chart (or prepare as an OHT). Each child will need a copy of 1–100 square (page 16).

LEARNING OUTCOMES

ORAL AND MENTAL STARTER
● Read whole numbers in figures and (say them) in words.

MAIN TEACHING ACTIVITY
● Order whole numbers to at least 100 and position them on a 100 square (Y2 revision).
● **Know what each digit represents,** and partition three-digit numbers into a multiple of 100, a multiple of 10 and ones (HTU).
● Read and begin to write the vocabulary of comparing and ordering numbers, including ordinal numbers to at least 100.

ORAL AND MENTAL STARTER

HTU CHART: Gather the children around the chart and read along the top row of numbers, using the pointer. Count this row in ascending order, then in descending order, then point to numbers at random. Ask particular children to confirm that they understand. Move on to the next row and get all the children joining in the count: '100, 200, 300...'. Combine numbers by, say, pointing to 200 and then 3; ask individual children to say the combinations. Move on to the penultimate row: 'tens' numbers with regular sounds. Work

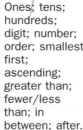

on these; combine them with other rows. Explain the final row as 'tens' numbers with irregular sounds (eg 'fifty' not 'five-ty').

MAIN TEACHING ACTIVITY

MIX, MATCH AND ORDER: Explain that this lesson is about ordering numbers. Select three different single-digit numbers and write them on the board. Ask the children to select two at a time to make a two-digit number (eg 3 and 4 can be combined to make 34). Show how several combinations are possible, then ask the children to arrange these numbers in ascending order. Focus on the language of ordinality: *Which number comes first, second, third? What numbers are greater than, between, next...?* Later work on this theme (Lesson 2, Unit 1, Term 2) will involve using an empty number line.

Set each group off working with a different set of three single-digit numbers (avoid 0). As you support individuals, you may want to say that it is acceptable to use one digit twice (eg 33). When they have found all nine possible combinations, ask them to re-record these in ascending order.

DIFFERENTIATION

Less able: Order a prepared set of two-digit numbers and stick them in place as a record.
More able: Record combinations on the 1–100 square. Is there always a pattern?

PLENARY

Present flashcards featuring two- and three-digit numbers. Ask questions such as: *What number is 10 more than this? What is the digit 2 worth in this number? What numbers make up this?* (eg 453 is 400 and 50 and 3.) Provide each child with a 1–100 square. Ask them to colour in the numbers they created and to identify the pattern in the arrangement.

LESSON 2

RESOURCES

Photocopiable page 23; scissors.

PREPARATION

Each pair of children will need a copy of page 23 on A4 card and a pair of scissors.

VOCABULARY

Same total; place value cards.

LEARNING OUTCOMES

ORAL AND MENTAL STARTER
● Understand the operations of addition and subtraction; use the related vocabulary.

MAIN TEACHING ACTIVITY
● **Read and write whole numbers to at least 1000** in figures and words.

ORAL AND MENTAL STARTER

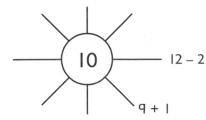

SPIDER SUMS: Write a target number (perhaps 10) in the middle of the board and ask the class to suggest different ways of making that amount. Draw up a spider diagram (see figure). You could ask more able pupils to give solutions involving multiplication, division, mixed numbers etc.

MAIN TEACHING ACTIVITY

MAKE IT: Explain that this lesson is about using 'place value cards'. Each pair should cut out their cards and arrange them neatly on the desk as two columns of ascending tens and units. Show the children how to make a given two-digit number by overlaying the single-digit card on top of the tens card and aligning the ends. Give individual children instructions or questions, and take opportunities to question more deeply: *Make 38. What is the tens digit worth? Make an odd number. Make the largest number you can. Make the number that is 10 more than this number. Did we change both cards?*

Next, say numbers for the children to make. They should write down how each number is made up (eg '68 is 60 and 8'). Alternatively, prepare a sheet of number names (eg 'sixty-eight') for children to assemble. This sheet could be made more appealing (and reusable) by separating the questions and presenting them as a set of cards per table.

DIFFERENTIATION

Less able: Work with numbers less than 50.
More able: Use photocopiable page 132 to extend the place value cards into hundreds.

PLENARY

Revise number facts of, say, 10. Ask the class why the cards they used are called 'place value cards' (because numerals take on different **values** according to where they are **placed** within a number). Save the cards for later use (Unit 9, Term 2).

RESOURCES

Two dice (1–6 and 1–10) per pair or small group; number flashcards or place value cards (photocopiable page 23); a 0–100 number line or 1–100 square (page 16)

LEARNING OUTCOMES

ORAL AND MENTAL STARTER

● Add a pair of numbers mentally by bridging through 10.

MAIN TEACHING ACTIVITY

● Round any two-digit number to the nearest 10.

VOCABULARY

Rounding up/down; nearest.

ORAL AND MENTAL STARTER

CROSS THE BRIDGE: Write 5 + 8 on the board. Discuss how we could break the 8 into 5 + 3 and then add the 5s first: 5 + 8 = 5 + 5 + 3 = 13. The children should typically have done this type of activity in Year 2. Consider similar examples where we have to 'bridge across 10'. When they are familiar with this idea, ask them how they would deal with 7 + 6. You might reinforce the idea using a simple number line (see figure).

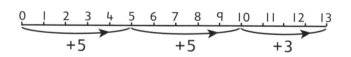

MAIN TEACHING ACTIVITY

ROUNDING GAME: Explain that this activity is about rounding numbers. Use a 0–100 number line (or 1–100 square) and a pointer to discuss rounding numbers up or down to the nearest 10. Revise the convention that when a number is halfway between, it is rounded **up** (eg 75 rounds to 80).

Organise the children into pairs (or groups of up to four) and give each group two standard dice. Players take turns to roll both dice and create a two-digit number (eg 3 and 2 makes either 23 or 32). This number is then rounded to the nearest 10. The challenge is to be the first person to round to every multiple of 10 from 10 to 70. Each player can create his or her 'scoreboard' by writing down these multiples of 10 and crossing them off.

DIFFERENTIATION

Less able: Work with teacher or partner support.
More able: Use 10-sided dice and numbers up to 100 to extend the range of numbers.

PLENARY

Conduct a rounding test. Hold up flashcards with two-digit numbers (or use place value cards) and ask the children to round each number up or down to the nearest 10. You might use a set of flashcards which includes some three-digit numbers.

Place value chart

1	2	3	4	5	6	7	8	9
100	200	300	400	500	600	700	800	900
			40	50	60	70	80	90
10	20	30						

Place value cards

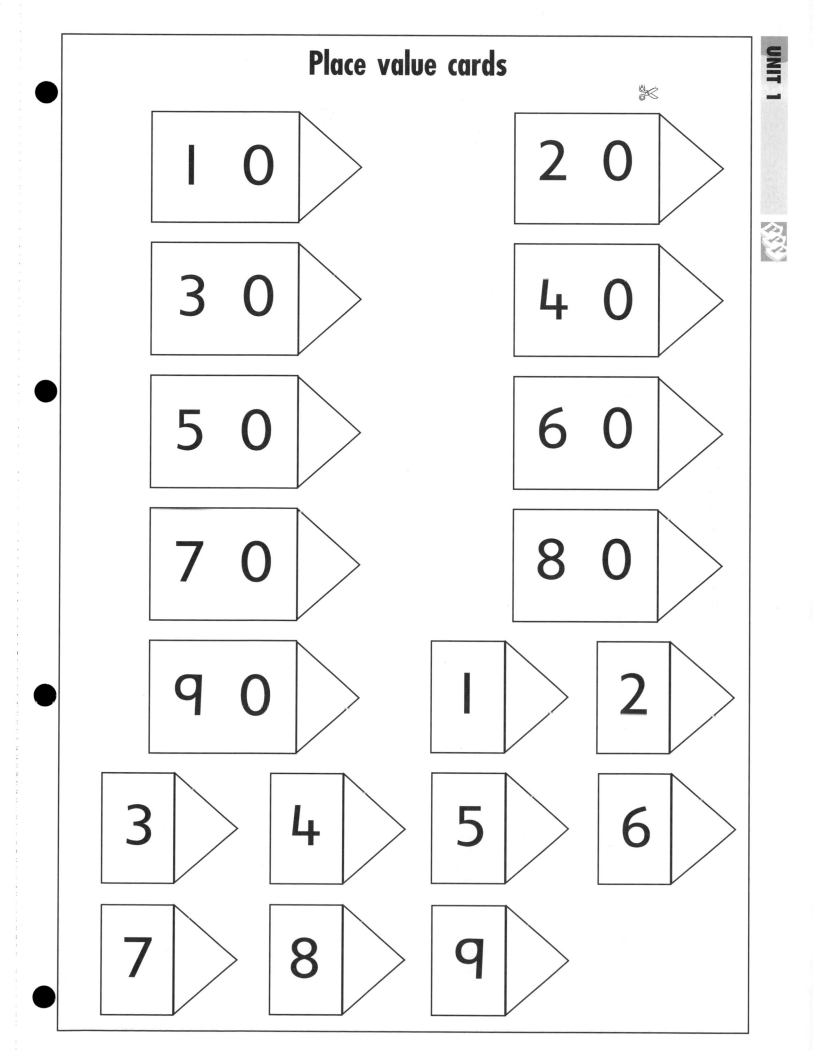

UNITS 2-3

ORGANISATION (10 LESSONS)

	LEARNING OUTCOMES	ORAL AND MENTAL STARTER	MAIN TEACHING ACTIVITY	PLENARY
LESSON 1	• Use patterns of similar calculations. • Use knowledge that addition can be done in any order to do mental calculations more efficiently. For example, put the larger number first and count on.	COUNT ON: Add by putting the larger number first.	10-STICKS: Make 10 in different ways.	How many ways are there of making 10? Is there a general rule?
LESSON 2	• **Know by heart all addition facts for each number to 20.** • Use knowledge that addition can be done in any order to do mental calculations more efficiently.	ADD THREE NUMBERS: By finding a convenient pairing.	2S AND 3S: Make various totals using 2s and 3s only.	Count in 10s.
LESSON 3	• Extend understanding that subtraction is the inverse of addition. • Use known number facts and place value to add/subtract mentally. • **Know by heart all subtraction facts for each number to 20.**	COUNT ON 2: Find difference by counting on.	MORE 10-STICKS: Practise recall of subtraction facts within 10.	Look for a generalisation.
LESSON 4	• Recognise all coins (to 20p). • Solve problems involving money, including finding totals and working out which coins to pay.	DOUBLE UP: Recall doubles to 10.	COINS AND COSTS: Find total costs of items, using coins.	Discuss strategies used.
LESSON 5	• **Know by heart all addition and subtraction facts for each number to 20.** • Extend understanding that subtraction is the inverse of addition. • Check subtraction with addition.	MORE DOUBLES: Recall doubles to 20.	NUMBER SENTENCES: Make statements with numeral and operation cards.	Revise number bonds within 10.
LESSON 6	• **Know by heart all addition and subtraction facts for each number to 20.** • Use patterns of similar calculations. • Derive quickly doubles of all whole numbers to at least 20 (eg 17 + 17 or 17 × 2).	COUNT ON: Repeat from Lesson 1 with higher numbers.	DOUBLES AND SUMS: Derive doubles to 40; explore bonds of 20.	Compare with bonds of 10.
LESSON 7	• Understand that more than two numbers can be added (Year 2 revision). • **Choose and use appropriate operations** and ways of calculating **to solve word problems.** • Use patterns of similar calculations.	NUMBER STRINGS: Extend from Lesson 2.	3S AND 5S: Make different totals with 3s and 5s only.	Look for a generalisation.
LESSON 8	• **Know by heart all subtraction facts for each number to 20.** • Extend understanding of the operation of subtraction and use the related vocabulary. • Check subtraction with addition.	100 SQUARE: Use 100 square for TU – TU subtraction.	TWO TOWERS: Use cubes to explore subtraction from 20.	Speed test of number bonds to 20.

MAIN TEACHING ACTIVITY

TWO TOWERS: Using the 20 cubes as in Lesson 1, investigate and record subtraction from 20. For example, take 6 cubes from 20. *How many are left? How might you record this?* Consider pictorial, word, tabular and symbolic methods of recording. Set this task for individuals and offer guidance where necessary.

DIFFERENTIATION

Less able: Use a prepared format for recording answers.
More able: Label both axes of a graph 0–20, to represent the possible heights of the two towers. A straight-line graph should result.

PLENARY

Try a speed test to see how well the children's knowledge of bonds to 20 is developing. Spend some time afterwards 'unpicking' the answers by sharing strategies used. Ask: *Did anyone use a visual image of the 2 towers of 10?*

LESSON 9

RESOURCES	Photocopiable page 32; coins with values to 50p; coin stamps (optional).
LEARNING OUTCOMES	**ORAL AND MENTAL STARTER** ● Derive quickly doubles of all numbers to at least 10 (Year 2 revision). **MAIN TEACHING ACTIVITY** ● Recognise all coins (to 50p). ● Solve problems involving money, including finding totals, giving change and working out which coins to pay.
ORAL AND MENTAL STARTER	MORE DOUBLES: Repeat from Lesson 5, extending to totals between 10 and 20. Initially, you may prefer to sequence your questions to provide a 'build-up': 5 + 5, 6 + 6, 7 + 7 etc.
MAIN TEACHING ACTIVITY	COINS AND TOTALS 2: Recap on Lesson 4 and introduce the 50p coin. Brainstorm different ways of making 50p using combinations of lower-value coins. Give each child an intact copy of page 32. They have to calculate the total cost of all 6 items and find different combinations of coins to that value (eg 20p + 10p + 5p + 2p + 2p).
DIFFERENTIATION	Less able: Work with a smaller number of items. More able: Add up a prepared shopping list with multiples of the items from page 32 (eg four oranges), or work out how to buy at least one of each item and spend exactly £1.00.
PLENARY	Share different ways of making 39p. Discuss the idea of giving change from 50p. and use this to introduce 'shopkeeper's addition' as a form of counting on.

LESSON 10

RESOURCES	Individual sets of numeral cards (page 13); a set of large numeral cards.
LEARNING OUTCOMES	**ORAL AND MENTAL STARTER** ● Derive quickly halves corresponding to doubles of all numbers to 10 (Year 2 revision). **MAIN TEACHING ACTIVITY** ● Extend understanding that more than two numbers can be added.
ORAL AND MENTAL STARTER	HALF TIME: Practise halves of numbers within 20, using the same approach as in 'Double up' in Lesson 4.
MAIN TEACHING ACTIVITY	TRIPLETS: Invite children to find different ways of making 20 by adding three or more numbers. This can be done by inviting two children to select and hold up a large numeral card each, then inviting a third child (and perhaps a fourth) to select a card or cards to make the total up to 20. Give each child or small group a set of numeral cards (page 13). They have to find number triplets that give a total of 20. As they only have one of each numeral, their choices are limited.
DIFFERENTIATION	Less able: Ask children to make a total of 10. Use numeral cards with spots or other images drawn on. More able: Use combinations of four, then five numeral cards.
PLENARY	Discuss the numeral cards that were not used. *Why was that?* (0, 1 and 2 cannot be used in triple bonds of numerals to make 20) *Could they be used if we tried quadruple bonds of 20?* (Yes.)

LEARNING OUTCOMES	ORAL AND MENTAL STARTER	MAIN TEACHING ACTIVITY	PLENARY
LESSON 9 ● Recognise all coins (to 50p). ● Solve problems involving money, including finding totals, giving change and working out which coins to pay.	MORE DOUBLES: Repeat from Lesson 5.	COINS AND COSTS 2. Find total costs of items, using several coins.	Introduce 'shopkeeper's addition'.
LESSON 10 ● Extend understanding that more than two numbers can be added.	HALF TIME: Halve numbers within 20.	TRIPLETS: Find triple bonds of 20.	Discuss unused numbers.

> **ORAL AND MENTAL SKILLS**   Understand the operation of addition and the related vocabulary. Understand that addition can be done in any order, and that more than two numbers can be added together. **Know by heart all addition facts for each number to 20.** Find a small difference by counting up. Derive quickly doubles of all whole numbers to at least 10 and corresponding halves.

Lessons 1, 2, 4, 5, 7 and 8 are given in full. Lessons 3, 6, 9 and 10 follow on from what has already been taught and are given in outline.

LESSON 1

RESOURCES

Interlocking cubes (ten per child or pair).

PREPARATION

Construct each set of ten cubes as indicated in the **Main teaching activity**.

LEARNING OUTCOMES

ORAL AND MENTAL STARTER
● Understand the operation of addition and the related vocabulary.
● Understand that addition can be done in any order.

MAIN TEACHING ACTIVITY
● Use patterns of similar calculations.
● Use knowledge that addition can be done in any order to do mental calculations more efficiently. For example, put the larger number first and count on.

> **VOCABULARY**
>
> How many;
> count on;
> total; record;
> predict;
> general rule.

ORAL AND MENTAL STARTER

COUNT ON: Ask the class: *What is 26 more than 3?* Ask those with answers how they worked it out, and use this to draw others into the discussion. Did they count on from 3? If not, how did they do it? Use this example to demonstrate that it is acceptable and often easier to put the larger number first and then count on by the smaller amount. Ask more addition questions, differentiated for particular individuals. Some children will need the sum written on the board if they find the mental reversal too difficult.

MAIN TEACHING ACTIVITY

10-STICKS: Call out single-digit numbers, asking the children to show you that number of cubes. Use the two-colour arrangement to emphasise how some numbers (eg 7) can be seen as '5 and a bit'. Now call out a number and ask the children to show the number needed to 'make it up' to 10.

  Give each child or pair a stick of ten interlocking cubes consisting of two sections of 5 in contrasting colours. This encourages children to look at the structure within 10: they can count out six cubes as 'a block of five and one more' without necessarily having to count out each cube. Ask them to break the stick in different ways and to record each arrangement in any way they wish. Explain that they will be able to 'show and tell' their recording methods later. As the children work on the task, ask questions such as: *Have you found them all? How do you know?* Focus on some strategies for checking answers. For example, with 2 and 8 it is easier to start with the larger number and count on to 10.

LEARNING OUTCOMES

ORAL AND MENTAL STARTER
● Understand the operation of addition and the related vocabulary.
● Understand that addition can be done in any order, and that more than two numbers can be added (Year 2 revision).

MAIN TEACHING ACTIVITY
● Understand that more than two numbers can be added (Year 2 revision).
● **Choose and use appropriate operations** and ways of calculating **to solve word problems.**
● Use patterns of similar calculations.

ORAL AND MENTAL STARTER
NUMBER STRINGS: Extend from Lesson 2. Look at adding strings of numbers, eg 3 + 6 + 5 + 4. Make sure the children appreciate that, although it is efficient to add 6 to 4 and 5 to 3, any ordering of the numbers gives the same answer.

MAIN TEACHING ACTIVITY
3S AND 5S: Ask oral questions to test the children's ability to add 5s and 3s, eg *How might you make 11 using 5s and 3s only?* Give each group either several towers of 3 and 5 cubes or several 3 and 5 numeral cards. Ask the class to investigate what different totals they can make by combining 3s and/or 5s (eg 10 = 5 + 5, 13 = 5 + 5 + 3).

DIFFERENTIATION
Less able: Use a number line, starting from 0, with numbers spaced to align with the cubes (typically 2cm). Work in mixed-ability groups or with teacher support.
More able: Work with 5s and 7s, extending to totals beyond 20.

PLENARY
Move toward a generalisation based on the evidence gathered: all counting numbers 8 and beyond can be created, as well as 3, 5 and 6. Forming a generalisation of this kind reinforces the underlying patterns of adding 3s and 5s.

RESOURCES
Interlocking cubes; 1–100 square (page 16).

PREPARATION
As for Lesson 1. Also make an enlarged copy of the 1–100 square on page 16.

LEARNING OUTCOMES

ORAL AND MENTAL STARTER
● Choose and use appropriate calculation strategies to solve problems (Year 2 revision).

MAIN TEACHING ACTIVITY
● **Know by heart all subtraction facts for each number to 20.**
● Extend understanding of the operation of subtraction and use the related vocabulary.
● Check subtraction with addition.

ORAL AND MENTAL STARTER
100 SQUARE: Explore subtraction problems of the type and order 100 – 86 to consider the efficiency of counting on from the smaller number. Use a large 100 square to demonstrate this, moving along a row and then down a column (jumps of 10). You might also demonstrate an alternative pathway, by moving down a column and then along a row.

Price cards

Potatoes
8p

Carrots
5p

Apples
6p

Bananas
7p

Oranges
4p

Lemons
9p

UNITS 4-6

ORGANISATION (13 LESSONS)

LEARNING OUTCOMES	ORAL AND MENTAL STARTER	MAIN TEACHING ACTIVITY	PLENARY
LESSON 1 +2 ● Classify and describe 2-D shapes (triangles), referring to properties (number and relative length of sides). ● Make and describe shapes and patterns.	TARGET TOTALS: Make various totals by adding and subtracting numbers from a given set.	GET INTO SHAPE: Make different triangles and quadrilaterals from straws.	Match shapes made to pictures on photocopiable sheet.
LESSON 3 ● **Identify** and sketch **lines of symmetry in simple shapes and recognise shapes with no lines of symmetry.**	20 QUESTIONS: Revise bonds of 20.	SYMMETRY: Arrange shapes in symmetrical patterns.	Recap names of triangles.
LESSON 4 ● **Identify** and sketch **lines of symmetry in simple shapes and recognise shapes with no lines of symmetry.**	TAKE IT AWAY: Revise subtraction from 20.	SYMMETRY 2: Identify and draw lines of symmetry.	Review the work.
LESSON 5 ● Classify and describe 3-D shapes, including the hemisphere and prism, referring to their properties (number of faces, edges and vertices). ● Make and describe shapes and patterns.	TARGET TOTALS: Extend from Lessons 1 and 2.	3-D SHAPES: Make solid shapes from squares and rectangles.	Solve a shape riddle.
LESSON 6 ● Classify and describe 2-D shapes, referring to their properties (number of sides and vertices).	QUICK ADDING: Practise addition bonds within 20.	MAKING SHAPES: Create polygons using squared and isometric paper.	Discuss shape names.
LESSON 7 ● Classify and describe 2-D shapes, referring to their properties.	QUICK SUBTRACTION: Practise subtraction bonds within 20.	SORT THE SHAPES: Identify and classify different shapes.	Revise names of triangles and quadrilaterals.
LESSON 8 ● Make and describe shapes and patterns. ● Relate solid shapes to pictures of them.	DOUBLE TIME: Practise doubles of numbers.	3-D SHAPES 2: Make solid shapes from triangles, squares and rectangles.	Identify shapes made on photocopiable sheet.
LESSON 9 + 10 ● Know the relationship between kilograms and grams. ● Suggest suitable units and measuring equipment to estimate or measure mass. ● Read scales to the nearest division (labelled or unlabelled).	NUMBER FAMILIES: Find related number facts. Make a given number using addition and/or subtraction.	MASSIVE MATHS: Estimate, measure and record the mass of different objects.	Order objects by estimated relative mass, then known mass.
LESSON 11 +12 +13 ● Begin to use decimal notation for metres and centimetres. ● Measure and compare using standard units (m, cm). ● Suggest suitable units and measuring equipment to estimate or measure length. ● Record estimates and measurements to the nearest whole/half unit, or in mixed units. ● Solve mathematical problems or puzzles, recognise simple patterns and relationships, generalise and predict. Suggest extensions by asking 'What if...?' ● Read scales to the nearest division (labelled or unlabelled).	MONEY PROBLEMS: Solve problems involving adding, subtracting, multiplying and dividing amounts of money.	HOW LONG?: Estimate and measure lengths. HOW MUCH LONGER?: Enlarge a picture by a factor of 2. HALF SIZE: Make an accurate half size sketch of a child.	Start a length wordbank. Share findings. Link 2-D and 3-D enlargement. Add to length wordbank.

cont...

...cont.

> **ORAL AND MENTAL SKILLS   Know by heart all addition and subtraction facts for each number to 20.** Use knowledge that addition can be done in any order. Understand that more than two numbers can be added. Extend understanding that subtraction is the inverse of addition. Check subtraction with addition. Use known number facts and place value to add/subtract mentally. Derive quickly: doubles of all numbers to 20 and corresponding halves. Solve word problems involving money, and explain how they were solved. Recognise all coins.

Lessons 1, 3, 5–7 and 9 are shown in full. Lessons 2, 4, 8 and 10 follow on from what has already been taught. Lessons 11–13 form a 'circus' of related activities.

LESSON 1 +2

RESOURCES

Photocopiable page 42; sets of two different lengths (with an approximate ratio of 5:3) of geostrips, artstraws or similar.

PREPARATION

Provide at least three long and three short strips per child, pair or trio. Copy the top half of page 42 twice and combine to make a master for further copying. Each child will need to be able to see the shapes; enlarging will help with this. For Lesson 2, provide at least four short and four long straws per child, pair or trio, and copy the bottom half of page 42.

LEARNING OUTCOMES

ORAL AND MENTAL STARTER
● **Know by heart all addition and subtraction facts for each number to 20.**
● Use knowledge that addition can be done in any order.
● Understand that more than two numbers can be added.

MAIN TEACHING ACTIVITY
● Classify and describe 2-D shapes (triangles), referring to properties (number and relative length of sides).
● Make and describe shapes and patterns.

VOCABULARY

Same;
different;
shape family;
triangles;
equilateral;
isosceles;
square;
rectangle;
quadrilateral.

ORAL AND MENTAL STARTER

TARGET TOTALS: Provide a set of numbers, clearly visible to the class (see figure below). Ask the class to use some or all of the numbers, along with addition and/or subtraction, to 'hit' given totals. Ask them to make 11, 17, 21, 16, 14 and 12.

6	8
3	7

MAIN TEACHING ACTIVITY

GET INTO SHAPE: Ask the class: *What is a shape?* Collect a range of answers, initially making little or no comment. Begin to refine thinking with questions such as: *Does it need to have straight sides? What if the shape is open? What if the sides are of different length? What if we don't know the name for it?* At this stage, the emphasis should be on developing a shared vocabulary and generating points for further consideration. It may be helpful to consult a mathematical dictionary to clarify some ideas. Conclude by discussing what a triangle is.

Provide the two different lengths of straws as described in **Preparation**. You can cut down on materials by making this a small-group task with a large work surface for placing or drawing the shapes. The task is to make different triangles using any three straws. Focus your teaching on the way that the relative length of the sides allows us to classify triangles by type (see vocabulary list).

DIFFERENTIATION

Less able: Use page 42 as a visual prompt.
More able: Tackle this challenge in a systematic manner. With teacher guidance, consider 'similar' and 'congruent' shapes. (The two equilateral triangles are similar shapes.)

PLENARY

Give each group a copy of the top half of page 42 and ask the children to match the featured shapes to the triangles they have created. Emphasise that **any** closed shape with three sides is a triangle. Clarify that the orientation of a shape is irrelevant (the idea of an upside down triangle' is nonsense). The children can use the sheet to help them label their own recorded triangles.

LESSON 2

Extend the **Oral and mental starter** from Lesson 1, this time using larger numbers: 8, 13, 12 and 4. Ask the children to make the totals 21, 24, 29 and 9. Extend the **Main teaching activity** from Lesson 1 by encouraging the children to make as many different four-sided shapes (quadrilaterals) as possible. Less able children could work in mixed-ability groups and/or with further adult support. More able children could write about those properties of the shapes that allow classification. For the **Plenary**, provide the lower section of photocopiable page 42 and develop as for Lesson 1.

RESOURCES

Photocopiable page 43; scissors; safety hand-mirrors; symmetrical pictures or patterns, or an OHT grid and projector (optional).

PREPARATION

Each child or pair will need to cut out each set of shapes (A and B) from a copy of page 43.

LEARNING OUTCOMES

ORAL AND MENTAL STARTER
● **Know by heart all addition facts for each number to 20.**

MAIN TEACHING ACTIVITY
● **Identify** and sketch **lines of symmetry in simple shapes and recognise shapes with no lines of symmetry.**

ORAL AND MENTAL STARTER

20 QUESTIONS: Revise the bonds of 20 found in Lesson 5, Unit 2. Target the more difficult combinations to more able pupils.

MAIN TEACHING ACTIVITY

SYMMETRY: Identify the children's recall of line symmetry from Year 2 by asking: *What is symmetry?* Accept examples initially, then push for more general ideas about what conditions are required for symmetry. You could demonstrate symmetry with pictures, examples drawn on an OHT grid, or patterns found in wallpaper or on fabric prints.

Provide copies of page 43, scissors and safety hand-mirrors. The children have to arrange the three pieces in each set to create different symmetrical images. The pieces must not overlap, and the edges should **align** (not just meet at a point). Note that each set has several solutions. For each solution, the line of symmetry should be drawn. The children should record on squared paper, or draw around the shapes themselves.

DIFFERENTIATION

Less able: Try making the same shapes from interlocking cubes; or use a simpler set with two pieces (see figure).
More able: Draw the line(s) of symmetry in each case.

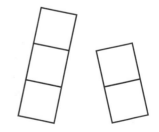

PLENARY

Use interlocking cubes (perhaps with an OHT) to demonstrate all solutions for both sets.

RESOURCES	Photocopiable page 42, adhesive labels (optional), hand-mirrors.
LEARNING OUTCOMES	**ORAL AND MENTAL STARTER** ● **Know by heart all subtraction facts for each number to 20.** **MAIN TEACHING ACTIVITY** ● **Identify** and sketch **lines of symmetry in simple shapes and recognise shapes with no lines of symmetry.**
ORAL AND MENTAL STARTER	TAKE IT AWAY: Revise subtraction from 20 (taught in Lesson 8, Unit 3). Target the more difficult questions to more able pupils, and reinforce the relationship between addition and subtraction.
MAIN TEACHING ACTIVITY	SYMMETRY 2: Revise the names of three- and four-sided plane shapes, perhaps using an enlarged or OHT copy of page 42 with the names obscured by adhesive labels (cut from memo sheets). Give each child a copy of page 42 and a hand-mirror. The task is to identify the line (or lines) of symmetry in each shape and draw them. You might test their understanding by asking, for example, why a diagonal (corner to corner) line through a rectangle is not a line of symmetry.
DIFFERENTIATION	Less able: Draw only a single line of symmetry on each shape. More able: Use card or plastic shapes as templates to examine before indicating the lines of symmetry.
PLENARY	Ask the class: *Are any of the shapes on the sheet unique?* (The square is the only one with four lines of symmetry.) *Do any of the shapes have no line symmetry? Can you think of a shape with no line symmetry?*

RESOURCES

Shapes for construction (eg Polydron) or skeletal framework kits; pictures or examples of a cube, prism, sphere and hemisphere; photocopiable page 42 (optional).

PREPARATION

Large amounts of construction materials will be needed.

LEARNING OUTCOMES

ORAL AND MENTAL STARTER
● **Know by heart all addition and subtraction facts for each number to 20.**
● Use knowledge that addition can be done in any order.
● Understand that more than two numbers can be added.

MAIN TEACHING ACTIVITY
● Classify and describe 3-D shapes, including the hemisphere and prism, referring to their properties (number of faces, edges and vertices).
● Make and describe shapes and patterns.

VOCABULARY

Cube; cuboid; parallel sides; vertices; edges; faces; solid shapes; closed shapes; open shapes; hemisphere; prism.

ORAL AND MENTAL STARTER

TARGET TOTALS: Extend from Lessons 1 and 2 by writing the numbers 11, 13, 19 and 7 on the board. The children try to make the totals 17, 5, 12, 1 and 25.

MAIN TEACHING ACTIVITY

3-D SHAPES: Explain that this section of the lesson is about 3-D shapes. Use a range of 3-D shapes to discuss features: edges, faces and vertices. Say that all 3-D shapes have these in varying numbers. Explain the difference between closed (solid) and open 3-D shapes. The vocabulary (see list) could be presented on the wall as part of a shape wordbank. Provide physical or pictorial representations of a sphere, hemisphere, cube, cuboid and prism, and explain these terms. Talk about the properties, or ask the children to match the shapes to 'What am I?' questions, eg *I have one curved face and no flat faces. What am I?*

   Provide groups with squares and rectangles for construction. Ask them to make different closed (solid) shapes, using 6 pieces each time. They will discover that the only possible solid shapes are **cuboids** (of which the **cube** is a special case with all faces the same). They should look carefully at each shape and note the number of vertices, edges and faces. All the shapes made should have 8 vertices, 12 edges and 6 faces.

DIFFERENTIATION

Less able: Build a solid shape and attach 'smiley face' stickers to the faces (supporting the vocabulary). Count the faces with adult help.
More able: Use a dictionary to find out more about the terms in the **Vocabulary** list.

PLENARY

Play a 'shape detective' game, starting with a riddle. Provide one clue at a time and invite discussion of the possibilities after each statement. For example: *I am a plane shape. I have four sides. I have sides of more than one length. I have no right-angled corners. My opposite sides are parallel.* If necessary, you could use an OHT of page 42, crossing out 'wrong' shapes as the clues develop.

LESSON 6

RESOURCES

Squared and isometric paper (one sheet of each per child); a range of 2-D shapes (see **Differentiation**); colouring pencils.

PREPARATION

Provide paper as indicated above.

LEARNING OUTCOMES

ORAL AND MENTAL STARTER
● **Know by heart all addition and subtraction facts for each number to 20.**
● Use known number facts and place value to add mentally.

MAIN TEACHING ACTIVITY
● Classify and describe 2-D shapes, referring to their properties (number of sides and vertices).

VOCABULARY
Polygon; hexagon; heptagon; pentagon; octagon; regular; irregular.

ORAL AND MENTAL STARTER

QUICK ADDING: Conduct a recall session for pairs of numbers with totals to 20. When recall is less than rapid, ask for strategies based on known facts (eg 9 + 6 is 15, based on 10 + 6 less 1).

MAIN TEACHING ACTIVITY

MAKING SHAPES: Recap on the different triangles and quadrilaterals made using an OHT copy of page 42. Introduce the terms **regular** and **irregular**. Say that a regular shape is one where all the sides are the same length and all the internal angles are the same. Explain that this lesson is about making regular and irregular shapes with up to eight sides.

Provide squared and isometric paper and ask the children to make different shapes, which must all have either five or six sides. When they have done this, they should colour all the shapes, using one colour for the **pentagons** and another for the **hexagons**. Ask the children whether any of their shapes fit the definition of regularity.

Divide the class into two. Ask one group to make a collection of **heptagons** and the other a set of **octagons**.

DIFFERENTIATION

Less able: Sort a given set of shapes by number of sides.
More able: Explore the names of other polygons using a CD-ROM or mathematical dictionary.

PLENARY

Talk about the names of shapes with more than 8 sides. Explain that we can simply use the phrase 'nine-sided shape' if we forget the technical term. Introduce the term **polygon**: any 2-D shape with straight sides.

LESSON 7

RESOURCES	Photocopiable page 44 (enlarged to A3 size if possible).
LEARNING OUTCOMES	**ORAL AND MENTAL STARTER** ● **Know by heart all addition and subtraction facts for each number to 20.** ● Check subtraction with addition. ● Extend understanding that subtraction is the inverse of addition. ● Use known number facts and place value to subtract mentally. **MAIN TEACHING ACTIVITY** ● Classify and describe 2-D shapes, referring to their properties.
ORAL AND MENTAL STARTER	QUICK SUBTRACTION: Practise rapid recall of subtraction facts using numbers within 20. Where recall is problematic, discuss the idea of using related facts (eg 17 – 8 is 17 – 7 less 1) and the inverse operation (eg 6 + 8 = 14 so 14 – 6 = 8).
MAIN TEACHING ACTIVITY	SORT THE SHAPES: Discuss with the children what they understand by 'regular' and 'irregular' shapes. Correct any misconceptions. 　Give out copies of page 44 and let the children work individually on them. The task is to cut out the shapes and sort one shape into each cell of the grid.
DIFFERENTIATION	Less able: Use a modified sheet with common or regular shapes only. Sort a mixture of shapes into circles, triangles, quadrilaterals and others. More able: Make another irregular shape to add to each cell in the right-hand column of the sheet.
PLENARY	Review the names of different triangles and quadrilaterals (see Unit 4).

LESSON 8

RESOURCES

Construction shapes (eg Polydron) or skeletal framework kit; photocopiable page 45.

PREPARATION

You will need a lot of construction materials. Make one copy per group (or an OHT) of page 45.

LEARNING OUTCOMES

ORAL AND MENTAL STARTER
● **Know by heart all addition and subtraction facts for each number to 20.**
● Derive quickly doubles of all numbers to 20 and corresponding halves.
● Use known number facts and place value to add mentally.

MAIN TEACHING ACTIVITY
● Make and describe shapes and patterns.
● Relate solid shapes to pictures of them.

ORAL AND MENTAL STARTER

DOUBLE TIME: Pick up on the idea of doubles, developed in Unit 3. Encourage rapid recall, and develop the idea of using known facts where necessary (eg 19 + 19 is 38 based on 20 + 20 less 2). Introduce the idea of corresponding halves by giving a double that has already been derived and 'working back' to the original number.

MAIN TEACHING ACTIVITY

3-D SHAPES 2: Explain that this lesson is about making solid shapes from 2-D shapes. Make a prism using two triangles and three rectangles. Discuss how the two end faces are the same (congruent) and how, if a cross-section were taken, that would also be the same.

Provide groups with squares, rectangles and triangles only. Their task is to make solid shapes using no more than six pieces each time. After they have finished each solid shape, they should sketch it before taking it apart.

DIFFERENTIATION

Less able: Work with squares and triangles only; or try to make the solids on page 45.
More able: Record how many sides, edges and vertices each solid shape has.

PLENARY

Give each group a copy of page 45, or present an OHT. Ask groups to identify any shapes they made, and to label their sketches accordingly. Introduce the word **polyhedron**: a solid shape with sides that are **all** polygons (so a cylinder, for example, is not a polyhedron).

NB Lessons 9 and 10 are intensive on materials and teacher input. You may wish to organise the week so that only one or two groups are engaged in measurement tasks at any one time, and the groups are rotated on a 'circus' basis.

LESSON 9 +10

RESOURCES

A range of equipment for measuring mass (see **Main teaching activity**); suitable objects for weighing, including a selection of packaged food items with printed weights.

PREPARATION

Bring in the food items needed.

LEARNING OUTCOMES

ORAL AND MENTAL STARTER
● Extend understanding that subtraction is the inverse of addition.
● **Know by heart all addition and subtraction facts for each number to 20.**

MAIN TEACHING ACTIVITY
● Know the relationship between kilograms and grams.
● Suggest suitable units and measuring equipment to estimate or measure mass.
● Read scales to the nearest division (labelled or unlabelled).

VOCABULARY

Addition; sum; total; subtraction; take away; difference; pan balance; kitchen scales; spring balance; bathroom scales; weight; weigh; grams; g; kilograms; kg.

ORAL AND MENTAL STARTER

NUMBER FAMILIES: Provide three numbers related by addition and subtraction (eg 6, 7 and 13). Invite individuals to say all four number statements (two for addition and two for subtraction). Repeat with larger numbers.

MAIN TEACHING ACTIVITY

MASSIVE MATHS: Explain that this lesson is about measuring **mass**. Record the masses of some of the food items on the board. Use different units to show how grams and kilograms are related, eg 500g = 0.5kg. Present a range of equipment for measuring mass, including a bucket balance, kitchen and bathroom scales, a spring balance and a pan balance. Discuss how each type of equipment is designed for a specific job, and where necessary, demonstrate this with actual objects.

Provide several items (eg a food can without a label, a book, a bag of marbles) for measurement, and focus each group on one type of measuring equipment. If a group is using a pan balance, a selection of plastic weights will be needed. Ask the groups to record their work using sketches and numbers.

DIFFERENTIATION

Less able: Order items by mass without recording mass; work in mixed-ability groups; work with additional teacher support or direction.

More able: With teacher guidance, use the conventions for recording a small mass in grams and as a fraction of a kilogram.

PLENARY

Show a selection of food packages, encouraging the children to suggest how you could arrange them in order of increasing mass. Ask them to give you an estimate of what each item weighs, given the nature of its contents. Now read and display the actual given weights, reordering the objects as necessary. Use this as an opportunity to discuss the units of mass (g, kg) and their relationship.

LESSON 10

For the **Oral and mental starter**, provide a target number such as 12. Invite quick suggestions for ways of making that answer using addition and/or subtraction. At this stage, you may also accept multiplication and division (these themes are developed further in Units 9 and 10 of this term). Continue the **Main teaching activity** from Lesson 9, rotating the groups. Repeat the **Differentiation** and **Plenary** from Lesson 9.

LESSON 11 +12 +13

RESOURCES

A range of instruments and items to measure (length only); squared paper; plain paper; rulers; a metre rule; measuring tapes; large sheets of paper at least half as big as a child.

LEARNING OUTCOMES

ORAL AND MENTAL STARTER

● Solve simple word problems involving money and explain how they were solved (Year 2 revision).
● Recognise all coins.

MAIN TEACHING ACTIVITY

● Begin to use decimal notation for metres and centimetres.
● Measure and compare using standard units (m, cm).
● Suggest suitable units and measuring equipment to estimate or measure length.
● Record estimates and measurements to the nearest whole or half unit, or in mixed units.
● Solve mathematical problems or puzzles, recognise simple patterns and relationships, generalise and predict. Suggest extensions by asking 'What if....?'
● Read scales to the nearest division (labelled or unlabelled).

ORAL AND MENTAL STARTER

MONEY PROBLEMS: In these three lesson starters, ideas developed in earlier units are applied in 'real' problems presented orally and/or in words. This skill prepares children for later work on the application of skills in money. Set the following problems, in order:
1. *I have four coins with a total value of 13p. What coins could I have?* Invite answers (there is more than one solution). If they cope well with this, ask similar questions with larger totals. If you have 'giant' coins, you can use these to represent the solutions.
2. *I have five coins. How much money could I have in total?* Accept and record a variety of answers. You may wish to organise the solutions so as to demonstrate a systematic approach (eg listing them in order of increasing total).
3. Ask questions such as: *If you have six identical coins, how much money might you have in total? How many 5p coins would be used to change three 20p coins? How did you work it out? Two girls have 45p altogether. One girl has twice as much as the other. How much money does each girl have?*
In each case, focus on the skills brought to the task. Emphasise that there is no single 'correct' way of finding the answer.

MAIN TEACHING ACTIVITY

The following activities are complex and resource-intensive. They may be taught in separate lessons, or prepared as a 'circus' of tasks for groups to carry out in rotation over three days. Suitable whole-class/group introductions are given for each task. You will need to introduce or revise the relevant teaching points each day.

HOW LONG?: Discuss the tools we use to measure length in the home and elsewhere. Outline the work for the next three days, drawing the children's attention to the intended learning outcomes.

Provide a range of measuring tools and some items to measure. The task is to decide what equipment is most appropriate for each object, and then to measure its length. Discuss which dimension of, say, a book constitutes its 'length' – remember that there are no hard and fast rules about this!

You may wish to offer a recording chart to enter the object being measured, the choice of measuring instrument, the estimated length and the measured length. Estimation will help the children to develop a 'feel' for measure. By observing, assess their use of the instruments and the accuracy of their recording. They should use standard units (cm, m). You may need to talk through the conventions for recording length, including the combination of units, eg '3m 20 cm' or '3.20 metres'.

HOW MUCH LONGER?: Ask: *What does 'twice as large' mean?* (All dimensions are doubled.) You might demonstrate this in two dimensions using, for example, grid paper shapes on an OHT. In three dimensions, you could show a simple tower or shape made of interlocking cubes and then a prepared enlargement of scale factor 2. (NB To be twice as large, the second shape will need 8 times as many cubes as the first.)

Prepare a picture made up of straight lines with right-angled corners (see figure). The task is to measure each length, then reproduce the picture at double size.

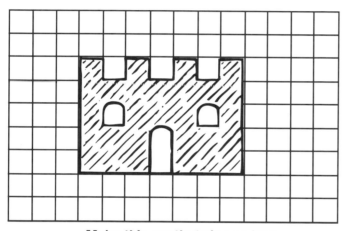

Make this castle twice as large.

HALF SIZE: Recap on the length wordbank (see **Plenary**), asking for definitions or explanations where appropriate. Extend with further words such as *smaller, half size, reduce, scale down*.

Groups of four children should elect one child to be measured, then produce a half-size representation of him or her on large sheets of plain paper (or wallpaper). Leave the task relatively open-ended, and observe their strategies for measuring and for halving the lengths. If the drawing becomes too much of a 'free-form' exercise, remind them of the need to make measurements of hands, feet etc. As the children work on this task, question them about the measurements they are making to see whether they can make sensible estimates.

DIFFERENTIATION

For HOW LONG?, less able children could work with a smaller range of instruments or a ruler with a simpler scale (marked in cm not mm); more able children could find lengths to the nearest mm and record them in different ways (eg 626mm, 0.626m). For HOW MUCH LONGER?, less able children could work on 2cm squared paper to enlarge a picture created on 1cm squares; more able children could enlarge the picture by a factor of 3, using line lengths that are not whole numbers of centimetres. HALF SIZE is well suited to mixed-ability grouping.

PLENARY

After HOW LONG?, start a wordbank of length vocabulary (see **Vocabulary** list) to be extended later. Recap on the recording of length. After HOW MUCH LONGER?, share results and discuss the effects of enlarging by a factor of 2 in 2-D and in 3-D. Some children may begin to grasp the generalisation that these enlargements involve using four and eight times as many cubes respectively. This can be demonstrated by looking at the enlargement of a one-unit square (2-D) or a one-unit cube (3-D). After HALF SIZE, add suitable further words to the wordbank. If you are working through the **Main teaching activities** as a circus, review the progress to date.

Assessment sheet 1b

Complete this addition grid. One number has already been done for you:

+	5	12	7	9
6				
8				
3		15		
7				

Fill in the missing numbers to make each statement correct:

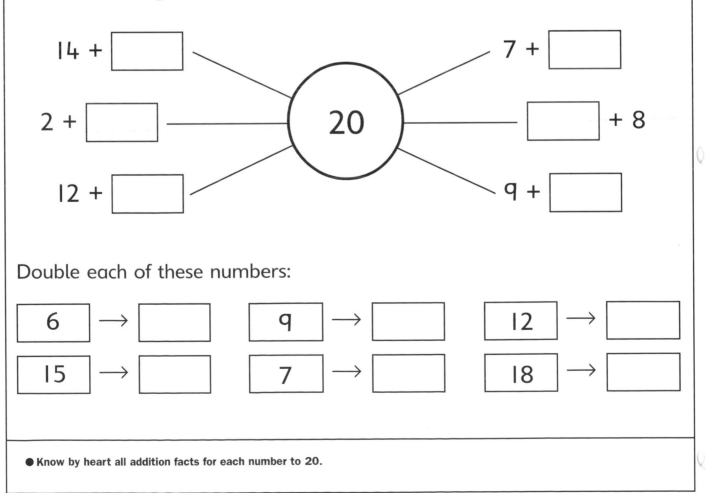

14 +   7 +

2 +   20   + 8

12 +   9 +

Double each of these numbers:

6	→			9	→			12	→	
15	→			7	→			18	→	

● Know by heart all addition facts for each number to 20.

UNIT 7

UNIT 8

ORGANISATION (5 LESSONS)

	LEARNING OUTCOMES	ORAL AND MENTAL STARTER	MAIN TEACHING ACTIVITY	PLENARY
LESSON 1	• Count larger collections by grouping them: for example, in tens, then other numbers. • Give a sensible estimate of up to about 100 objects.	ADDITION GRID: Explore number bond patterns.	HOW MANY?: Count many objects, using groups of numbers.	Use the 'five-bar gate' tallying method.
LESSON 2 +3	• Describe and extend number sequences: **count on or back in tens or hundreds, starting from any two- or three-digit number.**	ADDITION GRID 2: Explore the effect of odd + even addition. ADDITION GRID 3: Explore strategies for TU + TU addition.	SEQUENCES: Add units, tens or hundreds to various numbers. Subtract units, tens or hundreds from various numbers.	Use a 1–100 square to look at the effect of adding 10 repeatedly. Use a 1–100 square to add two-digit numbers.
LESSON 4	• Solve mathematical problems or puzzles, recognise simple patterns and relationships, generalise and predict. Suggest extensions by asking 'What if...?'	ADDITION GRID 4: Find missing numbers in an addition grid.	4S AND 5S: Make totals (below 20) by adding chains of 4s and 5s.	Discuss the results.
LESSON 5	• Solve mathematical problems or puzzles, recognise simple patterns and relationships, generalise and predict. Suggest extensions by asking 'What if...?'	ADDITION GRID 5: Find missing edge numbers in an addition grid.	NEXT IN LINE: Add three consecutive numbers – is the total odd or even?	Look for a general rule.

ORAL AND MENTAL SKILLS   Use patterns of similar calculations. Investigate a general statement about familiar numbers by finding examples that satisfy it. Check subtraction with addition. Extend understanding that subtraction is the inverse of addition.

Lessons 1, 2, 4 and 5 are given in full. Lesson 3 follows on from what has already been taught and are given in outline.

LESSON 1

RESOURCES

Photocopiable page 54; several hundred cubes, headless matchsticks or other objects for counting; OHP (optional).

PREPARATION

Make an enlarged copy of page 54 and place a large acetate sheet over the top. Alternatively, make an OHT of page 54.

LEARNING OUTCOMES

ORAL AND MENTAL STARTER
● Use patterns of similar calculations.

MAIN TEACHING ACTIVITY
● Count larger collections by grouping them: for example, in tens, then other numbers.
● Give a sensible estimate of up to about 100 objects.

Number; zero, one, two etc; how many; count; count up to; tally; every other; guess how many; exactly; group in pairs; threes... tens; equal groups of.

ORAL AND MENTAL STARTER

ADDITION GRID: Prepare a large addition table (see figure) for the class to see. Select cells out of sequence, seeking answers from targeted individuals. Use this as an opportunity to emphasise **commutativity** (eg 6 + 4 = 4 + 6). When the table is complete, talk about the number patterns.

+	1	2	3	4	5	6
1						
2						
3						
4						
5						
6						

MAIN TEACHING ACTIVITY

HOW MANY?: Explain that this lesson is about counting large numbers. Using the acetate or OHT (see **Preparation**), discuss how we could count the number of people in the scene. *If we just count in ones, how long will that take? Is it possible to count in twos, threes or more, crossing off groups as you go?* Wipe the cover after each count and invite other strategies. When you count in groups of 5 or 10, suggest making tally marks at the side as a precaution against miscounting.

Provide small groups with a significant number of counting objects each (45–70 per group, depending on ability). Ask them to count in ones first and then to try all the different ways of counting you have discussed. Remind them to try using tally marks for fives and tens.

DIFFERENTIATION

Vary the number of counting objects and the level of teacher/LSA support provided.

PLENARY

Discuss the methods used, encouraging children to evaluate their methods. Introduce the 'five-bar gate' for tallying: ask each child to say his or her name in register or positional order, and demonstrate the tallying method of four vertical strokes and a fifth diagonal stroke. You might reinforce this idea on occasions such as registration or going out at breaktime.

RESOURCES

Basic (arithmetic logic) calculators; an OHP calculator (optional); 1–100 square (page 16).

PREPARATION

Check that your calculators can perform a simple constant function by entering [0] [+] [2] [=] [=] [=]. In most cases, this will generate a sequence. Make an enlarged copy of the 1–100 square on page 16.

LEARNING OUTCOMES

ORAL AND MENTAL STARTER

● Use patterns of similar calculations.
● Investigate a general statement about familiar numbers by finding examples that satisfy it.

MAIN TEACHING ACTIVITY

● Describe and extend number sequences: **count on or back in tens or hundreds, starting from any given two- or three-digit number.**

VOCABULARY

What comes next?; predict; more; repeated addition; 2 more; 1 more; 10 more; 100 more.

ORAL AND MENTAL STARTER

ADDITION GRID 2: As for Lesson 1, prepare a large addition table (see figure) and ask individual children for answers. Emphasise that all the solutions in this grid are odd; discuss why this is. This activity extends the concept of odd and even (from Year 2) to arrive at a general statement about adding odd or even numbers.

+	1	3	5	7	9
2					
4					
6					
8					
10					

MAIN TEACHING ACTIVITY

SEQUENCES: Start by writing 1, 3, 5, 7 on the board. Invite pupils to say what number comes next. Talk about the idea of an 'adding on' or 'generating' rule: 'Add 2'. Try more challenging patterns with a constant 'adding on' rule. Ask children to add 1, 10 and/or 100 to several given starting numbers. Talk about how the units (ones) digit stays the same when you add 10 or 100, and how the tens and units digits stay the same when you add 100.

Demonstrate how to use the 'calculator constant' function, using an OHP calculator if available. Give the children calculators. Ask them to work in pairs, using a variety of start numbers, and investigate how they grow under constant addition. As they work on the task, ask them to predict the numbers that will follow.

DIFFERENTIATION

Less able: Try smaller start numbers and additions, eg [1] [+] [1] [0] [=] [=] [=].
More able: Try larger start numbers and additions, eg [1] [9] [3] [+] [1] [0] [0] [=] [=] [=].

PLENARY

Display a large 1–100 square and select a two-digit number. Use movement down the columns to emphasise the effect of adding 10 repeatedly.

LESSON 3

For the **Oral and mental starter**, ADDITION GRID 3, complete an addition table of larger (and more arbitrary) numbers (see figure). Use this exercise to develop and share strategies for calculation. For the **Main teaching activity**, extend Lesson 2: start with a number and count back in ones, tens and/or hundreds. Ask the children to write number sequences of their own, then recreate them on the calculator. Again, discuss which digits change or stay the same. Less able children could use the enlarged 1–100 square for counting back in tens (moving up a column of numbers). More able children should be able to count back in steps of 100 or 1000, and to recognise that such sequences can extend below zero. For the **Plenary**, use the 1–100 square to demonstrate how to add numbers such as 22 by moving along rows and down columns (or vice versa).

+	12	15	17	18
11				
17				
14				
19				

RESOURCES

Magnetic numerals (or numeral cards) showing 4 and 5; cubes grouped in 4s and 5s (optional).

PREPARATION

You will need a large supply of numeral 4s and 5s (the children could make their own).

LEARNING OUTCOMES

ORAL AND MENTAL STARTER
● Use patterns of similar calculations.
● Check subtraction with addition.
● Extend understanding that subtraction is the inverse of addition.

MAIN TEACHING ACTIVITY

● Solve mathematical problems or puzzles, recognise simple patterns and relationships, generalise and predict. Suggest extensions by asking 'What if...?'

ORAL AND MENTAL STARTER

ADDITION GRID 4: Prepare an incomplete addition grid (see figure). Use this problem to reinforce the relationship between addition and subtraction, and to develop further the notion of a 'missing number' (which is next extended in Unit 2, Term 2).

+	2	☐	7
6	☐	9	☐
7	☐	☐	☐
☐	☐	☐	19

MAIN TEACHING ACTIVITY

4S AND 5S: Explain that this lesson is about adding chains of numbers. Display a set of numeral 4s and 5s. Ask a child to select a combination of these to make a total less than 20 (eg 5 + 5 + 4 = 14). Invite further examples.

Ask the children (working individually) to use 4s and 5s to make as many different totals less than 20 as they can. Let them select a set of numeral cards if they wish to.

DIFFERENTIATION

Less able: Use cubes (in groups of 4 and 5) and draw a suitably-sized number line.
More able: Look for a pattern in the answers, and use this to predict which numbers can be made.

PLENARY

Discuss which numbers could and could not be made. *Could some numbers be made in more than one way? Is it possible to make every number greater than 11?*

RESOURCES

Sets of numeral cards (page 13) for each child, and a large set for demonstration.

PREPARATION

Prepare sets of numeral tiles, using copies of page 13.

LEARNING OUTCOMES

ORAL AND MENTAL STARTER
● Use patterns of similar calculations.

MAIN TEACHING ACTIVITY
● Solve mathematical problems or puzzles, recognise simple patterns and relationships, generalise and predict. Suggest extensions by asking 'What if...?'

VOCABULARY

Consecutive; total; pattern; calculate; calculation; describe the pattern; odd; even; numeral cards.

ORAL AND MENTAL STARTER

ADDITION GRID 5: Draw a large addition grid (see figure). Invite answers as before. Discuss how a problem like this can have several satisfactory solutions.

+	☐	☐
☐	8	19
☐	11	22

MAIN TEACHING ACTIVITY

NEXT IN LINE: Display a sequence of three consecutive numbers using large demonstration numeral cards, and ask the class for a total. Explain the term **consecutive**: numbers that follow directly in a sequence, such as the sequence of counting numbers.

Ask the children to investigate what happens when they add any three consecutive numbers. As they work (individually), observe how they are calculating their totals and note any informal jottings they are making. Ask them to think about why the answer is sometimes odd and sometimes even. Can they predict which it will be before adding the numbers?

DIFFERENTIATION

Less able: Add consecutive single-digit numbers; or add only two consecutive numbers (the answer will always be odd).
More able: Add four consecutive numbers (the answer will always be even).

PLENARY

Discuss the results of the investigation. See whether the children can realise that a set of three consecutive numbers where the middle number is even will always give an even total.

So many people

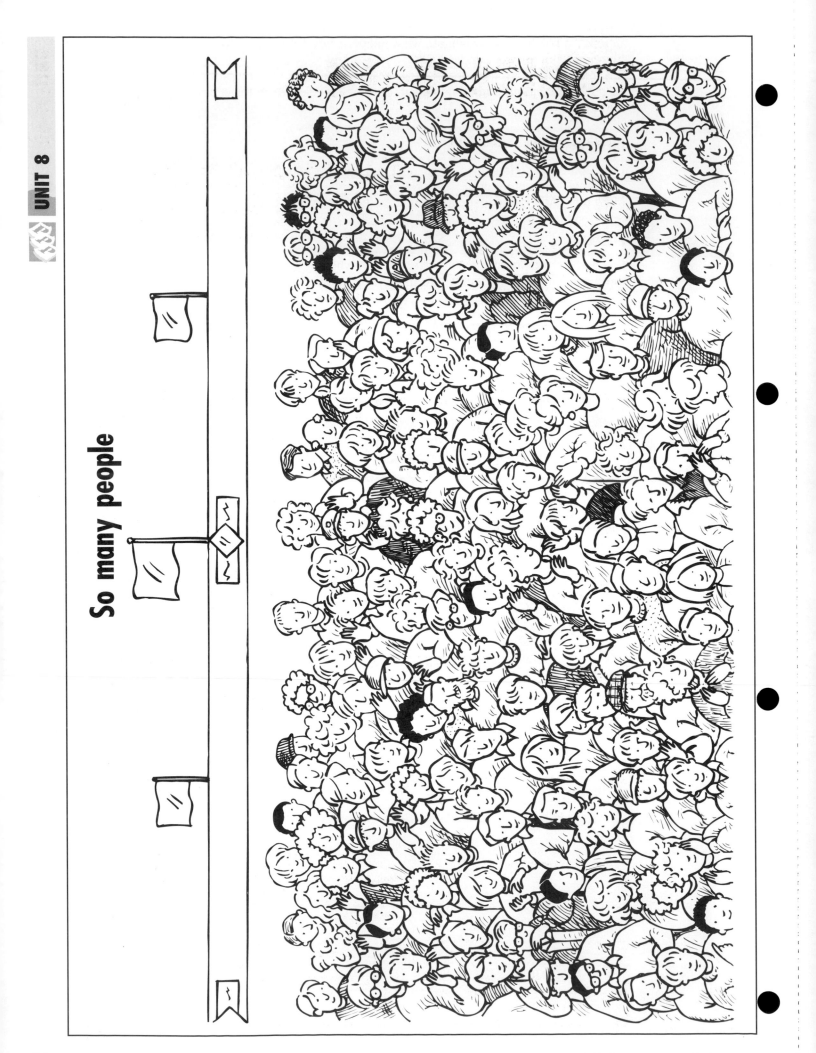

UNITS 9-10

ORGANISATION (10 LESSONS)

	LEARNING OUTCOMES	ORAL AND MENTAL STARTER	MAIN TEACHING ACTIVITY	PLENARY
LESSON 1	• Understand multiplication as repeated addition. Read and begin to write the associated vocabulary. • Extend understanding that multiplication can be carried out in any order.	SILVER START: Make 50p using combinations of 'silver' coins.	COUNTING SHAPES: Arrange 24 objects in rectangular arrays.	Consolidate using multiplication grid and number line.
LESSON 2	• Understand multiplication as repeated addition. Read and begin to write the associated vocabulary. • Extend understanding that multiplication can be carried out in any order.	TARGET 50: Make 50 by adding pairs of numbers.	MORE 24: Find factors of 24 using repeated addition.	Draw links with Lesson 1.
LESSON 3	• Understand multiplication as repeated addition. Read and begin to write the associated vocabulary. • Extend understanding that multiplication can be carried out in any order.	TARGET 100: Make 100 by adding pairs of numbers.	GRID FACTS: Read facts from multiplication grid and record them (eg 12 × 2).	Relate multiplication facts to division facts.
LESSON 4	• **Understand division** as sharing. Read and begin to write the associated vocabulary. • Check division with multiplication.	CASH COUNT: Make £5 using combinations of coins.	FAIR SHARES: Use counters to explore division as sharing.	Use multiplication to check division.
LESSON 5	• **Understand division** as grouping (repeated subtraction). Read and begin to write the associated vocabulary.	QUICK CASH: Make £1 quickly using combinations of coins.	TAKE THAT: Use a calculator to explore division as grouping.	Explore division as the inverse of multiplication.
LESSON 6	• Solve word problems involving numbers in 'real life'. Explain how the problem was solved. • Use known number facts and place value to multiply and divide mentally.	MULTIPLES OF 5: Look at odd and even multiples.	ADD AND MULTIPLY: Solve word problems involving addition and multiplication (as repeated addition).	Guess a secret number (to 50) when told whether guesses are 'higher' or 'lower'.
LESSON 7	• Solve word problems involving numbers in 'real life'. Explain how the problem was solved. • Use known number facts and place value to multiply and divide mentally.	MULTIPLES OF 3: Look for patterns in multiples.	SUBTRACT AND DIVIDE: Solve word problems involving subtraction and division (as repeated subtraction).	Guess a secret number (as above, to 100).
LESSON 8 +9	• Recognise all coins.	MULTIPLES OF 2: Relate to doubles. MULTIPLES OF 4: Relate to 2 times table.	MAKING MONEY: Find coin combinations equivalent to 10p, then to 20p.	Discuss mental calculations with money in real life. Repeat from Lessons 6 and 7.
LESSON 10	• Recognise all coins and notes. • Solve word problems involving money. Explain how the problem was solved.	DOUBLE, DOUBLE: Use repeated doubling to multiply by 4.	MONEY TALK: Solve word problems involving money.	Discuss relationships between different coin values.

cont...

LESSON 1

...cont.

Lessons 1, 2, 4, 8 and 10 are given in full. Lessons 3, 5–7 and 9 follow on from what has already been taught and are given in outline.

RESOURCES

Counters and/or squared paper; photocopiable page 62; a number line; OHP (optional).

PREPARATION

You will need 24 counters per group. Prepare an enlargement or OHT of page 62, and a large 0–100 number line.

LEARNING OUTCOMES

ORAL AND MENTAL STARTER
● Recognise all coins.

MAIN TEACHING ACTIVITY
● Understand multiplication as repeated addition. Read and begin to write the associated vocabulary.
● Extend understanding that multiplication can be carried out in any order.

VOCABULARY

Column; row; array; lots of; groups of; equal groups of; arrange; rearrange; find all; describe; same way; different way.

ORAL AND MENTAL STARTER

SILVER START: This activity, and those in Lessons 4 and 5 consolidate and extend some of the money problems explored in Unit 6, preparing for work in Unit 10. Ask the class: *How could you spend 50p using 'silver' coins only?* Focus on systematic recording. Although you may not have time to list all the different possibilities, you might want to discuss whether a sequence in a different order (eg 20p + 20p + 10p and 20p + 10p + 20p) is actually 'different' (there is no 'correct' answer to this).

MAIN TEACHING ACTIVITY

COUNTING SHAPES: Explain that this lesson is about organising groups of objects. Demonstrate how to count out 12 counters in twos. Ask the children to suggest ways of arranging the 12 counters in rows to create rectangular shapes (eg two rows of 6). You may choose to project the counters directly on an OHP. Discuss various arrangements. Do the children consider two rows of 6 to be the same as six rows of 2? Again, there is no 'correct' answer to this.

Set the task: to investigate ways of making rectangular arrangements using 24 counters. You might offer squared paper as an alternative to counters, or as a means of recording.

DIFFERENTIATION

Less able: Use gummed squares and/or a smaller total number of counters (eg 12 or 16).
More able: Label their pictures with sentences, including the words 'columns' and 'rows'.

PLENARY

Look up 24 on an enlarged copy of the multiplication grid (page 62) to reinforce the learning. Identify the cells where 24 can be found on the grid. In each case, show how this cell represents the bottom right-hand corner of a rectangle with an area of 24 square units. Demonstrate 'jumps' along a 0–100 number line to parallel the children's findings (eg 8 jumps of 3).

LESSON 2

RESOURCES

Calculators; an OHP and OHP calculator (optional).

PREPARATION

Provide enough calculators for at least one per pair of children.

LEARNING OUTCOMES

ORAL AND MENTAL STARTER
● Use patterns of similar calculations.
● Use known number facts and place value to add/subtract mentally.

MAIN TEACHING ACTIVITY
● Understand multiplication as repeated addition. Read and begin to write the associated vocabulary.
● Extend understanding that multiplication can be carried out in any order.

VOCABULARY

Multiple of; repeated addition; remainder; divided into.

ORAL AND MENTAL STARTER

TARGET 50: Write 50 in the centre of the board (or OHT). Invite children to offer quickfire pairs of numbers to make that total. Emphasise how some new pairs can be derived from earlier successful pairs (eg 19 +31 can be changed to 11 + 39 by swapping the units digits).

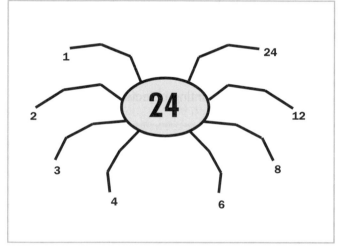

MAIN TEACHING ACTIVITY

MORE 24: Remind the class of the work they did in Lesson 2, Unit 8 using the calculator's constant facility. Tell them that they are going to use this facility to investigate the properties of 24 again (see previous lesson). Use an OHP calculator or a mental method to see whether counting in ones from 0 'hits' the number 24. Next, investigate whether counting in twos 'hits' 24. Tell the children that 1 and 2 are both **factors** of 24.

Provide calculators and ask the children to find out which other numbers are factors of 24. They should record by sketching a spider and writing each factor they find on one of its legs. Challenge them to find a factor for each leg (see figure).

DIFFERENTIATION

Less able: Use a smaller number and equal groups of cubes to place along a labelled number line (as in Lesson 4, Unit 8).
More able: Investigate for other numbers.

PLENARY

Draw links with what was found in Lesson 1.

Word problems 2

	Show your working	Answer
Six eggs fit in one box. How many boxes are needed for 28 eggs?		
Start with 36 apples and share them between four people. How many apples do they have each?		
A bag holds 29 nuts. If each person takes four nuts, how many people will one bag serve?		
Can you share 28 grapes equally between three people? (You are not allowed to cut up the grapes.)		
A box of chocolates has two layers of 30 chocolates. How many chocolates each can 12 people take from the box?		

Money problems

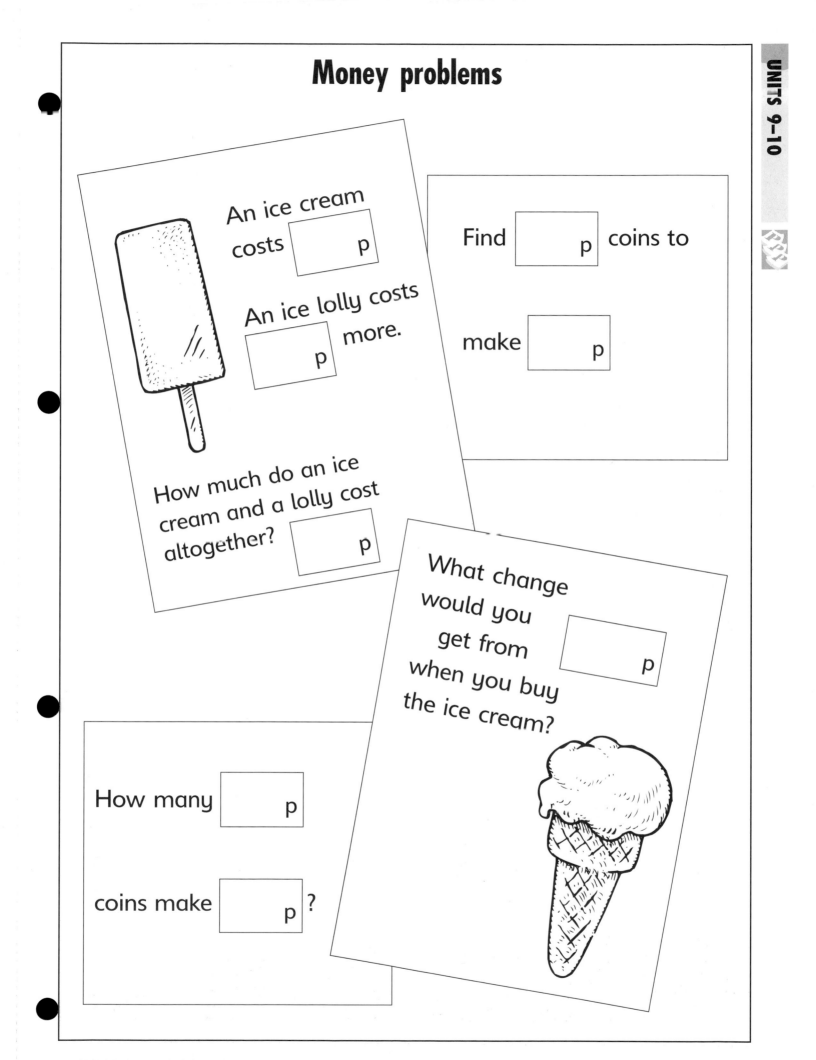

An ice cream costs ☐ p

An ice lolly costs ☐ p more.

How much do an ice cream and a lolly cost altogether? ☐ p

Find ☐ p coins to

make ☐ p

What change would you get from ☐ p when you buy the ice cream?

How many ☐ p

coins make ☐ p ?

UNIT 11

ORGANISATION (5 LESSONS)

	LEARNING OUTCOMES	ORAL AND MENTAL STARTER	MAIN TEACHING ACTIVITY	PLENARY
LESSON 1 +2	● Recognise unit fractions such as $1/2$ and $1/4$ and use them to find fractions of shapes.	MAGIC SQUARE: Solve an addition problem. ODD SET: Another addition problem.	SHAPE HALVES: Divide a square into $1/2$. SHAPE QUARTERS: Divide a rectangle into $1/4$.	Share findings.
LESSON 3 +4	● Begin to recognise simple equivalent fractions. ● Recognise unit fractions such as $1/2$ and use them to find fractions of shapes or numbers. ● Use doubling to multiply, starting from known facts.	STEPS OF 5: Count on in 5s to 50. TWO FACTS: Solve problems involving two simultaneous number facts.	DIVIDING AREAS: Find $1/2$ and $1/4$ of a shape and a quantity.	Find half an area by multiplication. Use doubling to multiply by 4.
LESSON 5	● Recognise unit fractions such as $1/2$ and use them to find fractions of shapes or numbers. ● Begin to recognise simple fractions that are several parts of a whole, eg $3/4$. ● Use halving to divide, starting from known facts.	STEPS AND MULTIPLES: Count on in various steps; relate to multiples.	FRACTIONS: Word problems involving fractions.	Use halving to divide by 4.

ORAL AND MENTAL SKILLS   Solve mathematical problems or puzzles, recognise simple patterns and relationships, generalise and predict. Count on in steps of 3, 4 or 5 from any small number to at least 50, then back again. Recognise two-digit multiples of 2, 5 or 10.

Lessons 1, 3 and 5 are shown in full. Lessons 2 and 4 follow on from what has already been taught and are given in outline.

RESOURCES

A set of numeral floor tiles (1–9); squared paper.

PREPARATION

Each child will need one sheet of squared paper for each lesson.

LEARNING OUTCOMES

ORAL AND MENTAL STARTER
● Solve mathematical problems or puzzles, recognise simple patterns and relationships, generalise and predict.

MAIN TEACHING ACTIVITY
● **Recognise unit fractions such as $1/2$ and $1/4$ and use them to find fractions of shapes.**

VOCABULARY

Divide;
partition;
equal; area;
half; halve;
quarter.

ORAL AND MENTAL STARTER

MAGIC SQUARE: Present a set of numeral floor tiles (1–9). Place 5 in the middle; invite individual children to try and create a 'magic square' in which each row, column and diagonal gives a total of 15. Encourage the idea of working by trial and improvement. There are many possible solutions.

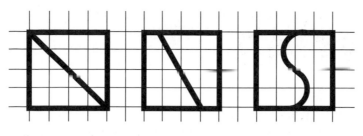

MAIN TEACHING ACTIVITY

SHAPE HALVES: Draw a large 4 × 4 square on the board, or project it on an OHP grid. Ask the children how they could divide the square in **half** using a single unbroken line. Most children will suggest a straight line through the centre of the square, running from corner to corner or through the mid-points of two opposite sides. Draw the three examples shown above, and discuss how each line divides the square into two sections of equal area. Emphasise that the two halves do not have to be exactly the same, but that they must have the same **area** (in this case, 8 square units each).

Provide the children with squared paper. Ask them to draw several 4 × 4 squares, then try to find different ways of dividing them in half.

DIFFERENTIATION

Less able: Use sheets with squares already drawn on, and/or use larger squares.

More able: Use pairs of compasses to partition using curved lines (see figure).

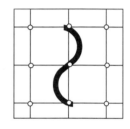

PLENARY

Share findings and draw some of the shapes on the board. Emphasise the idea of being able to find half of a shape. Complete or repeat the **Oral and mental starter**.

LESSON 2

For the **Oral and mental starter**, ODD SET, ask the children for a set of four odd numbers with a total of 20. Accept any successful solutions. Go on (if necessary) to encourage the use of deriving solutions from earlier examples. This will encourage a systematic approach, as well as revising multiple addition bonds. For the **Main teaching activity**, SHAPE QUARTERS, extend Lesson 1 by dividing a 6 × 4 rectangle into four sections of equal area.

Draw and discuss the two solutions shown below, then ask the children to investigate further solutions on squared paper. Less able children could simply find half of the rectangle in various ways. More able children could go on to divide the shape into eight equal parts. In the **Plenary**, share findings as in Lesson 1.

RESOURCES

Squared paper; a graduated counting stick.

PREPARATION

Each child will need one sheet of squared paper for each lesson.

LESSON 3 + 4

LEARNING OUTCOMES

ORAL AND MENTAL STARTER

- Count on in steps of 5 from any small number to at least 50, then back again.
- Recognise two-digit multiples of 5.
- Solve mathematical problems or puzzles, recognise simple patterns or relationships, generalise and predict.

MAIN TEACHING ACTIVITY

- Begin to recognise simple equivalent fractions.
- **Recognise unit fractions such as $1/2$ and use them to find fractions of shapes and numbers.**
- Use doubling to multiply, starting from known facts.

VOCABULARY

Divide; partition; equal; area; half; halve; quarter; fraction; amount.

ORAL AND MENTAL STARTER

STEPS OF 5: Use a graduated counting stick (see Unit 1) to revise Year 2 work on counting in fives. Point to the markers to revise the sequence of multiples of 5 from 0 to 50. Now point to them out of sequence, to encourage derivation or quick recall. Model counting back from the end of the scale to derive 9×5 as '50 less 5'.

MAIN TEACHING ACTIVITY

DIVIDING AREAS: Recap on the concept of area and the units used to measure it. Ask children to describe half of a football pitch or the school playground in terms of visual indicators. Demonstrate how to divide a circle and a square in half.

Give out sheets of squared paper. Ask the children to draw some different-sized squares and rectangles of their own, shade half of each shape, then count the area of each whole and half shape. They should record this as 'Half of... is...'. If they are using cm squared paper, they can record using the units 'square centimetres' or 'cm^2'.

DIFFERENTIATION

Less able: Use prepared shape drawings.
More able: Find both half and quarter of the area of each shape. (This should result in work involving fractional parts.)

PLENARY

Sketch some rectangles on the board and label the side lengths. Record the area of each rectangle as a multiplication sentence. By halving the product, the children can halve the area numerically without modelling on paper. Try this technique with some 'large' rectangles, eg 12×8.

LESSON 4

For the **Oral and mental starter**, TWO FACTS, set problems involving two simultaneous number facts: *My two numbers have a sum of 14 and a difference of 2. What are my numbers? I have two numbers with a sum of 8 and a product of 12. What are my numbers?* Explain that it is sometimes a useful strategy to attack half of the problem, listing possible outcomes, then see whether any of these satisfy the second condition.

Extend the **Main teaching activity** from Lesson 3: the children draw shapes and find quarter of the area of each shape. Less able children could be given a set of paper shapes to find a quarter of the area by marking or folding. More able children could investigate an eighth of the area of their shapes. For the **Plenary**, ask children to report back on the work they have done. Consider how we might calculate an eighth of (say) 64, using strategies such as repeated halving. Revisit 'Double, double' from Lesson 10, Unit 10; extend the range of numbers where possible.

RESOURCES

A graduated counting stick; photocopiable page 70.

PREPARATION

Copies of page 70 will need to have suitable numbers inserted to meet the needs of different ability groups (see **Differentiation**).

LEARNING OUTCOMES

ORAL AND MENTAL STARTER

● Count on in steps of 3, 4 or 5 from any small number to at least 50, then back again.
● Recognise two-digit multiples of 2, 5 or 10.

MAIN TEACHING ACTIVITY

● **Recognise unit fractions such as $^1/_2$ and use them to find fractions of shapes or numbers.**
● Begin to recognise simple fractions that are several parts of a whole, eg $^3/_4$.
● Use halving to divide, starting from known facts.

VOCABULARY
Word problems; fraction.

ORAL AND MENTAL STARTER

STEPS AND MULTIPLES: Recap on counting in 5s to 50 using the counting stick (as in Lesson 3). Select a multiple of 5 (eg 35) and ask the children to count on to 50 using the stick: '40, 45, 50... that's 15 more'. Try this with multiples of 2, 3, 4 and 10. Ask the class whether they have any strategies for solving these problems without the aid of the counting stick.

MAIN TEACHING ACTIVITY

FRACTIONS: Ask the class some real life fraction questions, eg *In a class of 36, half are boys. How many boys is that? Of these boys, half are nine years old. How many are **not** nine years old?* Ask similar questions involving $^1/_4$, leading to $^3/_4$ if possible (eg *What is $^3/_4$ of 24?*).

Provide copies of photocopiable page 70 with suitable numbers inserted. The problems on the sheet are 'closed', however, the children are also invited to write two problems of their own. Groups could work collaboratively to create questions to ask in the **Plenary**; or individuals could create and exchange questions within their group.

DIFFERENTIATION

Less able: Answer questions involving $^1/_2$ and $^1/_4$, with numbers up to 100, eg *Is it better to have half of 12 or a quarter of 20?*
More able: Answer questions involving other fractions (eg $^1/_8$, $^1/_5$, $^3/_4$), with numbers up to 1000.

PLENARY

Exchange and share some of the children's own questions. Also, select a number which can be halved and then halved again (eg 28) and explain that this is sometimes a useful strategy for finding quarter of a number.

Fraction problems

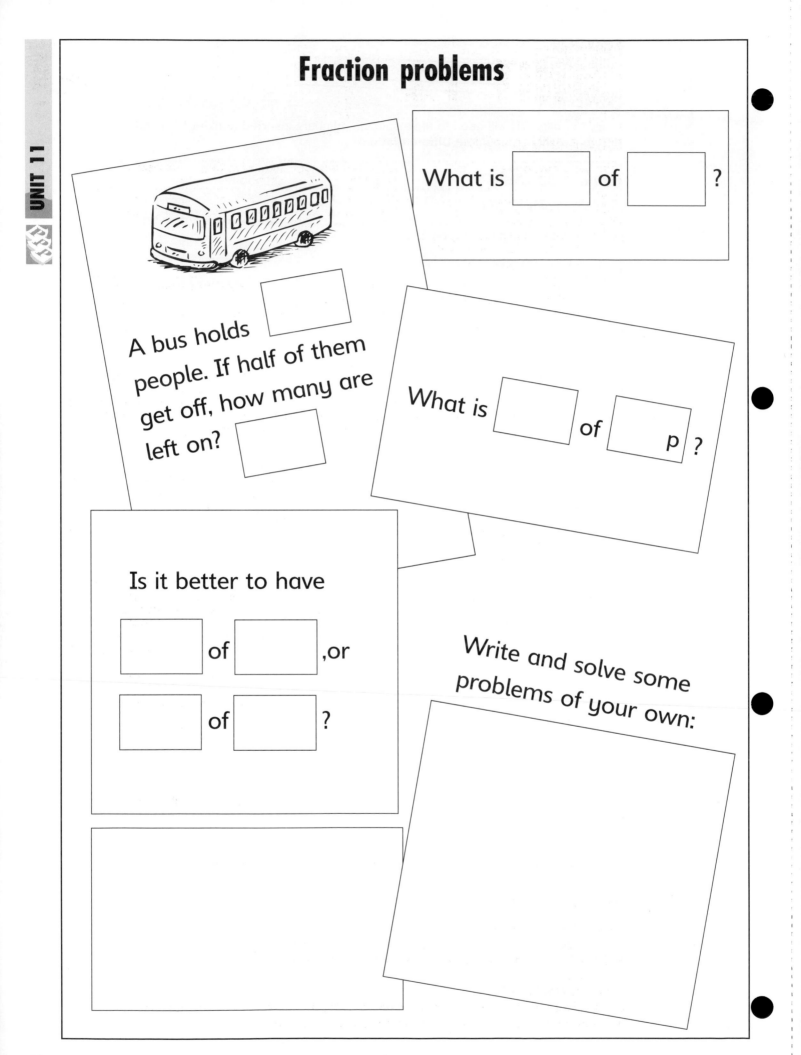

What is ☐ of ☐ ?

A bus holds ☐ people. If half of them get off, how many are left on? ☐

What is ☐ of ☐ p ?

Is it better to have

☐ of ☐ ,or

☐ of ☐ ?

Write and solve some problems of your own:

UNIT 12

ORGANISATION (5 LESSONS)

	LEARNING OUTCOMES	ORAL AND MENTAL STARTER	MAIN TEACHING ACTIVITY	PLENARY
LESSON 1	● Use informal pencil and paper methods to support, record or explain addition. ● Count on in steps of 3, 4 or 5 from any small number to at least 50, then back again.	DERIVE DOUBLES: Extend beyond 20.	JUMPS: Count along a number line, eg 42, 47, 52, 57...	Play a 'multiples of 5' game.
LESSON 2	● Use informal pencil and paper methods to support, record or explain addition. ● Bridge through a multiple of 10, then adjust. ● Use the +, – and = signs.	NUMBER SENTENCES: Make + and – sentences using given numbers.	GIANT JUMPS: Use a number line to add two-digit numbers.	Play a 'multiples of 3' game.
LESSON 3 +4	● Understand and use the vocabulary related to time. ● **Use units of time and know the relationships between them.**	DERIVE DOUBLES: Extend to larger numbers. NEAR DOUBLES: Use for addition.	ABOUT TIME: Record times and calculate time differences. Estimate and measure time taken for various short activities.	Review calculation of time differences. Estimate a minute.
LESSON 5	● Understand and use the vocabulary related to time. ● **Use units of time and know the relationships between them.** ● Read the time to 5 minutes on an analogue clock and a 12-hour digital clock.	NUMBER SENTENCES: Make × sentences using given numbers.	5 MINUTES: Record analogue time in 5-minute intervals.	Record digital time.

ORAL AND MENTAL SKILLS   Say or write a subtraction statement corresponding to a given addition statement, and vice versa. Use doubling or halving to multiply or divide, starting from known facts. Derive quickly: doubles of multiples of 5 to 100; doubles of all whole numbers to at least 20 (eg 17 + 17 or 17 × 2). Check halving with doubling. Identify near doubles, using doubles already known. Understand multiplication as repeated addition, and use the related vocabulary. Extend understanding that multiplication can be carried out in any order.

Lessons 1–3 are given in full. Lessons 4 and 5 follow on from what has already been taught, and are given in outline.

RESOURCES
Cards with 'start' and 'jump' numbers (see below); calculators or number lines (optional).

PREPARATION
Provide sets of number cards for each group as detailed in **Differentiation**.

LEARNING OUTCOMES

ORAL AND MENTAL STARTER
● Use doubling or halving to multiply or divide, starting from known facts.
● Derive quickly doubles of all whole numbers to at least 20 (eg 17 + 17 or 17 × 2).

MAIN TEACHING ACTIVITY
● Use informal pencil and paper methods to support, record or explain addition.
● Count on in steps of 3, 4 or 5 from any small number to at least 50, then back again.

LESSON 2

VOCABULARY

Sequence; rule; number line; continue.

ORAL AND MENTAL STARTER

DERIVE DOUBLES: Revisit the idea of knowing and, where necessary, deriving doubles (see Lesson 7, Unit 5). Extend the children's repertoire to include doubles beyond 20, using partitioning strategies (eg 14 + 14 = 10 + 10 + 4 + 4). Show doubles in an alternative format (eg 14 × 2). This links back to work in Unit 3, Term 1.

MAIN TEACHING ACTIVITY

JUMPS: Explain that this lesson is about counting on from any number in different steps. Engage the children in chanting sequences of numbers, counting in steps of 2, 3 and 5 from small numbers to at least 50 and back again. Do they notice patterns of repetition in the units digit? (For example, when adding on 4 from 3, the '3' repeats at 23, 43, 63 etc.)

Draw an empty number line on the board. Write a starting number at the left-hand end of the line. State the size of 'jump' you want to record, and use this to generate 'stopping points' (see figure below). Stop when you reach the right-hand end of the line.

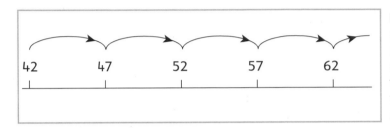

Set groups a range of 'jumping' tasks (see **Differentiation**). A useful approach is to prepare a selection of 'start' and 'jump' number cards. Each group can place a set of each type of cards in the centre of the desk, then mix and match the cards to produce a variety of number sequences. They should use an empty number line to record each sequence.

DIFFERENTIATION

Less able: Use start numbers 6, 9, 12, 15 and jump sizes 2, 3, 5. They could also use calculators or ready-labelled number lines.
Average: Use start numbers 16, 24, 27, 32 and jump sizes 4, 6, 9.
More able: Use start numbers 34, 67, 93, 104 and jump sizes 11, 15, 29.

PLENARY

Play this game with the whole class. Take turns to count in counting order, but with the rule that multiples of a certain given number (eg 5) must be replaced with a given word (eg 'buzz'). If an error occurs, start the sequence again – perhaps from a number other than 0.

RESOURCES

Cards with 'start' and 'jump' numbers (see **Differentiation**).

PREPARATION

Provide sets of number cards for each group as detailed in **Differentiation**.

LEARNING OUTCOMES

ORAL AND MENTAL STARTER
● Say or write a subtraction statement corresponding to a given addition statement, and vice versa.

MAIN TEACHING ACTIVITY
● Use informal pencil and paper methods to support, record or explain addition.
● Bridge through a multiple of 10, then adjust.
● Use the +, – and = signs.

VOCABULARY

Adding on; counting on; addition.

ORAL AND MENTAL STARTER

NUMBER SENTENCES: Present the numbers 12, 14, 26, 28 and 40. Ask the children to suggest correct number sentences using these numbers. Discuss examples such as: 14 + 12 = 26; 12 + 28 = 14 + 26; 40 – 14 = 26. The second example is particularly important, as it emphasises = as an 'equaliser' rather than as an 'instruction'. Emphasise the relationship between addition and subtraction by showing an example such as 40 –☐ = 14. The answer can be found by subtracting 14 from 40, or by counting on from 14 to 40.

MAIN TEACHING ACTIVITY

GIANT JUMPS: This activity builds on Lesson 1. Draw an empty number line alongside a linear addition statement (eg 24 + 35). Write the first number at the left-hand end. Demonstrate how a jump of 30 takes you to 54, and a further jump of 5 to 59 (see figure).

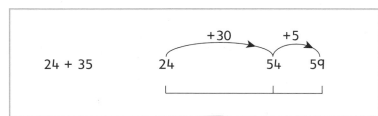

As for Lesson 1, provide groups with sets of cards with 'start' and 'jump' numbers. Ask the children to combine these to create a range of sequences, recorded on empty number lines.

DIFFERENTIATION

Less able: Use start numbers 8, 6, 9 and jump sizes 8, 6, 9.
Average: Use start numbers 12, 16, 13 and jump sizes 22, 13, 34.
More able: Use start numbers 26, 67, 38 and jump sizes 23, 34, 19. The complexity of this set arises not only from the range of numbers, but also from the need to bridge across multiples of 10. You should cover this point with everyone at some point in the session.

PLENARY

Repeat the **Plenary** from Lesson 1, this time using multiples of 3 as a cue.

LESSON 3 +4

RESOURCES

Timers; access to the school hall (or further teaching resources); a geared clock.

PREPARATION

You will need one timer per group.

LEARNING OUTCOMES

ORAL AND MENTAL STARTER
● Use doubling or halving to multiply or divide, starting from known facts.
● Derive quickly doubles of multiples of 5 to 100.
● Check halving with doubling.
● Identify near doubles, using doubles already known.

MAIN TEACHING ACTIVITY
● Understand and use the vocabulary related to time.
● **Use units of time and know the relationships between them.**

VOCABULARY

Timer; estimate; minute; second; nearest.

ORAL AND MENTAL STARTER

Extend DERIVE DOUBLES from Lesson 1, using concepts of place value with which the children should already be familiar, eg *What is double 16?* (This may be seen as double 15 plus 2.) *What is double 19?* (May be seen as double 20 less 2.) Use the inverse nature of multiplication and division to revise the corresponding halves (eg half of 38). Work with larger numbers to expose the class to doubles of multiples of 5 (up to 200), eg double 75 by combining the totals of 70 × 2 and 5 × 2.

MAIN TEACHING ACTIVITY

ABOUT TIME: Start by playing 'Estimate a minute'. The children stand up and then sit down when they think a minute has passed. Try this for two or three attempts, giving feedback each time.

Identify the actual time to the nearest quarter-hour and record this in both digital and analogue forms (eg '10:45' and 'quarter to 11'). Explain that both forms present the time in hours and minutes, but the former always gives the minutes **past** the hour, whereas the latter sometimes indicates the minutes **to** the hour. Identify another time (eg the end of the school day) and use a geared clock to demonstrate how the difference in time can be calculated by counting on: the minutes first, then the hours. Practise this, then consider other methods.

Ask groups to estimate how much time some short activities will take, then carry them out and time them using a simple timer. Suitable tasks could include PE activities in the hall, writing the alphabet three times over or filling in the numbers on a 1–100 square. Let the children decide how best to record the results (alternatively, you might want to provide a prepared grid).

DIFFERENTIATION

The children should work in mixed-ability groups.

PLENARY

Recap on time differences (see **Main teaching activity**), identifying some significant daily events for calculation.

LESSON 4

For the **Oral and mental starter**, NEAR DOUBLES, pose some 'near doubles' additions such as 8 + 9, 49 + 50, 35 + 36. Discuss the strategies used (or suggest them if necessary): doubling the larger number and compensating down; doubling the smaller number and compensating up. For the **Main teaching activity**, ABOUT TIME 2, continue from Lesson 3; keep the same mixed-ability groups, but rotate them to vary the activities. For the **Plenary**, play 'Estimate a minute' three more times.

LESSON 5

RESOURCES	A teaching clock; clock stamps or prepared sheets of blank clocks.
LEARNING OUTCOMES	**ORAL AND MENTAL STARTER** ● Understand multiplication as repeated addition, and use the relevant vocabulary. ● Extend understanding that multiplication can be carried out in any order. **MAIN TEACHING ACTIVITY** ● Understand and use the vocabulary related to time. ● **Use units of time and know the relationships between them.** ● Read the time to 5 minutes on an analogue clock and a 12-hour digital clock.
ORAL AND MENTAL STARTER	NUMBER SENTENCES: Repeat from Lesson 2, this time with a different set of numbers (2, 4, 6, 8, 16 and 24) and the operation of multiplication, eg 2 × 8 = 4 × 4.
MAIN TEACHING ACTIVITY	5 MINUTES: Demonstrate the passage of an hour in 5-minute intervals using a teaching clock, revising vocabulary from Year 2. Provide clock stamps and/or a prepared sheet of empty clocks. Ask the children to record the passage of time in 5-minute intervals by drawing in the hands, then writing each time in words ('five past ten', 'quarter to eleven' etc).
DIFFERENTIATION	Less able: Work with further teaching support and/or record in 15-minute intervals only. More able: Record times in both analogue and digital format.
PLENARY	Demonstrate how digital time (within 12 hours) is written. Let the children add digital times alongside their recording from the **Main teaching activity**.

UNIT 13

ORGANISATION (5 LESSONS)

	LEARNING OUTCOMES	ORAL AND MENTAL STARTER	MAIN TEACHING ACTIVITY	PLENARY
LESSON 1	● Solve a given problem by organising and interpreting numerical data in simple lists, tables and graphs, eg Venn diagrams (one criterion).	COUNT IN 5S: Count on from multiples of 5 beyond 50.	VENN DIAGRAMS: Use to sort shapes and numbers.	Discuss findings.
LESSON 2	● Solve a given problem by organising and interpreting numerical data in simple lists, tables and graphs, eg Carroll diagrams.	COUNT IN 4S: Count on from multiples of 4 beyond 40.	CARROLL DIAGRAMS: Use to sort shapes and numbers.	Compare with Lesson 1.
LESSON 3	● Solve a given problem by organising and interpreting numerical data in simple lists, tables and graphs, eg simple frequency tables.	COUNT IN 3S: Count on from multiples of 3 beyond 30.	FREQUENCY: Conduct a survey and draw a frequency table.	Give a brief presentation of results.
LESSON 4	● Solve a given problem by organising and interpreting numerical data in simple lists, tables and graphs eg simple frequency tables.	TABLE TALK: Recap on known multiplication facts.	PREFERENCE: Use order of preference to conduct a more meaningful survey. Record results.	Give a brief presentation of results and method used.
LESSON 5	● Solve a given problem by organising and interpreting numerical data in simple lists, tables and graphs, eg block graph (Year 2 revision).	UNTOUCHABLES: Find out which numbers 1–50 are not times table products.	BLOCK GRAPH: Draw a block graph to record results of Lesson 3 or 4 survey.	Review work done in this unit.

ORAL AND MENTAL SKILLS **Know by heart the 2, 5 and 10 times tables.** Begin to know the 3 and 4 times tables. Count on and back in steps of 3, 4 or 5.

Lessons 1–4 are shown in full. Lesson 5 follows on from what has already been taught.

LESSON 1

RESOURCES

Photocopiable page 80; copies of 1–100 square (page 16); cut-out numbers and shapes; adhesive; scissors; marker pen, OHP (optional).

PREPARATION

Create enlarged or OHT versions of pages 16 and 80. Prepare cut-out numbers and shapes to use with the Venn diagram (see **Main teaching activity**). Make one copy per child of page 80 and insert targeted criteria and numbers according to ability (see **Differentiation**).

LEARNING OUTCOMES

ORAL AND MENTAL STARTER
● **Know by heart the 5 times table.**
● Count on and back in steps of 5.

MAIN TEACHING ACTIVITY
● **Solve a given problem by organising and interpreting numerical data in simple lists, tables and graphs**, eg Venn diagrams (one criterion).

Ask the children to replicate this activity in groups of up to eight. Provide them with a theme (eg fast food), and explain that the task has five stages: 1. Identify five examples of fast food; 2. Label the chart; 3. Conduct a 'secret ballot' within the group; 4. Collate the results to make up a frequency table; 5. Write about the results.

DIFFERENTIATION

The children should work in mixed-ability groups.

PLENARY

Each group should give a brief presentation of their work.

LESSON 4

RESOURCES

Blank A4 tables (or lined paper); various graphs from school or other sources.

PREPARATION

Draw a simple blank table and make an A4 copy for each child. (Alternatively, the children could draw their own tables on lined paper.)

VOCABULARY

Order; first, second, third etc; most; least.

LEARNING OUTCOMES

ORAL AND MENTAL STARTER
● **Know by heart the 2, 5 and 10 times tables.**
● Begin to know the 3 and 4 times tables.

MAIN TEACHING ACTIVITY
● **Solve a given problem by organising and interpreting numerical data in simple lists, tables and graphs**, eg simple frequency tables.

ORAL AND MENTAL STARTER

TABLE TALK: Ask the children to provide you with multiplication facts they know with totals up to 10. Progress to facts known up to 20, then to 50. Elicit facts from the 2, 3, 4 and 5 times tables, eg *What facts give answers in the 20s?* (6 × 4, 7 × 3 etc) *In the 30s?*

MAIN TEACHING ACTIVITY

PREFERENCE: Review the findings of Lesson 3. Ask whether anyone it difficult to choose a favourite and why. Hopefully someone will say that they liked more than one option. Explain that today they will conduct a survey with the same choices, but this time the choices should all be numbered in **order of preference**. Give each child a blank grid, and ask them to write the choices in the left-hand column and, in the other column, to write '1st', '2nd' and so on according to their individual preference.

Now the groups from Lesson 1 should reform (or form two smaller groups) and find a way of collating the new information to find the 'true favourite'. Some children may find this idea confusing at first, and you may need to offer support. The most obvious strategy is to count 1st as 1 mark, 2nd as 2 marks and so on; the winner has the **lowest** total.

DIFFERENTIATION

See Lesson 3. Provide adult support as necessary.

PLENARY

Ask each group to give a brief presentation of their findings, and to explain how they tackled the problem. This is a good opportunity to demonstrate some graphical forms (including bar charts and pictograms), using work from other years and/or enlargements from books or magazines. Recap on some of the conventions for these graphs.

RESOURCES	An enlarged copy or OHT of 1–100 square (page 16), a block graph (see below), 2cm squared paper; gummed paper.
LEARNING OUTCOMES	**ORAL AND MENTAL STARTER** ● **Know by heart the 2, 5 and 10 times tables.** ● Begin to know the 3 and 4 times tables. **MAIN TEACHING ACTIVITY** ● **Solve a given problem by organising and interpreting numerical data in simple lists, tables and graphs**, eg block graphs (Year 2 revision).
ORAL AND MENTAL STARTER	UNTOUCHABLES: Present the 1–100 square with the numbers above 50 concealed. Tell the children they are looking for numbers that are not 'touched' by multiplication. Recap on the previous starter by striking off numbers representing known products. Able children may 'touch' more products, eg 49 = 7 × 7. The class may begin to see that certain numbers seem unlikely ever to be 'touched'.
MAIN TEACHING ACTIVITY	BLOCK GRAPH: Provide an enlargement of a block graph from one of the following sources: a reference book or textbook, some pupils' own recorded work or a data handling program. Use this to demonstrate the conventions of a block graph. Ask the children to create a block graph of their own, based on the data accumulated in Lessons 3 and 4. Their work should follow the conventions demonstrated.
DIFFERENTIATION	Less able: Use squared paper with pre-marked axes; use gummed paper to create the blocked columns. More able: Present their block graph using a data handling program.
PLENARY	Recap on the themes covered in this unit. Focus on any points which caused difficulty.

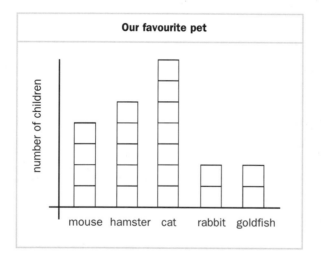

Our favourite pet

Venn diagram

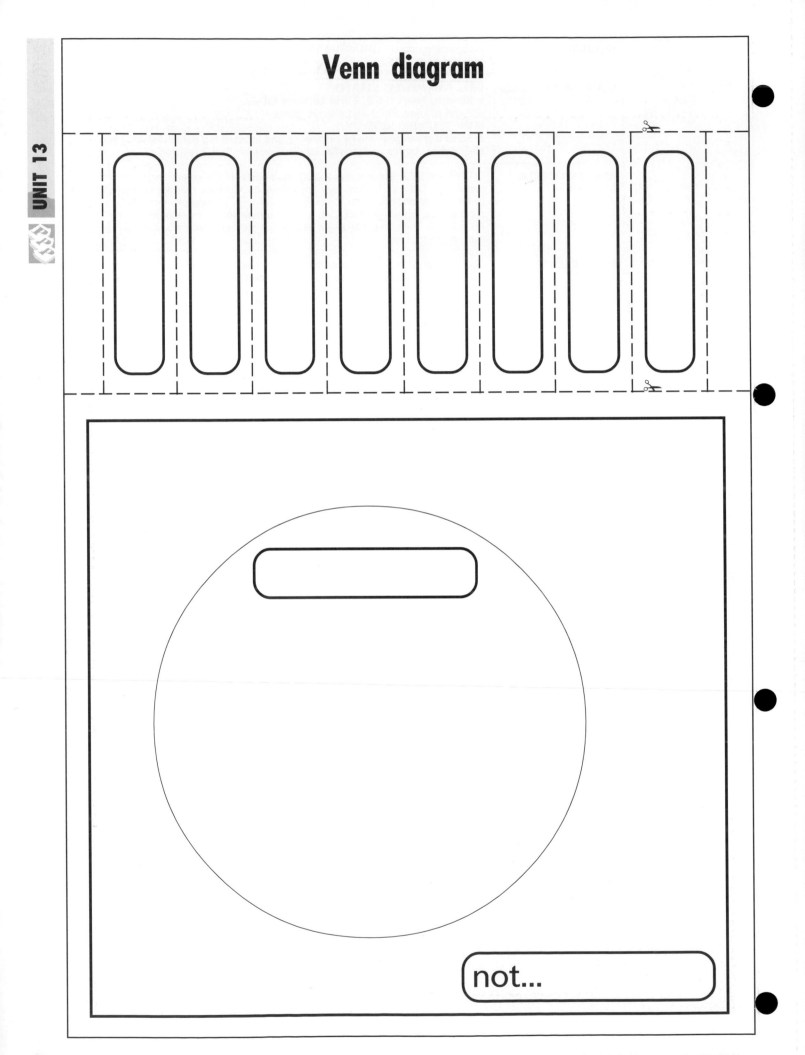

not...

Carroll diagram

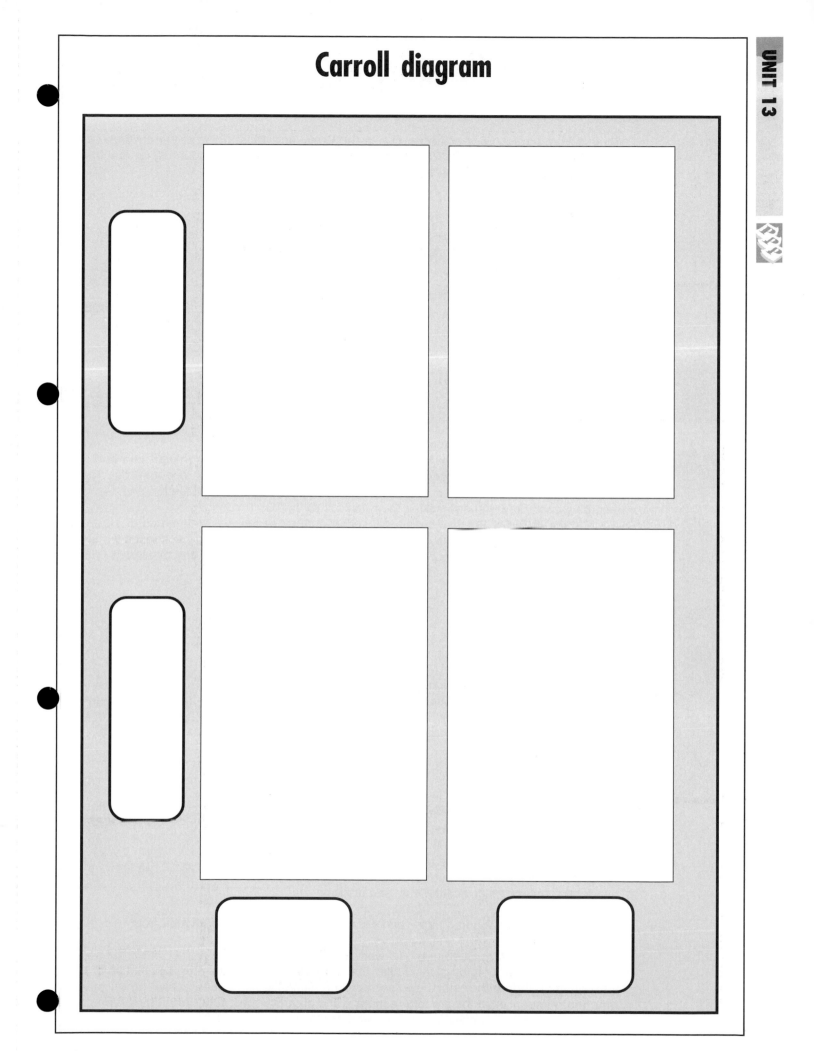

UNIT 14: Assess & Review

Choose from the following activities. During the **Group activities**, some of the children can complete assessment sheets 2a and 2b, which assess their skills in counting on and back in tens or hundreds and telling the time.

RESOURCES

A set of large numeral cards 0–10; recording sheets (see below); copies of assessment sheets 2a and 2b; cut-out triangles (see below); timers; squared paper.

PREPARATION

Prepare one copy per group of the table (see figure). Allow space for an entry from each group member.

	Event			
Name				

ORAL AND MENTAL STARTER

ASSESSMENT

Do the children:

● **Know by heart multiplication facts for the 2 and 10 times tables?**

● **Count on or back in tens or hundreds, starting from any two- or three-digit number?**

MULTIPLICATION TABLES: Present each of the 0–10 numeral cards in a random order. The children should multiply each number by 2. Allow a few seconds for calculation and recording each time. Repeat, asking them to multiply by 10.

COUNTING ON/BACK: Practise chanting together number sequences with jumps of 10 and then 100, starting with various small numbers and counting on. Use these sequences in reverse to practise counting back. Practise counting back in tens from any three-digit number, crossing multiples of 100.

GROUP ACTIVITIES

ASSESSMENT

Do the children:

● **Understand division?**

● **Know by heart multiplication facts for the 5 times table?**

● **Recognise unit fractions such as $1/2$ and $1/4$ and use them to find fractions of shapes?**

● **Use units of time and know the relationships between them?**

● **Solve a given problem by organising and interpreting numerical data in simple lists, tables and graphs?**

MULTIPLICATION AND DIVISION: Provide cut-out triangles marked with 5 in one corner, a number from 0–10 in another corner and the third corner left blank. Ask the children to copy the triangle on paper, write the product of the two given numbers in the blank corner, then write four multiplication and division facts relating to these numbers. If the children are not ready to record division facts, restrict the task to multiplication only and discuss division as sharing.

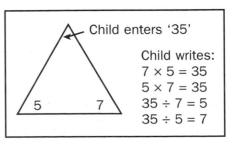

Child enters '35'

Child writes:
$7 \times 5 = 35$
$5 \times 7 = 35$
$35 \div 7 = 5$
$35 \div 5 = 7$

FRACTIONS: Provide squared paper and repeat the **Main teaching activities** from Lessons 3 and 4 of Unit 11.

TIME/HANDLING DATA: Extend Unit 12 work to include timing of various activities, such as speed reading or writing, physical challenges or mathematical puzzles (eg completion of an addition grid). Before they start, give each child a recording sheet (see above) on which to write their times. Leave the group to generate and organise their data. When they have completed a table, ask questions to see whether they can interpret it.

Assessment sheet 2a

Count **on** in tens:

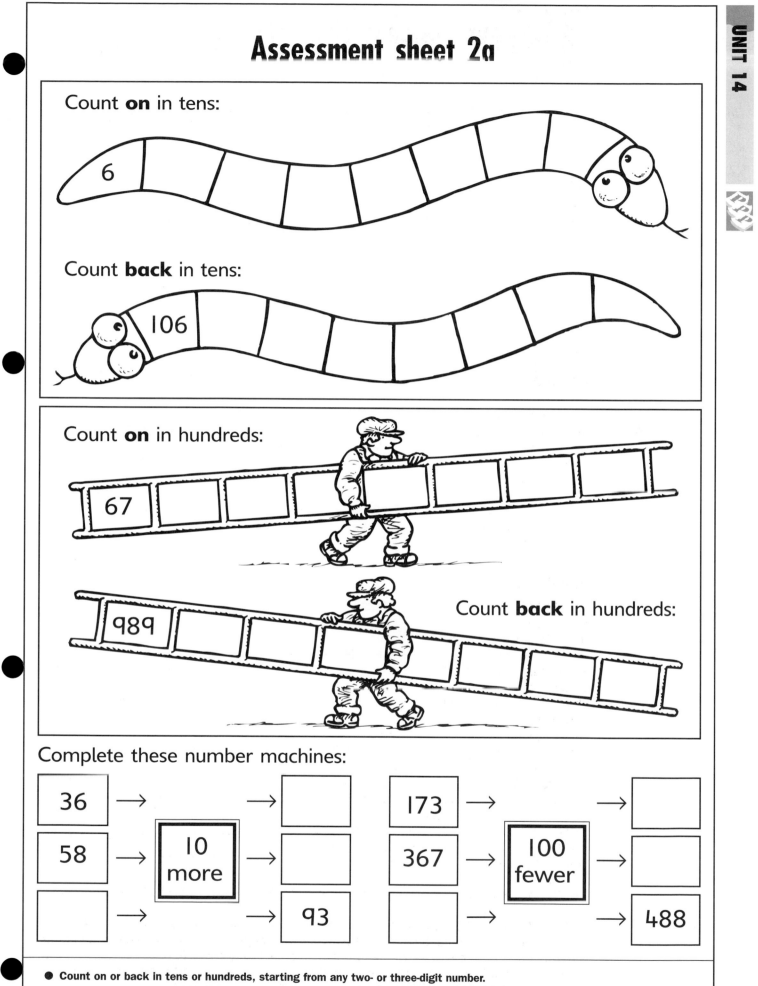

6

Count **back** in tens:

106

Count **on** in hundreds:

67

Count **back** in hundreds:

989

Complete these number machines:

36	→		→	
58	→	10 more	→	
	→		→	93

173	→		→	
367	→	100 fewer	→	
	→		→	488

● Count on or back in tens or hundreds, starting from any two- or three-digit number.

Assessment sheet 2b

What time is shown on each clock? One has already been done for you.

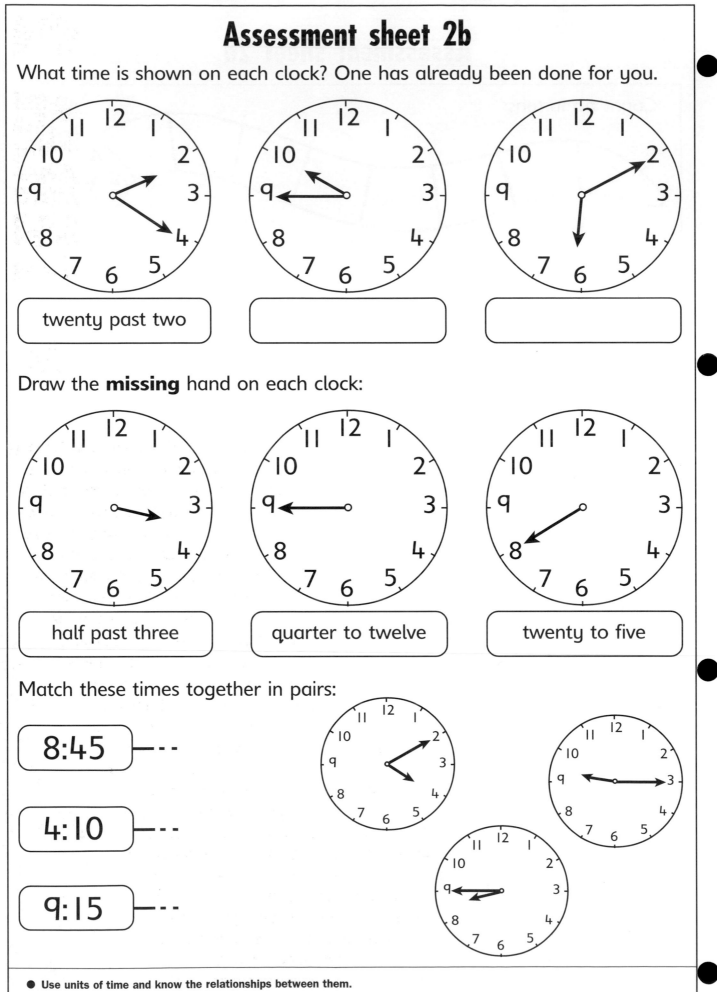

twenty past two

Draw the **missing** hand on each clock:

half past three

quarter to twelve

twenty to five

Match these times together in pairs:

8:45 ---

4:10 ---

9:15 ---

● Use units of time and know the relationships between them.

The nature of the *Framework for Teaching Mathematics* requires that many of the themes of this term parallel those of the first term. These ideas are consolidated and extended. A wider range of table facts are investigated, and division is explored both as repeated subtraction and as the inverse of multiplication. Work involving money requires the use of the full range of coin values, and develops related skills such as 'shopkeeper's addition' for giving change. In measures, attention is given to the types of equipment used for particular applications, along with the associated vocabulary and standard units. Work on time includes the months of the year. Shape and space tasks continue to explore properties of 2-D and 3-D shapes, and children are introduced to location on a simple grid network. Data handling skills taught at the end of the first term are applied in new and challenging contexts, with an opportunity to create and gather information through a short questionnaire.

ENLARGE THIS SHEET TO A3 AND USE IT AS YOUR MEDIUM-TERM PLANNING GRID.

ORAL AND MENTAL SKILLS   **Know by heart all addition and subtraction facts for each number to 20.** Bridge through a multiple of 10, then adjust. Recall doubles of numbers to 10. Identify near doubles. Understand the operation of subtraction and the related vocabulary. Understand that subtraction is the inverse of addition. Check subtraction with addition. Use known number facts and place value to add/subtract mentally. **Choose and use appropriate operations** and ways of calculating **to solve problems.** Use doubling or halving to multiply or divide. Find a small difference by counting up from the smaller to the larger number. Repeat addition or multiplication in a different order. **Recognise unit fractions such as** $^1/_2$, $^1/_4$. Begin to recognise simple equivalent fractions. **Know by heart multiplication facts for the 2, 5 and 10 times tables.** Derive corresponding division facts. Recognise two-digit multiples of 2 and 5. Know by heart all pairs of multiples of 100 with a total of 1000.

Unit	Topic	Objectives: Children will be taught to:
1	Place value, ordering and rounding. Reading numbers from scales.	● Say the number that is 1, 10 or 100 more or less than any given two-digit or three-digit number. ● **Add and subtract mentally a 'near multiple of 10' to or from a two-digit number...** by adding or subtracting 10, 20, 30... and adjusting. ● Compare two given three-digit numbers, say which is more or less, and give a number which lies between them. ● **Order whole numbers to at least 1000**, and position them on a number line. ● Use and understand the vocabulary of estimation and approximation. ● Read scales to the nearest division (labelled or unlabelled).
2–3	Understanding + and –. Mental calculation strategies (+ and –). Money and 'real life' problems. Making decisions and checking results.	● Extend understanding of the operation of addition and recognise that addition can be done in any order. ● Extend understanding that subtraction is the inverse of addition. ● Extend understanding that more than two numbers can be added; add three or four single-digit numbers mentally, or three or four two-digit numbers with the help of apparatus or pencil and paper. ● Solve word problems involving money, including finding totals and giving change, and working out which coins to pay. ● Solve word problems involving numbers in 'real life'. Explain how the problem was solved. ● Recognise all coins. ● **Choose and use appropriate operations (including multiplication and division) to solve word problems.**
4–6	Shape and space. Reasoning about shapes. Measures, and time, including problems.	● Make and describe shapes and patterns: for example, explore the different shapes that can be made from four cubes. ● Read and begin to write the vocabulary relating to position, direction and movement. ● **Identify** and sketch **lines of symmetry in simple cases, and recognise shapes with no lines of symmetry.** ● Read and begin to write the vocabulary related to length, mass and capacity. ● Know the relationships between m and cm, kg and g, l and ml. ● **Use units of time and know the relationships between them (second, minute, day, week, month, year).** ● Read and begin to write the vocabulary related to time. ● Investigate a general statement about familiar shapes by finding examples that satisfy it. ● Classify and describe 3-D and 2-D shapes. ● Know the relationships between km and m, m and cm, kg and g, l and ml. ● To multiply by 10/100, shift the digits one/two places to the left. ● Classify and describe 2-D shapes, referring to their properties.
7	Assess and review.	

ORAL AND MENTAL SKILLS   Solve mathematical problems or puzzles, recognise simple patterns and relationships, generalise and predict. Suggest extensions by asking 'What if...?' **Explain methods and reasoning** orally and, where appropriate, in writing. Investigate a general statement about familiar numbers by finding examples that satisfy it. Use knowledge that addition can be done in any order. Find a small difference by counting up. **Add or subtract mentally a 'near multiple of 10' to or from a two-digit number...** by adding or subtracting 10, 20, 30... and adjusting. Use patterns of similar calculations. Repeat addition or multiplication in a different order. Use doubling or halving, starting from known facts, to multiply or divide. **Know by heart multiplication facts for the 5 times table.** Say the number that is 1, 10 or 100 more or less than any given three-digit number. To multiply by 10, shift the digits of a number one place to the left. **Recognise that division is the inverse of multiplication.** Begin to know the 3 and 4 times tables. Understand and use the vocabulary of comparing and ordering numbers. Compare two given three-digit numbers, say which is more or less, and give a number which lies between them. Round any two-digit number to the nearest 10 and any three-digit number to the nearest 100.

Unit	Topic	Objectives: Children will be taught to:
8	Counting and properties of numbers. Reasoning about numbers.	● Count on or back in twos starting from any two-digit number, and recognise odd and even numbers to at least 100. ● Count on in steps of 3, 4 or 5. ● **Count on or back in tens or hundreds, starting from any two- or three-digit number.** ● Recognise three-digit multiples of 50 and 100. ● Count on in steps of 3, 4 or 5 from any small number to at least 50, then back again.
9–10	Understanding + and –. Mental calculation strategies (+ and –). Understanding × and ÷. Mental calculation strategies (× and ÷). Money and 'real life' problems. Making decisions and checking results.	● **Recognise that division is the inverse of multiplication.** ● **Understand division** as grouping (repeated subtraction). ● Extend understanding of the operation of subtraction. ● Recognise all coins and notes. ● Solve word problems involving money, including finding totals and giving change, and working out which coins to pay. Explain how the problem was solved. ● Extend understanding that more than two numbers can be added. ● Use knowledge that addition can be done in any order to do mental calculations more efficiently. For example: put the larger number first and count on; add three or four small numbers by putting the largest number first and/or finding pairs totalling 9, 10 or 11; partition into '5 and a bit' when adding 6, 7, 8 or 9. ● Partition into tens and units, then recombine. ● Derive quickly all pairs of multiples of 5 with a total of 100. ● Say or write a subtraction statement corresponding to a given addition statement.
11	Fractions.	● **Recognise unit fractions such as** $^1/_2$ **and** $^1/_4$, **and use them to find fractions of shapes and numbers.** ● Estimate a simple fraction. ● Recognise that halving is the inverse of doubling. ● Begin to recognise simple equivalent fractions. ● Compare familiar fractions. ● Begin to recognise simple fractions that are several parts of a whole, such as $^3/_4$. ● Derive quickly halves corresponding to doubles of all whole numbers to at least 20.
12	Handling data.	● **Solve a given problem by organising and interpreting numerical data in simple lists, tables and graphs,** for example: Carroll diagrams, Venn diagrams.
13	Assess and review.	

UNIT 1

ORGANISATION (3 LESSONS)

LEARNING OUTCOMES	ORAL AND MENTAL STARTER	MAIN TEACHING ACTIVITY	PLENARY
LESSON 1 ● Say the number that is 1, 10 or 100 more or less than any given two-digit or three-digit number. ● **Add and subtract mentally a 'near multiple of 10' to or from a two-digit number**... by adding or subtracting 10, 20, 30... and adjusting.	ADDITION BONDS: Focus on bonds with numbers to 10.	NEARLY NUMBERS: Add near multiples of 10; add 1, 10 or 100 repeatedly.	Sate the number 1, 10 or 100 more or fewer than a given number.
LESSON 2 ● Compare two given three-digit numbers, say which is more or less, and give a number which lies between them. ● **Order whole numbers to at least 1000**, and position them on a number line. ● Use and understand the vocabulary of estimation and approximation.	SUBTRACTION BONDS: Focus on bonds with numbers to 10.	GOING UP: Order two-digit numbers on an unstructured number line.	Order three-digit numbers on a number line with markings.
LESSON 3 ● Read scales to the nearest division (labelled or unlabelled).	ADDITION BONDS 2: Focus on bridging through multiples of 10.	SCALES: Read from various scales.	Measure using scales; record using correct units.

ORAL AND MENTAL SKILLS **Know by heart all addition and subtraction facts for each number to 20.** Bridge through a multiple of 10, then adjust.

All lessons in this unit are given in full.

LESSON 1

RESOURCES

A selection of number lines, calculators, counting apparatus and number grids; a set of prepared flashcards (see **Plenary**); copies of 1–100 square (page 16); plain paper.

PREPARATION

Make an enlarged copy of page 16. Prepare flashcards as detailed in **Plenary**.

LEARNING OUTCOMES

ORAL AND MENTAL STARTER
● **Know by heart all addition facts for each number to 20.**

MAIN TEACHING ACTIVITY
● Say the number that is 1, 10 or 100 more or less than any given two-digit or three-digit number.
● **Add and subtract mentally a 'near multiple of 10' to or from a two-digit number**... by adding or subtracting 10, 20, 30... and adjusting.

ORAL AND MENTAL STARTER

ADDITION BONDS: Recap on addition bonds, focusing on rapid recall. By questioning, try to confirm that the children are using strategies such as counting on from the larger number and/or re-ordering the numbers. Take facts for numbers to 10 as your 'bottom line' for the class, though you may extend to numbers to 20 with some children.

VOCABULARY

More; less; sequence; pattern; count on/back; count in ones, twos, threes, fours, fives and so on...; continue.

MAIN TEACHING ACTIVITY

NEARLY NUMBERS: Explain that this lesson is about addition. Highlight a number on the 1–100 square and ask what number is 9, 19 and 29 more than that number. Discuss strategies used (eg going down a column and back one place along a row to add 9). Try for other 'near-multiples' of 10, eg 11, 21, 28, 38. Encourage the class to visualise these as movements on the 1–100 square, without pointing or touch counting.

Talk about number patterns that grow (eg times tables). Start at a number other than 0 (eg 1), and do a 'nearly times table' (eg 6, 11, 16...). Talk about how you might use the various resources to continue adding a constant amount from a given number. Working mentally, add on from some three-digit numbers (eg 135, 139, 143...).

Ask the children to select a starting number and add on 1, 10 or 100 to it several times. They can use any of the resources provided to help with this. They could also start with a larger number and count back in one of these steps. They should record their work on plain paper as a number chain, snake or ladder.

DIFFERENTIATION

You may wish to allocate appropriate starting numbers, steps and even calculating aids to individuals or groups, based on prior attainment. Alternatively, you may leave the choice more open, discussing the relative merits of different practical aids and/or moderating up or down the complexity of work which individuals have chosen.

PLENARY

Use flashcards with numbers of varying scale: one side showing a bold number with the instruction '1 more', '10 more' or '100 more', and the reverse showing the solution in bold, with the inverse instruction ('1 fewer', etc). Target individuals and assess their counting on/back skills.

LESSON 2

RESOURCES

Numeral cards and 1–100 square (pages 13 and 16); blank cards; Blu-tack.

PREPARATION

Make an enlarged copy of the 1–100 square, and cut nine blank square cards to cover cells on the grid. (Alternatively, use a washable marker to highlight numbers.)

LEARNING OUTCOMES

ORAL AND MENTAL STARTER
● **Know by heart all subtraction facts for each number to 20.**

MAIN TEACHING ACTIVITY
● Compare two given three-digit numbers, say which is more or less, and give a number which lies between them.
● **Order whole numbers to at least 1000**, and position them on a number line.
● Understand and use the vocabulary of estimation and approximation.

ORAL AND MENTAL STARTER

SUBTRACTION BONDS: Recap as in Lesson 1, focusing on quick recall of subtraction facts for all numbers to 10.

MAIN TEACHING ACTIVITY

COMBINATIONS: Provide three digits (eg 3, 6 and 8). Ask the children to suggest (and say in words) three-digit numbers they can make with these digits. Write combinations on the board (eg 386, 863, 836). Ask which numbers are the largest and the smallest. Write the numbers **in between** in ascending order. Talk about the different two-digit numbers that can be made (eg 38, 63). Highlight these on the 0–99 grid; the numbers should form a

<table>
<tr><td>**VOCABULARY**</td></tr>
<tr><td>Units; ones; tens; hundreds; digit; one-, two- or three-digit number; place value.</td></tr>
</table>

pattern with line symmetry. You might also allow double digits (eg 33). Repeat with another three digits. Ask: *Why does that happen?* (Because there is a 'closed set' of digits.)

Ask the children (working in pairs) to select three digits and repeat the activity on plain paper, then present the numbers in ascending order as a number snake, train or ladder.

DIFFERENTIATION

Less able: Use numeral tiles to make the numbers.
More able: Make three-digit numbers and order them within 1000. Very able pupils could try to arrange these numbers on a number line marked only at its ends (0 and 1000).

PLENARY

Repeat the first part of the **Main teaching activity** with a new set of digits. This time, draw a 0–1000 number line with numbered markings at 100, 200, 300 etc. Ask children to generate three-digit numbers and place them in their approximate positions on the line.

RESOURCES

A counting stick; photocopiable page 90; an OHT of page 90; a dry-wipe marker; a selection of scales and items to measure (see page 90 for ideas); OHP (optional).

PREPARATION

Make one copy per child of page 90, with measurements and dial readings inserted to match different abilities (see **Differentiation**). Make an OHT of the unmodified page 90.

LEARNING OUTCOMES

ORAL AND MENTAL STARTER
● Bridge through a multiple of 10, then adjust.

MAIN TEACHING ACTIVITY
● Read scales to the nearest division (labelled or unlabelled).

VOCABULARY

Measure;
measuring
scale; division.

ORAL AND MENTAL STARTER

ADDITION BONDS 2: Extend from Lesson 1 by focusing on addition bonds that take the total over 10, 20 or 30. Ask individuals how they solved the problems, making the point that 'bridging the 10' (eg 6 + 5 = 6 + 4 + 1 = 10 + 1) is one of several possible strategies. Use a counting stick as a visual aid. Some children may recall these bonds directly.

MAIN TEACHING ACTIVITY

SCALES: Talk about where dials and other scales can be found in everyday life. Why do we need to measure speed, capacity etc? Show the OHT of page 90. Discuss where and why we might see and use these devices, referring to them by their names. Use a non-permanent marker to set readings of increasing difficulty on the OHT.

When the children seem to be confident in reading scales, give modified copies of page 90 to groups, and monitor their progress.

DIFFERENTIATION

The sheets might be graded at 3 levels: aligning directly to a number, at a mid-point interval, and anywhere between markers (perhaps including fractions of the basic unit).

PLENARY

Group the class around you. Display a selection of measuring equipment and items to measure. Ask volunteers to measure the items (ie their length, mass or capacity). Consider what units are used, and record these in a written form.

Measuring scales

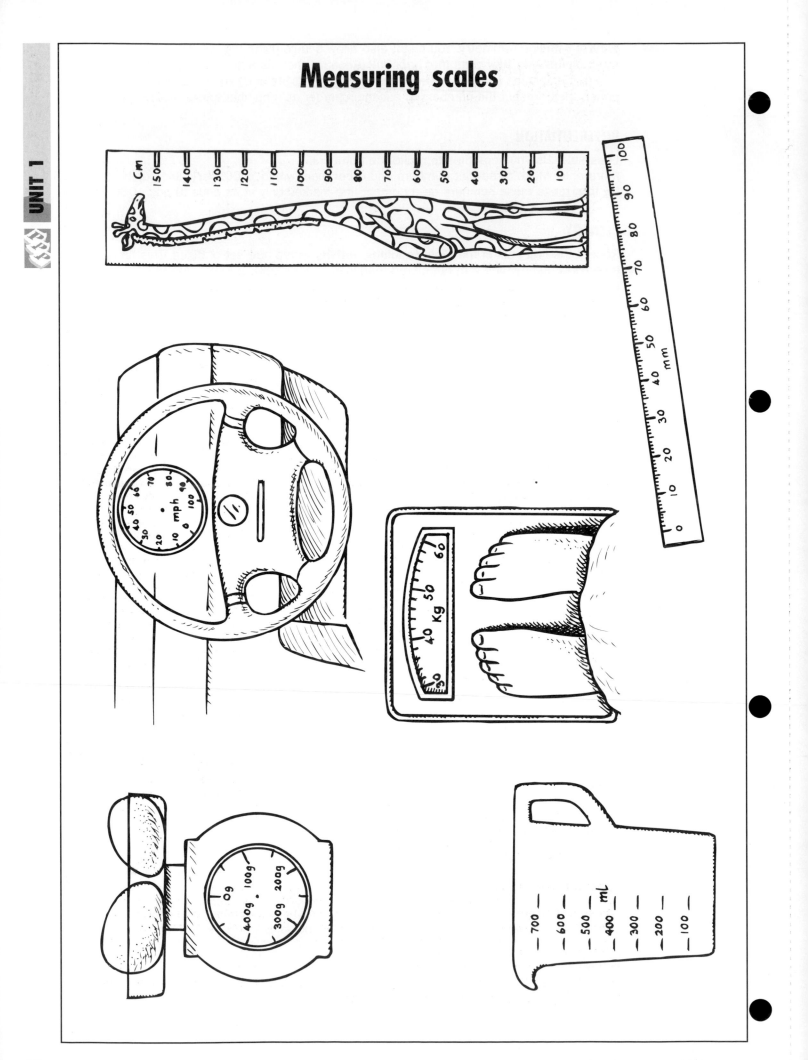

UNITS 2-3

ORGANISATION (10 LESSONS)

LEARNING OUTCOMES	ORAL AND MENTAL STARTER	MAIN TEACHING ACTIVITY	PLENARY
LESSON 1 • Extend understanding of the operation of addition and recognise that addition can be done in any order. • Extend understanding that subtraction is the inverse of addition.	COUNTING ON: Subtract by counting on.	+ AND −: Discuss addition and subtraction methods; answer written questions.	Create an addition and subtraction wordbank.
LESSON 2 +3 • Extend understanding of the operation of addition and recognise that addition can be done in any order. • Extend understanding that more than two numbers can be added; add three or four single-digit numbers mentally, or three or four two-digit numbers with the help of apparatus or pencil and paper.	MORE DOUBLES: Recall or calculate doubles within 20. NEAR DOUBLES: Recall or calculate within 20.	NUMBER PAIRS: Make different totals with pairs of numbers. Extend to making different totals with two or more numbers.	Compile a class grid of results. Compile a class grid of results.
LESSON 4 • Solve word problems involving money, including finding totals and giving change, and working out which coins to pay.	TAKE AWAY: Flashcard test and discussion on subtraction.	BURGER BAR: Solve money problems involving addition.	Review work and methods of converting and recording money.
LESSON 5 • Solve word problems involving numbers in 'real life'. Explain how the problem was solved.	BREAKDOWN: Addition and subtraction involving larger numbers.	STAMPS: Solve money problems involving multiplication and/ or division.	Discuss equivalence between different coin values.
LESSON 6 +7 • Recognise all coins.	WORK IT OUT: Solve word problems by identifying operations. NEAR DOUBLES: Extend to 'not so near' doubles.	MAKING MONEY: Find equivalent coins to 50p. Find equivalent coins to £1.00.	Discuss relationships between different coin values.
LESSON 8 • Solve word problems involving money. Explain how the problem was solved.	STRATEGIES: Discuss strategies for mental addition, subtraction and multiplication.	HARD CASH: Word problems involving money.	Discuss money calculation skills and their real-life uses.
LESSON 9 +10 • Solve word problems involving numbers in 'real life'. Explain how the problem was solved. • **Choose and use appropriate operations (including multiplication and division) to solve word problems.**	HALFWAY THERE: Discuss strategies for doubling and/or halving a number.	WORD PROBLEMS: Create separate word problems involving + and −, then × and ÷.	Challenge the class with word problems written by groups.

ORAL AND MENTAL SKILLS   Recall doubles of numbers to 10. Identify near doubles. Understand the operation of subtraction and the related vocabulary. Understand that subtraction is the inverse of addition. Check subtraction with addition. Use known number facts and place value to add/subtract mentally. **Choose and use appropriate operations** and ways of calculating **to solve problems**. Use doubling or halving to multiply or divide. Find a small difference by counting up from the smaller to the larger number. Repeat addition or multiplication in a different order.

Lessons 1, 2, 4, 6, 8 and 9 are given in full. Lessons 3, 5, 7 and 10 follow on from what has already been taught and are given in outline.

LEARNING OUTCOMES
ORAL AND MENTAL STARTER
● Understand the operation of subtraction and the related vocabulary.

MAIN TEACHING ACTIVITY
● Solve word problems involving money, including finding totals and giving change, and working out which coins to pay.

VOCABULARY
Money; coin; price; cost; spend; spent; how much; total; amount; value.

ORAL AND MENTAL STARTER

TAKE AWAY: Use the prepared flashcards for a 'question and answer' session. At times, take stock by asking the children to describe their strategies and mental models.

MAIN TEACHING ACTIVITY

BURGER BAR: Explain that this lesson is about adding up prices. Recap on coin values. Ask: *Why are coins often called 'loose change'?* Practise adding up amounts below £1.00, calculating change from £1.00 and deciding which coins could make that much change.

Provide a visual representation of the prices shown below (or develop your own version). Set the children the following challenges: *Select one item from each category to make your favourite meal, then work out the total cost. How much is the cheapest meal? How much is the most expensive meal? Find a meal costing as close to £1.60 as you can.* Let them work individually.

Drinks	Orange juice	32p
	Fizzy drink	44p
	Milk shake	35p
Snacks	Baked potato	58p
	Hot dog	65p
	Burger	82p
Desserts	Apple pie	70p
	Ice cream	62p
	Ice lolly	54p

DIFFERENTIATION

Less able: Choose from a smaller range of cheaper items; use money (say 10p and 1p coins) as counting equipment.
More able: Try to find all 27 price combinations, perhaps working together in a group and using a strategic (logical) approach.

PLENARY

Discuss the findings of different groups. Confirm methods of converting pounds to/from pence, and demonstrate the conventional forms of recording. Let the children make any necessary adjustments to their own work. Discuss what coins would be used. Consider the change from £5.00, £10.00 etc.

RESOURCES	Coins; counting apparatus (optional).
LEARNING OUTCOMES	**ORAL AND MENTAL STARTER** ● Check subtraction with addition ● Use known number facts and place value to add/subtract mentally. **MAIN TEACHING ACTIVITY** ● Solve word problems involving numbers in 'real life'. Explain how the problem was solved.
ORAL AND MENTAL STARTER	BREAKDOWN: Ask questions of the order 54 + 6, 97 – 8. Discuss how breaking the task down can make it more manageable, eg 54 + 6 = 50 + 4 + 6 = 50 + 10. With subtraction, consider the value of checking with addition, eg 97 – 8 = 89, check using 89 + 8.
MAIN TEACHING ACTIVITY	STAMPS: Provide a calculation task, organised as in Lesson 4. A suggested starting point is: *Stamps cost 28p or 24p. How many 24p stamps could you buy with just £1.00? If you could buy them in combination, find a way of spending exactly £2.00.*
DIFFERENTIATION	Less able: Offer more closed questions involving stamps of lower value. More able: Find how many 24p stamps match a set of six 28p stamps. Find other matching sets of different stamps.
PLENARY	Talk about equivalence between coins (eg *How many 20p coins make £1.00?*).This will prepare the children for related work in Unit 3.

RESOURCES

Photocopiable page 100; real coins (as required); other counting apparatus (including calculators); large sheets of paper; coin stamps (optional).

PREPARATION

Create giant card coins using page 100. These will support teaching on many future occasions. You will need multiple copies of the smaller values.

LEARNING OUTCOMES

ORAL AND MENTAL STARTER
● **Choose and use appropriate operations** and ways of calculating **to solve problems**.
● Identify near doubles.

MAIN TEACHING ACTIVITY
● Recognise all coins.

VOCABULARY

How many?;
same as;
multiple of.

ORAL AND MENTAL STARTER

WORK IT OUT: Provide some word problems that do not overtly state what mathematical operation is needed, eg *I have £2.00 to give to four children. How much should I give each child so that they all have the same amount?* Discuss how the children identified the necessary operation and how they worked it out.

MAIN TEACHING ACTIVITY

MAKING MONEY: Display a giant 5p coin and invite pupils to total an equivalent amount using a combination of 2p and 1p coins. Go on to making 50p with 10p and 20p coins.

Ask the children to find as many different ways of making 50p as they can. They should write '50p' in the centre of a blank page, then draw the combinations as a spider diagram. They can work in groups on large sheets of paper, perhaps using multiple copies of page 100 to cut and paste some combinations.

DIFFERENTIATION

Organise the class into two or three groups, based on your judgement of their money skills. You might ask them to choose the level of difficulty and modify it if problems arise.
Less able: Make 20p or 10p instead of 50p. Use coin stamps to help with recording.

More able: Make £1.00 although it would be difficult and unrealistic to show **all** the possible combinations.

PLENARY

Discuss the relationships between different coin values, eg *How many 20p coins are equivalent to six 10p coins?*

LESSON 7

For the **Oral and mental starter**, recap on NEAR DOUBLES from Lesson 3, and increase the range of numbers used. You might also look at 'not so near doubles' (eg 16 + 18) which involves compensation of both numbers (ie 17 + 17). For the **Main teaching activity**, extend Lesson 6 to making a total of £1.00 or £2.00. Less able children could work to 50p. More able children could record in a table, with coin values as headings and a combination of coins in each row. Use the **Plenary** from Lesson 6, with higher coin values.

RESOURCES

Photocopiable page 101; OHP (optional).

PREPARATION

Prepare an OHT of the unmodified page 101. Modify copies of page 101 to suit the needs of specific individuals or groups (see **Differentiation**).

LEARNING OUTCOMES

ORAL AND MENTAL STARTER
● Repeat addition or multiplication in a different order.

MAIN TEACHING ACTIVITY
● Solve word problems involving money. Explain how the problem was solved.

VOCABULARY

Answer; how did you work it out?; money; costs more; calculate; cost; show your working.

ORAL AND MENTAL STARTER

STRATEGIES: Present some written problems involving two-digit addition and subtraction and/or single-digit multiplication, eg 62 + 17 or 4 × 5 × 2. Discuss the strategies used, asking whether the order of the numbers is important. Emphasise that, in multiplication and addition, re-ordering the numbers for calculation can be helpful (eg 4 × 5 × 2 may be easier to work out as 5 × 2 × 4).

MAIN TEACHING ACTIVITY

HARD CASH: Conduct a class discussion of the language of money. Use a prepared OHT of the unmodified page 101, inserting and replacing numbers as you go through the questions in order. Discuss appropriate strategies for calculation. If you develop this whole-class teaching fully, the task below should be largely consolidatory and relatively brief.

   Distribute the modified sheets (see **Differentiation**), and give support as required. To encourage use of mathematical vocabulary, you might allow collaboration.

DIFFERENTIATION

Less able: Answer oral questions based on a simple version of page 101. Work with additional support.
Average: Shopping totals up to £10; pocket money in convenient multiples of 50p (eg £3.50 per week); swimming fees in mixed units (£ and p).
More able: Extend beyond £10 and/or answer questions involving more than one step.

PLENARY

Ask children to identify situations in which they might be required to make mental calculations involving money. Discuss useful strategies, such as rounding up and then compensating.

LESSON 9 +10

RESOURCES

No specific resources needed.

PREPARATION

Prepare some word problems involving addition and subtraction, eg *I think of a number and subtract 42. If the answer is 16, what number was I thinking about originally? I ate 13 raisins and had 37 left. How many did I start with? I have 26p but I need 62p. How much more do I need?* For Lesson 10, prepare some similar questions involving multiplication and division.

LEARNING OUTCOMES

ORAL AND MENTAL STARTER
● Use doubling or halving to multiply or divide.

MAIN TEACHING ACTIVITY
● Solve word problems involving numbers in 'real life'. Explain how the problem was solved.
● **Choose and use appropriate operations (including multiplication and division) to solve word problems.**

VOCABULARY

Listen, think; imagine; number sentence; word sentence; write; question; explain; lots of; groups of; times; double; halve; divide; divided by.

ORAL AND MENTAL STARTER

HALFWAY THERE: Present some numbers and ask the children to halve and/or double them. Discuss how each answer was derived. Use this to emphasise links between addition and multiplication, and between subtraction and division.

MAIN TEACHING ACTIVITY

WORD PROBLEMS: Set some problems orally for the class. Develop examples of the type suggested in **Preparation**, and explain some appropriate methods and strategies for calculation.

The children work collaboratively in groups to create a word problem, suitably illustrated, for addition and another for subtraction.

DIFFERENTIATION

Less able: Focus on a single operation, using a given set of key words and phrases as prompts.
More able: Work with numbers to 1000 and/or add more than two numbers.

PLENARY

Each group presents its 'best' question for the class to solve. These could be displayed as interactive posters, with the answers on the reverse side.

LESSON 10

Continue the **Oral and mental starter** from Lesson 9. Repeat Lesson 9s **Main teaching activity**, with problems involving multiplication and/or division. Groups who were less successful last time could build on their experience and repeat the exercise for addition and subtraction, or try to create a word problem involving repeated addition. More able groups could create two-step problems: addition or subtraction first, then multiplication or division. Develop the **Plenary** as for Lesson 9.

Word problems

1. What is the total of _____ and _____ ?

2. Add _____ to _____ .

3. How many more is _____ than _____ ?

4. Find the difference between _____ and _____ .

5. What is the sum of _____ and _____ ?

6. I think of a number. I add _____ . The answer is _____ .
   What is my number?

7. What must you add to _____ to give _____?

8. The total of _____ and _____ is _____ .

9. What number is _____ fewer than _____ ?

10. What is the number halfway between _____ and _____ ?

1–50 grid

1	2	3	4	5	6	7	8	9	10
11	12	13	14	15	16	17	18	19	20
21	22	23	24	25	26	27	28	29	30
31	32	33	34	35	36	37	38	39	40
41	42	43	44	45	46	47	48	49	50

Coin cards

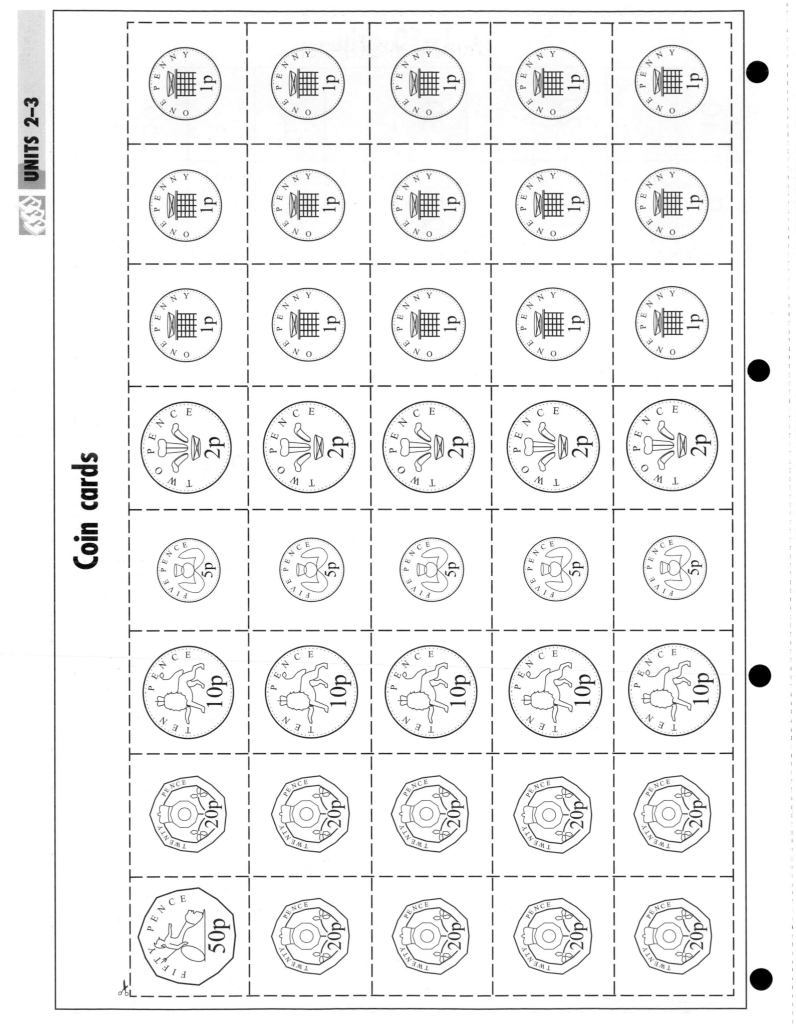

Money problems

Shopping list

Eggs

Bread

Milk

How much altogether?

Pocket money

[   ] per week

Computer game

How many weeks to save?

Swimming Sunday

Opens 10am

Adult swim

Junior swim

How much for _____,

_____ and _____?

Chocolate bar

Ice cream

Toothbrush

Pen

Birthday card

Buy some of these items to spend exactly £

UNITS 4-6

ORGANISATION (13 LESSONS)

	LEARNING OUTCOMES	ORAL AND MENTAL STARTER	MAIN TEACHING ACTIVITY	PLENARY
LESSON 1 +2	• Make and describe shapes and patterns. • Read and begin to write the vocabulary relating to position, direction and movement.	$1/2$: Relate the symbol $1/2$ to ×2. $1/4$: Relate the symbol $1/4$ to ×4.	PENTOMINOES: Make different shapes with five interlocking cubes. Combine the shapes in a jigsaw.	Share solutions. Play a game using co-ordinates.
LESSON 3	• **Identify** and sketch **lines of symmetry in simple cases, and recognise shapes with no lines of symmetry.**	NUMBER FRACTIONS: Find $1/4$ and $1/2$ of a set.	LINE SYMMETRY: Investigate using cubes and mirror.	Share the solution. Play a modified version of the co-ordinate game.
LESSON 4	• Read and begin to write the vocabulary related to length, mass and capacity. • Know the relationships between m and cm, kg and g, l and ml. • **Use units of time and know the relationships between them (second, minute).**	PIECES OF 8: Divide a shape into eighths; explore equivalent fractions.	MEASURES: Mix and match words and images relating to different measures.	Consider equivalent metric units.
LESSON 5	• Read and begin to write the vocabulary related to time. • **Use units of time and know the relationships between them (day, week, month, year).**	SHAPE FRACTIONS: Use fractions of shapes to explore equivalence.	TIME: Explore units of time using calendars.	Learn a rhyme about the calendar year.
LESSON 6 +7	• Investigate a general statement about familiar shapes by finding examples that satisfy it.	2× AND 5×: Count in 2s and 5s. 2 TIMES: Recite the 2× table.	FOUR SIDES: Sort quadrilaterals by their properties. Name and define quadrilaterals.	Discuss the names of polygons. Share and refine definitions of shapes.
LESSON 8	• **Identify** and sketch **lines of symmetry in simple cases, and recognise shapes with no lines of symmetry.**	5 TIMES: Recite the 5× table.	AXIS: Identify line symmetry in quadrilaterals.	Share findings and discuss any misconceptions.
LESSON 9	• Make and describe shapes and patterns: for example, explore the different shapes that can be made from four cubes. • Classify and describe 3-D and 2-D shapes.	MORE 2×: Recall or derive 2× table facts.	TANGRAM: Create various 2-D shapes from four triangles.	Make 2-D shapes with four cubes.
LESSON 10	• Read and begin to write the vocabulary related to position, direction and movement.	MORE 5×: Recall or derive 5× table facts.	INTO SPACE: Create a picture from a set of co-ordinates.	Play a modified version of the co-ordinate game. Consider strategies.
LESSON 11	• Know the relationships between km and m, m and cm, kg and g, l and ml. • To multiply by 10/100, shift the digits one/two places to the left.	HOW MANY TENS?: Count in 10s to 100 and in 100s to 1000.	UNITS: Explore relationships between metric units of measure.	Discuss units used to measure in different contexts.

	LEARNING OUTCOMES	ORAL AND MENTAL STARTER	MAIN TEACHING ACTIVITY	PLENARY
LESSON 12	● Read and begin to write the vocabulary related to position, direction and movement.	10 TIMES: Recall the 10× table and derive ÷10 facts.	INTO SPACE 2: Write a set of co-ordinates which create a picture.	As for Lesson 10. Discuss effective strategies.
LESSON 13	● Classify and describe 2-D shapes, referring to their properties.	2 AND 5 TIMES: Recall the 2× and 5× tables. Derive ÷2 and ÷5 facts.	SHAPE REVIEW: Draw 2-D shapes, given only their names.	Discuss and name some common 3-D shapes.

ORAL AND MENTAL SKILLS   Recognise unit fractions such as $^1/_2$, $^1/_4$. Begin to recognise simple equivalent fractions. **Know by heart multiplication facts for the 2, 5 and 10 times tables.** Derive corresponding division facts. Recognise two-digit multiples of 2 and 5. Know by heart all pairs of multiples of 100 with a total of 1000.

Lessons 1, 3–6, 9–11 and 13 are shown in full. Lessons 2, 7, 8 and 12 follow on from what has already been taught and are given in outline.

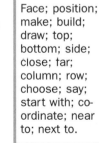

RESOURCES

Cards marked $\frac{1}{2}$ and **× 2**; interlocking cubes; plain or squared paper.

PREPARATION

Each group (up to four children) will need 60 cubes.

LEARNING OUTCOMES

ORAL AND MENTAL STARTER
● Recognise unit fractions such as $^1/_2$, $^1/_4$.

MAIN TEACHING ACTIVITY
● Make and describe shapes and patterns.
● Read and begin to write the vocabulary relating to position, direction and movement.

VOCABULARY
Face; position; make; build; draw; top; bottom; side; close; far; column; row; choose; say; start with; co-ordinate; near to; next to.

ORAL AND MENTAL STARTER

$^1/_2$: Present the symbols $\frac{1}{2}$ and **× 2** on cards, and repeat the doubling and halving exercise from Lessons 9 and 10, Unit 3. Hold up either card, without speaking, and write a number on the board. The children have to say the answer.

MAIN TEACHING ACTIVITY

PENTOMINOES: Explain that this lesson is about making shapes. Ask each group to make a flat (2-D) shape using five cubes. Now ask them to conceal the shape under the table, and invite a group to describe their shape in words for the class to build. Repeat with a couple more groups. Explain that the shapes they have made are collectively known as **pentominoes**.

Set the groups the task of finding 12 different pentominoes using 60 cubes. Note that the last couple can be quite hard to find, but that one shape involves a reflection of the other. Some shapes may appear to differ, but are simply orientated in a different way. Towards the end of the session, provide paper for recording. Squared paper can be used, although plain paper tends to give more diagnostic information about children's visual perception.

DIFFERENTIATION

Less able: Use fewer cubes (leading to fewer arrangements).
More able: Compare the number of edges on different arrangements.

PLENARY

Discuss the children's findings. Build up a collection of pentominoes on the board, working towards the full set (see figure below). Point out the 'letter' shapes.

LESSON 2

For the **Oral and mental starter**, ¼, present the symbol $\frac{1}{4}$ as in Lesson 1. Talk about strategies for finding quarter of a number, such as halving twice. For the **Main teaching activity**, use the children's recording from Lesson 1 to recreate the pentominoes with cubes. Ask groups to arrange all of them like a jigsaw so that they occupy a 5 × 12 rectangle. This is not an easy task, but the solution is very rewarding! Less able children could be given the 12 pentominoes ready prepared, and an outline of a 5 × 12 rectangle (perhaps with some shapes already drawn in place). More able children could type 'pentominoes' in to a World Wide Web search engine to investigate some of the many interesting sites. For the **Plenary**, share the solution (see figure). Use the idea of a grid to lead into a co-ordinates game: provide a large 8 × 8 grid, pick a 'target' co-ordinate and ask children to volunteer locations as co-ordinates. After each attempt, say *You are cold, lukewarm, warm, hot, boiling* to indicate how near they are.

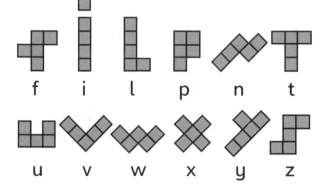

u	u	x	v	v	v	i	i	i	i	t
u	x	x	x	f	v	y	z	z	t	t	t
u	u	x	f	f	v	y	y	z	w	w	t
p	p	n	n	f	f	y	l	z	z	w	w
p	p	p	n	n	n	y	l	l	l	l	w

LESSON 3

RESOURCES

Interlocking cubes; safety mirrors; plain paper.

PREPARATION

Each individual or pair will need an initial set of about 50 cubes.

LEARNING OUTCOMES

ORAL AND MENTAL STARTER
● Begin to recognise simple equivalent fractions.

MAIN TEACHING ACTIVITY
● **Identify** and sketch **lines of symmetry in simple cases, and recognise shapes with no lines of symmetry.**

VOCABULARY

Symmetry; symmetrical; line of symmetry; mirror line; reflection; match; grid; horizontal; vertical.

ORAL AND MENTAL STARTER

NUMBER FRACTIONS: Draw a picture of 8 small shapes (eg triangles). Ask a child to circle a quarter of them. Circle another quarter and ask the class what fraction is now circled, to establish the idea that $^1/_4 + ^1/_4 = ^1/_2$. Repeat the activity with pictures of 12 and 16 shapes.

MAIN TEACHING ACTIVITY

LINE SYMMETRY: Discuss the idea of line symmetry to gain an idea of the range of levels of understanding. At one level, we might expect children to talk about mirror images. At a higher level, they may talk about a point being matched at the equivalent point on the other side of the line of symmetry. Explain this idea if necessary. The further idea that a line joining two corresponding points will cross the line of symmetry at right angles may be too advanced at this stage.

Give individuals or pairs hand mirrors and sets of 50 cubes. Ask them to create a shape with line symmetry using six cubes connected together. Now ask them to make as many such shapes as possible, using the mirror to test for symmetry. Use the time to work intensively with those needing support in using the mirror. The idea is to arrange it across the middle of the shape, so that the shape you see in the mirror matches what you see when it is taken away.

Each successful arrangement should be drawn (freehand) on plain paper. Encourage the children to draw a line showing where to place the mirror. The solutions are shown on the left.

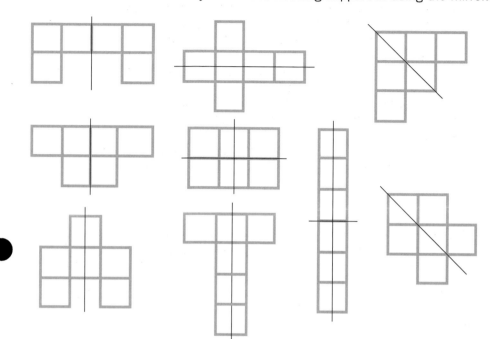

DIFFERENTIATION

Arrange the children in mixed-ability pairs or small groups, making use of peer support. You may need to assign some children as 'recorders' to support their involvement.

PLENARY

Share solutions. Use the ideas of position and direction to lead into a modified version of the co-ordinate game from Lesson 2: instead of using words to give an idea of proximity, specify the number of 'streets' each guess is from the target. A target of (5, 5), for example, is 'three streets away' from a guess of (7, 6). Start a wordbank of position words.

LESSON 4

RESOURCES

Photocopiable page 112; scissors; adhesive; a selection of scales for measuring length; mass; capacity and time.

PREPARATION

Make one copy per child of page 112.

LEARNING OUTCOMES

ORAL AND MENTAL STARTER
● Begin to recognise simple equivalent fractions.

MAIN TEACHING ACTIVITY
● Read and begin to write the vocabulary related to length, mass and capacity.
● Know the relationships between m and cm, kg and g, l and ml.
● Use units of time and know the relationships between them (second, minute).

ORAL AND MENTAL STARTER

PIECES OF 8: Draw a large circle divided into eighths. Label one section $\frac{1}{8}$ and invite individuals to do the same on the other seven. Ask related questions, eg *How many eighths altogether? How many eighths are in half/quarter of a shape?*

VOCABULARY

Capacity; kilogram; gram; mass; litre; millilitre; balance; time; weight; scales; equivalent.

MAIN TEACHING ACTIVITY

MEASURES: Present a range of different scales (see **Resources**). Discuss how they are graduated, looking carefully at the intervals between marked points. Sketch some parts of scales on the board and use them to explore number steps, fractional parts and rounding to the nearest marked point. Recap on the units and their abbreviated forms (eg cm, g).

Give each child a copy of page 112. Explain that the four 'windows' have their panels muddled up. Ask them to cut out all 16 pieces, then sort them into four new windows, each window showing one kind of measure only.

DIFFERENTIATION

Less able: Reduce the number of windows to 8, focusing on two aspects of measure only.
More able: Extend their windows to six panels, using additional units and/or pictures (they could use a mathematical dictionary).

PLENARY

Discuss the solutions. Draw attention to the fact that the two units in each window are **equivalent**. Make the point that, with the exception of time, the units all follow our metric system. Remind the children that the prefix 'kilo' means 1000 of something.

LESSON 5

RESOURCES

A 'year-at-a-glance' sheet or wall calendar; small calendars.

PREPARATION

You will need one small calendar per child.

LEARNING OUTCOMES

ORAL AND MENTAL STARTER
● Begin to recognise simple equivalent fractions.

MAIN TEACHING ACTIVITY
● Read and begin to write the vocabulary related to time.
● Use units of time and know the relationships between them (day, week, month, year).

VOCABULARY
Recite; time; day; week; fortnight; month; year; calendar; date.

ORAL AND MENTAL STARTER

SHAPE FRACTIONS: Draw various shapes cut into halves, quarters and eighths. Ask children to shade various fractional quantities of each shape. Use this as an opportunity to reinforce the equivalence of, say, two quarters and one half.

MAIN TEACHING ACTIVITY

TIME: Discuss the relationship between smaller units of time (second, minute, hour). Go on to talk about larger units of time, perhaps developing wordbank (see **Vocabulary**).

Provide individuals or groups with calendars. Ask them to: find and record the number of days in each month; calculate the total number of days in that year; calculate how many days, and how many weeks, there are until a major school or national event.

DIFFERENTIATION

Less able: Use a calculator.
More able: Convert their answers into minutes or seconds. Look at when leap years arise; use a reference book or CD-ROM to find out why they are necessary.

PLENARY

Tell the children the following poem, and encourage them to commit it to memory: *Thirty days has September, / April, June and November. / All the rest have 31, / Except February alone, / which has 28 days clear / And 29 in each leap year.*

LESSON 6 + 7

RESOURCES

Photocopiable pages 113 and 114; a selection of large shapes for demonstration (square, oblong, rhombus, diamond, parallelogram, kite, trapezium); adhesive (optional); a number line and pointer; a mathematical dictionary (optional); OHP (optional).

PREPARATION

Each child will need a copy of pages 113 and 114 (enlarged, OHT or floor versions would also be useful).

LEARNING OUTCOMES

ORAL AND MENTAL STARTER
● Recognise two-digit multiples of 2 and 5.
● **Know by heart multiplication facts for the 2 and 5 times tables.**

MAIN TEACHING ACTIVITY
● Investigate a general statement about familiar shapes, finding examples that satisfy it.

VOCABULARY

Right angle; corner; edge; square; rectangle; oblong; quadrilateral; rhombus; diamond; parallellogram; kite; trapezium.

ORAL AND MENTAL STARTER

2× AND 5×: Practise counting in twos and fives from 0 (as in Unit 11 of Term 1). Stop at 20 and 50 respectively. Break up the counting sequence in several places and ask: *How many twos/fives was that?* Emphasise the repetitive pattern of the 5× table and the 'even' nature of the 2× table.

MAIN TEACHING ACTIVITY

FOUR SIDES: Ask the question *What is a shape?* (as in Unit 4 of the Autumn term). Discuss what is meant by a **quadrilateral** and talk about the properties of the four-sided shapes on page 114, using an enlarged or OHT version to demonstrate if possible.

Give out copies of pages 113 and 114. Explain that each shape has to be taken through the 'Shape trail'. Each child should cut out the shapes from page 114 and follow the trail with each one. They should end up with one shape correctly 'posted' (redrawn) in each space on the trail. Alternatively, you could create a giant floor version of the trail and work with a large group or the whole class, using questions to guide children through the trail with a large drawing of each shape.

DIFFERENTIATION

Less able: Work in pairs, sharing the sheet (perhaps using an A3 version, and sticking down photocopies of the shapes). The completed sheet can be photocopied for recording purposes.
More able: Use the shape trail to write a definition for each shape, eg 'A rhombus has four sides of equal length, but no right angles'.

RESOURCES
None required.

PREPARATION
Make sure that you are comfortable with the relationships between metric units, eg the fact that 1 litre (1000ml) of water has a mass of 1000g and a volume of 1000cm^3.

LEARNING OUTCOMES

ORAL AND MENTAL STARTER
● **Know by heart: multiplication facts for the 10 times table**; all pairs of multiples of 100 with a total of 1000 (eg 300 + 700).

MAIN TEACHING ACTIVITY
● Know the relationships between km and m, m and cm, kg and g, l and ml.
● To multiply by 10/100, shift the digits one/two places to the left.

VOCABULARY

Kilometre; metre; kilogram; gram; millilitre; litre; length; relationship; tape measure; ruler; metre stick; mile.

ORAL AND MENTAL STARTER
HOW MANY TENS?: Practise counting in tens from 0 to 100, and perhaps beyond. Ask the children how many tens make 100. Present some contextual questions such as: *How many 10p coins make a total of 50p?* Extend by asking *How many 10p coins are needed to make (say) £1.30?* Go on to consider tens in relation to mass: ask questions involving multiples of 100 with a total of 1000, eg *I have 1kg of rice and I use 300g. How much do I have left?* Reinforce the links with complements of 10: 3 + 7 = 10 parallels with 300 + 700 = 1000.

MAIN TEACHING ACTIVITY
UNITS: Begin by talking about distance: *About how far is 6cm? What if the distance was 10 times that amount?* Write the distance before and after in the chosen units: 6cm and 60cm. Write the headings T and U above both distances, and explain how multiplying by 10 has the effect of moving the digits to the left, with 0 acting as a place holder. Demonstrate the same thing for multiplication by 100. Extend the idea of the relationship between units by discussing length, mass and capacity (eg 10mm = 1cm, 100cm = 1m, 1000m = 1km). Practise converting between units (eg 1500g = 1.5kg).

Provide a set of word problems involving the use of standard measures, eg *A bottle of orange squash holds 500ml. I need 6 litres for a party. How many bottles do I need? A 15m ball of string is cut into 4 equal lengths. Write the length of each piece in metres and centimetres. A cat drinks 100ml of milk a day. How long will it take to drink 3 litres? If you use 400g of flour, 250g of milk and 250g of butter, what will be the total mass of the mixture in kg?*

DIFFERENTIATION
Adapt the range and scale of the units in the word problems to broad groupings of ability within the class. Less able children could work within one standard unit (eg *Shorten 1 metre by 25 centimetres*).

PLENARY
Talk about 'fitness for purpose', eg *If I had to measure the playground, what equipment might I use and what would be sensible units of measure? What about a trip to another country... the weight of a pencil... the capacity of a teaspoon?* You may need to distinguish and compare imperial and metric units of measure (eg a kilometre is a little over $^1/_2$ mile).

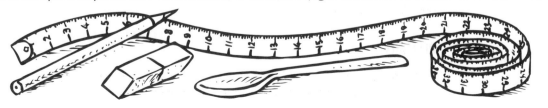

RESOURCES	Squared paper.
LEARNING OUTCOMES	**ORAL AND MENTAL STARTER** ● Know by heart multiplication facts for the 10 times table. Derive corresponding division facts. **MAIN TEACHING ACTIVITY** ● Read and begin to write the vocabulary related to positions, direction and movement.
ORAL AND MENTAL STARTER	10 TIMES: Provide single-digit numbers (eg 7) for the class to multiply by 10. Aim for rapid recall. Reverse by giving a multiple of 10 and inviting the corresponding division sentence (eg '70' is a prompt for '70 ÷ 10 = 7').
MAIN TEACHING ACTIVITY	INTO SPACE 2: Recap on the work done in Lesson 10. Provide squared paper and ask the children to create an 8 × 8 grid. They should draw a very simple picture and note down the set of co-ordinates that make it, then swap with a partner to draw the picture.
DIFFERENTIATION	Less able: Work in pairs; or draw a picture from a given set of co-ordinates. More able: Ask the children to create a picture and 'decorate' the points as ordered pairs.
PLENARY	Play a final game of 'Co-ordinates' (as in Lesson 3). Explain how the solution can be found quickly by selecting a reference point at the origin and an extreme point on the horizontal or vertical axis.

RESOURCES

Some 3-D shapes (see **Plenary**) and/or pictures of them; squared paper.

PREPARATION

Prepare a list from the **Vocabulary** section.

LEARNING OUTCOMES

ORAL AND MENTAL STARTER
● **Know by heart multiplication facts for the 2 and 5 times tables.** Derive corresponding division facts.

MAIN TEACHING ACTIVITY
● Classify and describe 3-D and 2-D shapes, referring to their properties.

VOCABULARY

Triangle; square; rectangle; oblong; pentagon; hexagon; heptagon; octagon; nonagon; decagon.

ORAL AND MENTAL STARTER

2 AND 5 TIMES: Present a series of questions involving the 2× and 5× tables (9 × 2 = ?, 7 × 5 = ?), or deal with them separately. Expect rapid recall or the use of appropriate strategies to derive the answers. Include some corresponding division facts, (35 ÷ 5 = ?).

MAIN TEACHING ACTIVITY

SHAPE REVIEW: Review the work on 2-D shapes in Units 4–6. Use this session as consolidation by revisiting ideas that caused difficulty.

Provide a list of shape names, selected from those given in **Vocabulary**, and ask the children to draw them (based on what they have learned). Some children may find squared paper helpful for drawing the sides of shapes.

DIFFERENTIATION

Less able: Work with a narrower range of shapes.
More able: Extend the list of shapes (including 3-D shapes), using a maths dictionary.

PLENARY

Discuss the names of some common 3-D shapes: prism, pyramid, cuboid, cube, sphere, cylinder, cone. Display real shapes or pictures of them.

Measure windows

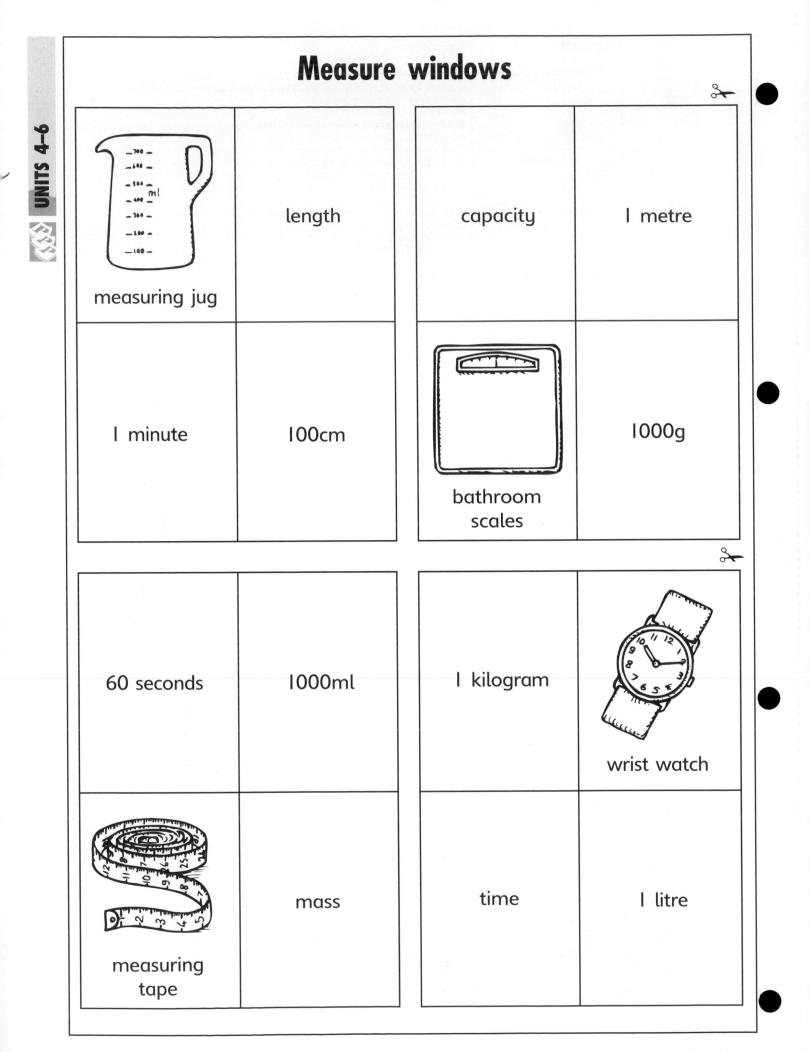

measuring jug	length	capacity	I metre
I minute	100cm	bathroom scales	1000g
60 seconds	1000ml	I kilogram	wrist watch
measuring tape	mass	time	I litre

Shape trail

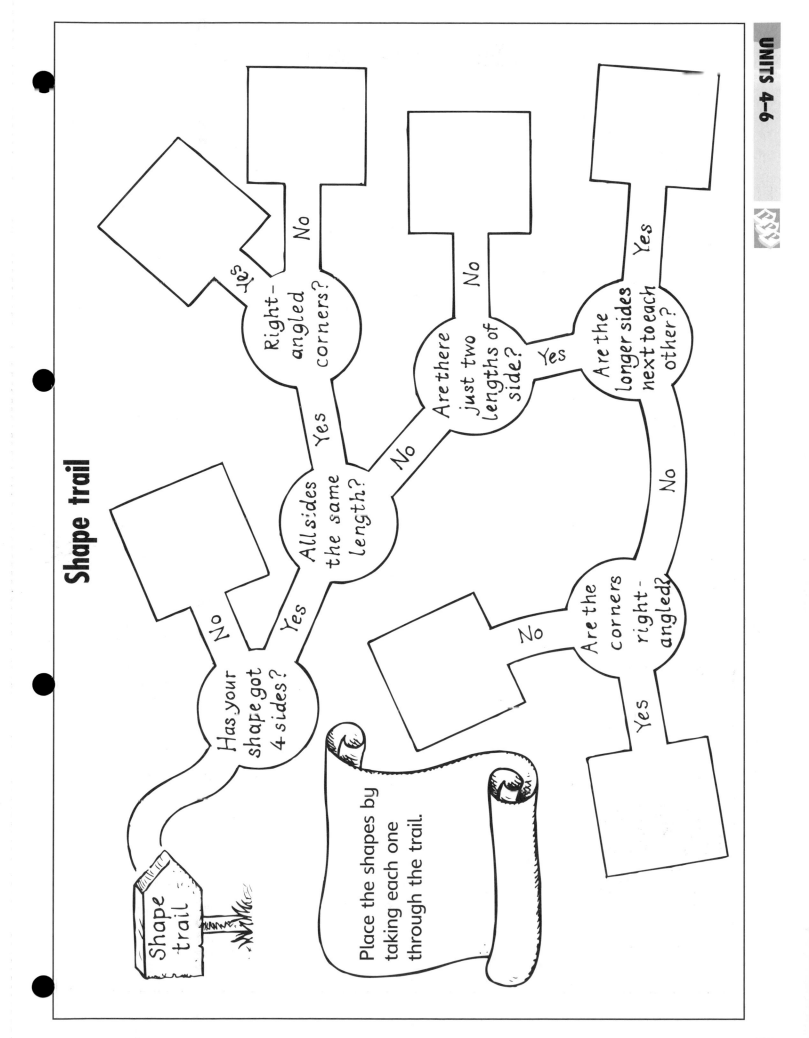

Has your shape got 4 sides?

No

Yes

All sides the same length?

Yes

No

Right-angled corners?

Yes

No

Are there just two lengths of side?

No

Yes

Are the longer sides next to each other?

Yes

No

Are the corners right-angled?

No

Yes

Place the shapes by taking each one through the trail.

Shape trail

Quadrilaterals and other shapes

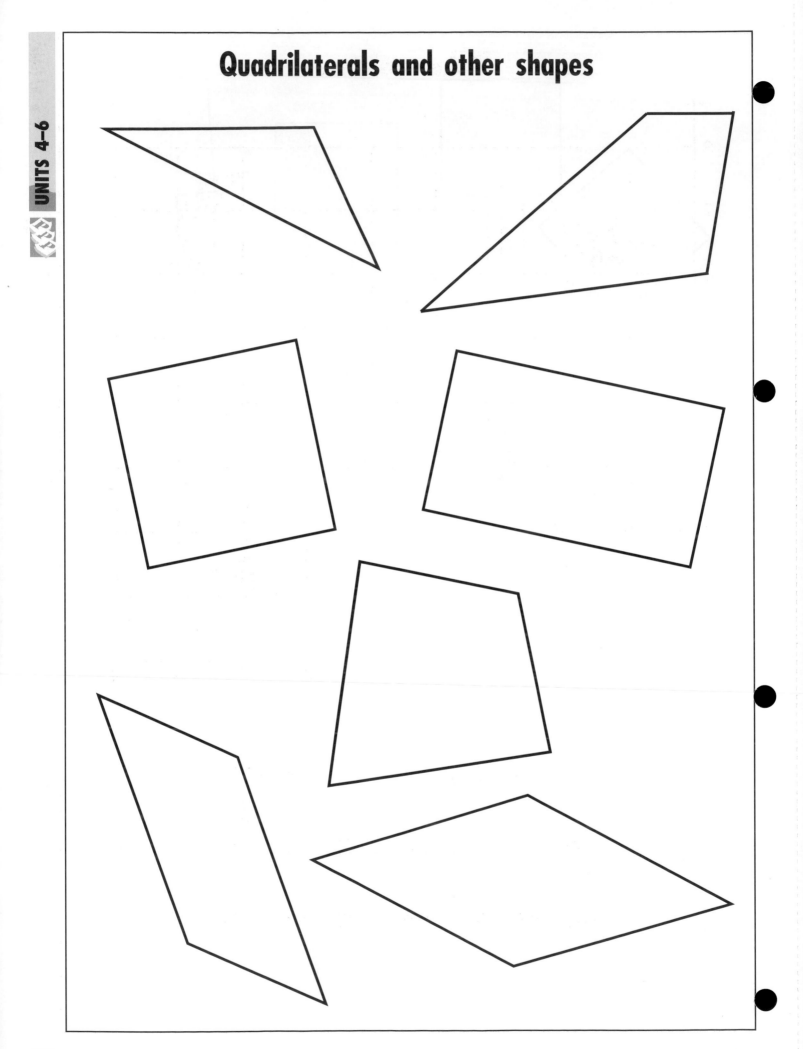

114

Make a picture

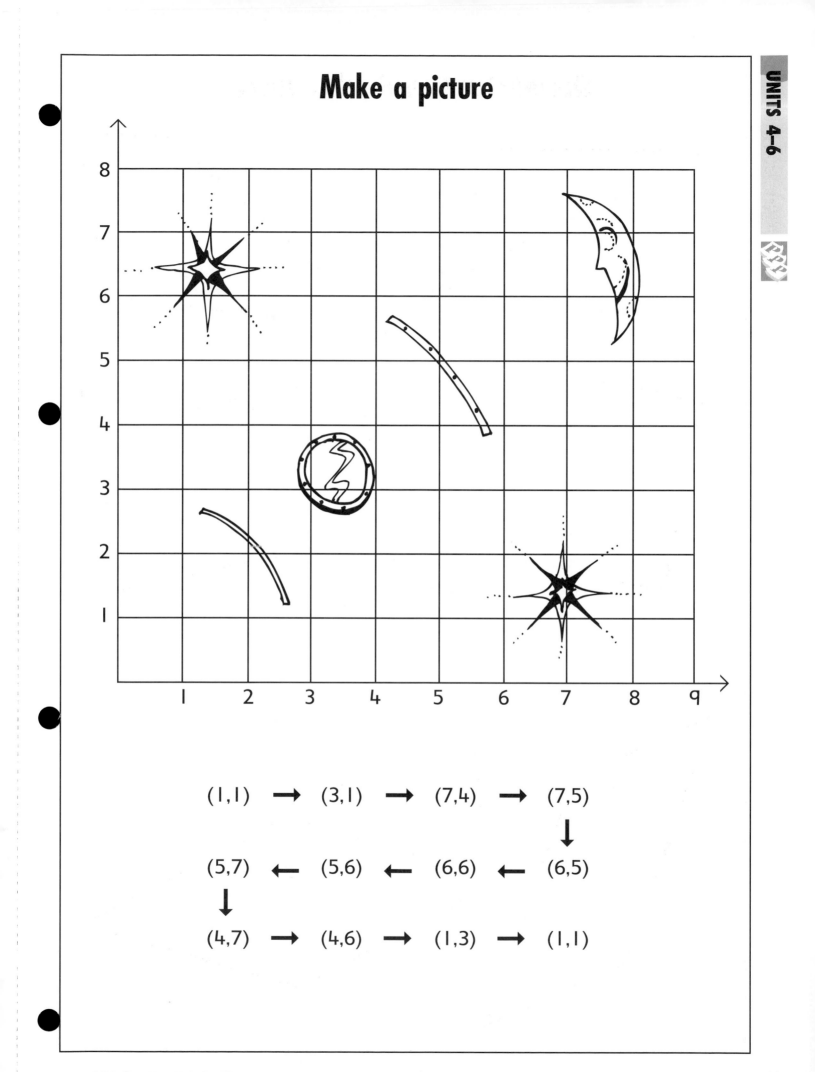

(1,1) ➔ (3,1) ➔ (7,4) ➔ (7,5)

⬇

(5,7) ⬅ (5,6) ⬅ (6,6) ⬅ (6,5)

⬇

(4,7) ➔ (4,6) ➔ (1,3) ➔ (1,1)

UNIT 7: Assess & Review

Choose from the following activities. During the **Group activities**, some of the children can complete assessment sheets 3a and 3b, which assess their skills in identifying line symmetry and right angles, and in choosing and using appropriate operations to solve word problems. The Learning outcomes for each sheet are given at the bottom of the page.

RESOURCES

Two labelled dice (see **Preparation**); numeral cards 0–9; assessment sheets 3a and 3b.

PREPARATION

Label two dice using stickers: one with +9, +19, +29, –9, –19, –29; the other with ×2, ×2, ×5, ×5, ×10, ×10.

ORAL AND MENTAL STARTER

ASSESSMENT

Do the children:
- **Use units of time and know the relationships between them?**
- **Recognise unit fractions such as $1/2$ or $1/4$, and use them to find fractions of numbers?**

TIME: Prepare a series of questions, of increasing difficulty, about the relationships between different units of time, for example:
- *How many days in two weeks?*
- *How many seconds in three minutes?*
- *How many days in November?*
- *Can you say the poem that helps us remember the number of days in each month?*

FRACTIONS: Ask children to halve and quarter given numbers, using the 'halving once' and 'halving twice' methods respectively. Present some of the questions in 'real-life' contexts, eg *What is quarter of £1.00?* Encourage children to look at the remaining fraction, eg *If one quarter of 24 is 6, then what is three quarters of 24?*

GROUP ACTIVITIES

ASSESSMENT

Do the children:
- **Add and subtract mentally a 'near multiple of 10' to or from a two-digit number?**
- **Order whole numbers to at least 1000?**
- **Know by heart multiplication facts for the 2, 5 and 10 times tables?**

ADDITION AND SUBTRACTION: Each child in the group draws two numeral cards at random to create a two-digit number, then rolls the first labelled dice and adds or subtracts according to the outcome. Make the activity into a game by seeing who 'scores' the largest number to win a point. The first person to collect eight points wins the game.

ORDERING: Ask each child to select three different numeral cards, then use the digits to create as many different three-digit numbers as possible, and arrange these numbers in ascending numerical order. As a broader assessment, you could ask the children to write their numbers in words.

MULTIPLICATION: Each player takes turns to roll the second labelled dice and select a random numeral card, then calculate the product of the two numbers and write down the number sentence. They should take turns around the group. Collect in the recorded work for assessment.

Assessment sheet 3a

Name: Date:

Draw **all** the lines of symmetry (some letters have more than one):

Which of these shapes have line symmetry?

Mark the right angles (if any) on the following shapes:

● **Identify** and sketch **lines of symmetry in simple shapes, and recognise shapes with no lines of symmetry.**
● **Identify right angles** in 2-D shapes.

Assessment sheet 3b

Name: _____   Date: _____

Solve these problems and say how you worked them out:

	Answer:	Method:
102 – 94		
47 – 18		
124 – 25		
1000 – 499		

Which one was the easiest? Why was it easy?

Choose the correct operation for each number sentence:

16 ☐ 2 = 32   42 ☐ 19 = 23

17 ☐ 44 = 61   3 ☐ 16 = 48

36 ☐ 12 = 3   21 ☐ 7 = 3

● Choose and use appropriate operations (including multiplication and division) to solve word problems. Explain methods and reasoning.

UNIT 8

ORGANISATION (5 LESSONS)

	LEARNING OUTCOMES	ORAL AND MENTAL STARTER	MAIN TEACHING ACTIVITY	PLENARY
LESSON 1	● Count on or back in twos starting from any two-digit number, and recognise odd and even numbers to at least 100.	COMBINATIONS: Make totals by combining given numbers using any operation.	UNITS PATTERNS: Count on in twos from various numbers. Look for units digit patterns.	Repeat COMBINATIONS and look at patterns of odd/ even numbers.
LESSON 2	● Count on or back in twos starting from any two-digit number, and recognise odd and even numbers to at least 100.	ADDITION: Consider and discuss mental addition methods.	ODD AND EVEN: Investigate addition of odd and even numbers.	Play an 'odds and evens' addition game.
LESSON 3	● Count on in steps of 3, 4 or 5. ● **Count on or back in tens or hundreds, starting from any two- or three-digit number.** ● Recognise three-digit multiples of 50 and 100.	PUZZLES: Make a target number by combining given numbers using any operation.	SEQUENCES: Count on in constant steps; look for patterns.	Play an 'odds and evens' subtraction game.
LESSON 4	● Count on in steps of 3, 4 or 5 from any small number to at least 50, then back again.	SUBTRACTION: Adapt from Lesson 2.	STEPS: Look at step patterns on different grids.	Play an 'odds and evens' multiplication game.
LESSON 5	● Count on in steps of 3, 4 and 5 from any small number to at least 50, then back again.	NEW ORDER: In which operations does order of numbers matter?	UNITS PATTERNS 2: Look for units digit patterns in multiples of 3, 4 and 5.	Use a rule to identify large multiples of 3.

ORAL AND MENTAL SKILLS Solve mathematical problems or puzzles, recognise simple patterns and relationships, generalise and predict. Suggest extensions by asking 'What if...?' **Explain methods and reasoning** orally and, where appropriate, in writing. Investigate a general statement about familiar numbers by finding examples that satisfy it.

Lessons 1, 2 and 4 are shown in full. Lessons 3 and 5 follow on from what has already been taught and are given in outline.

LESSON 1

RESOURCES

Paper; a class number line (optional).

PREPARATION

A class 0–100 number line may be useful.

LEARNING OUTCOMES

ORAL AND MENTAL STARTER
● Solve mathematical problems or puzzles, recognise simple patterns and relationships, generalise and predict. Suggest extensions by asking 'What if...?'

MAIN TEACHING ACTIVITY
● Count on or back in twos starting from any two-digit number, and recognise odd and even numbers to at least 100.

VOCABULARY

Number; sequence; rule; every other; odd; even; pattern.

ORAL AND MENTAL STARTER

COMBINATIONS: Write the numbers 2, 3 and 6 on the board. Ask the class to combine these mentally, using one or more operations. Discuss which combination would give the largest answer. Ask questions such as: *Is it possible to make 20?*

MAIN TEACHING ACTIVITY

UNITS PATTERNS: Ask the class a series of questions about 5 times table facts. Ask the questions in a random pattern; write answers ending in 0 on the left of the board and answers ending in 5 on the right. Ask the class why you have sorted the answers into two subsets. Reinforce the point by underlining each units digit. Confirm that the subsets are numbers with the same units digit.

Ask the children (working individually) to select any number in the 2 times table, and to create a sequence by adding 2 to it ten times. Then they should try to describe the pattern of the units digit. They can go on to create other 'adding 2' patterns, starting at different multiples of 2.

DIFFERENTIATION

Less able: Identify the pattern by drawing 'hops' along a number line.
More able: Investigate what happens when you start from a number which is not in the 2 times table (ie an odd number).

PLENARY

Repeat the **Oral and mental starter**, stressing ways to make odd and even numbers.

RESOURCES

Numeral cards 1–9 (page 13); two large dice.

PREPARATION

Each child or pair will need a set of numeral cards.

LEARNING OUTCOMES

ORAL AND MENTAL STARTER
● **Explain methods and reasoning** orally and, where appropriate, in writing.

MAIN TEACHING ACTIVITY
● Count on or back in twos starting from any two-digit number, and recognise odd and even numbers to at least 100.

VOCABULARY

Relationship; rule; equation.

ORAL AND MENTAL STARTER

ADDITION: Write two or three addition problems on the board (of the type 17 + 24 =). Ask the children to think about them quietly for a minute. Note those who seem unable or unwilling to engage in this task (they may need support at a more opportune time). Gather answers, and discuss how the children worked them out mentally. Stress that there are no 'right' approaches, but some methods tend to be more efficient (eg dealing with the units digits first).

MAIN TEACHING ACTIVITY

ODD AND EVEN: Review the work of Lesson 1, drawing attention to the notion of odd and even numbers. Discuss what makes a number even, in terms of both the multiples of 2 (the 'adding on 2 from 0' sequence) and the numbers which can be divided into two equal (whole number) parts.

Give each child or pair a set of numerals from 1–9. Ask the children to sort these into two piles: 'odds' and 'evens'. They should then investigate whether the answer is odd or even when two evens, two odds or a mixed pair are added. (Look for the answers: two evens or two odds always gives an even total, and that the total of an even and an odd is always odd. If you have included 0, remember that it is an even number.)

DIFFERENTIATION

Less able: Divide a set of 1–10 or 1–20 number cards into two sets, odd and even. Arrange both sets in ascending order and record them.
More able: Investigate whether there are general rules for what happens when odd and even numbers are combined using subtraction, multiplication or division. Start to use general equations, eg odd + odd = even.

PLENARY

Divide the class into two teams, one representing 'odds' and the other 'evens'. Roll two large dice and find the total. Which team gets a point depends on whether the total is odd or even. Play continuously until one team has scored 10 points. Use this as a context to demonstrate that odd + odd is even, even + odd is odd and so on.

RESOURCES	As for Lesson 1.
LEARNING OUTCOMES	**ORAL AND MENTAL STARTER** ● Solve mathematical problems or puzzles, recognise simple patterns or relationships, generalise and predict. Suggest extensions by asking 'What if..?' **MAIN TEACHING ACTIVITY** ● Count on in steps of 3, 4 or 5. ● **Count on or back in tens or hundreds, starting from any two- or three-digit number.** ● Recognise three-digit multiples of 50 and 100.
ORAL AND MENTAL STARTER	PUZZLES: Write three numbers on the board (different from those used for 'Combinations' in Lesson 1). Set puzzles such as: *I have a score of 26. How did I make that with these three numbers?*
MAIN TEACHING ACTIVITY	SEQUENCES: Starting at 0, practise counting in steps of 50 and 100. Ask questions such as: *What are 7 lots of 50?* Use partitioning to show how this relates to the 5 times table, eg $7 \times 50 = 7 \times 5 \times 10 = 35 \times 10 = 350$. Ask groups of children to focus on other (smaller) steps, building up sequences of multiples as in Lesson 1. Work with the groups, discussing whether there is a cyclical repeating pattern in the units and/or tens digits (eg adding on 4 results in the digit repeating every fifth number). Towards the end of the session, gather the children together to compare outcomes. Emphasise the different possible approaches to recording.
DIFFERENTIATION	Less able: Work with multiples of 5 (building on Lesson 1). More able: Work with multiples of 7.
PLENARY	Repeat from Lesson 2, this time finding the difference between the two dice outcomes. Use this as a context to demonstrate that odd – odd is even,

RESOURCES

A class number line; photocopiable page 123; coloured pencils.

PREPARATION

Make one copy per child of page 123.

LEARNING OUTCOMES

ORAL AND MENTAL STARTER
● **Explain methods and reasoning** orally and, where appropriate, in writing.

MAIN TEACHING ACTIVITY
● Count on in steps of 3, 4, or 5.

VOCABULARY

Equivalent;
coins; notes;
same; all
solutions/
answers;
systematic;
represent.

LEARNING OUTCOMES

ORAL AND MENTAL STARTER

● Use patterns of similar calculations.

MAIN TEACHING ACTIVITY

● Recognise all coins and notes.
● Solve word problems involving money, including finding totals and giving change, and working out which coins to pay. Explain how the problem was solved.

ORAL AND MENTAL STARTER

ADDITION GRID: Display a 1–10 addition grid. Talk about the symmetry of its layout, and ask questions to confirm understanding of this. Ask the class how it could be used to derive answers which lie outside the grid (eg 12 + 12 could be thought of as '10 + 10 and 2 + 2' or 'double 6 + 6').

MAIN TEACHING ACTIVITY

FIVE COINS: Discuss the children's knowledge of money, including the range of coin values in circulation from 1p to £2 coins. Use these values to revise counting in 1s, 2s, 5s, 10s, 20s and 50s. Begin to discuss equivalence with £5.00 and £10.00 (eg *How many 50p coins are equivalent to £5.00?*).

  Ask the children to investigate how much money you might have if you are holding five coins of the same value. Tell the groups to try to find all the possible answers, and to represent the work in their own way. During the session, encourage systematic working by drawing on examples of good practice. Afterwards, discuss change from £5.00, £10.00 and £20.00, using some of the larger totals made with five coins as a starting point.

DIFFERENTIATION

Less able: Use coin stamps and/or counting apparatus.
More able: Consider which sets of five equal-value coins are/are not equivalent to another coin or note. Can they see a pattern?

PLENARY

Use place value cards to add multiples of 10 to a given number. The children could work individually or in pairs with their own sets, or answer questions demonstrated with an enlarged set of numeral cards (eg adding multiples of 10 to 324, 415 or 296).

RESOURCES

A large 1–100 square (page 16); numeral cards (page 13).

PREPARATION

Each child or group will need a set of five numeral cards (see below).

LEARNING OUTCOMES

ORAL AND MENTAL STARTER

● Use patterns of similar calculations.

MAIN TEACHING ACTIVITY

● Extend understanding that more than two numbers can be added.
● Use knowledge that addition can be done in any order to do mental calculations more efficiently. For example: put the larger number first and count on; add three or four small numbers by putting the largest number first and/or finding pairs totalling 9, 10 or 11; partition into '5 and a bit' when adding 6, 7, 8 or 9.

VOCABULARY
Number bonds; how many ways?

ORAL AND MENTAL STARTER

A CHOICE: Use the 1–100 grid to investigate adding a number such as 27. Note that two clear strategies arise, and the best choice depends on the starting number: for 22 + 27, start at 22, then go down 20 to 42, then go along 7 to 49, but for 38 + 27, start at 38, go down 30 to 68, then compensate by going back 3 to 65.

MAIN TEACHING ACTIVITY

ADDITION SKILLS: Display a set of five single-digit numbers. Invite individuals to give you the total of any three. Ask: *If you only use each number once, what is the largest/smallest total you can make? Can you make an even/odd total? A multiple of 5?*

Use the set of numbers 14, 9, 6, 7 and 12 to teach the following skills: putting the largest number first (eg 14 + 7 + 6); finding convenient pairs to make up multiples of 10 (eg 14 + 6); partitioning into '5 and a bit' (eg 9 + 7 = 5 + 4 + 5 + 2 = 10 + 6).

Provide each group with a set of five two-digit numbers, and ask them to find as many different triple bond totals as possible.

DIFFERENTIATION

Less able: Use single-digit numbers; work with teacher support; use number apparatus.
More able: Use two- and three-digit numbers, working systematically.

PLENARY

Ask each group how they approached the task. Note that the number of possible combinations for any five numbers should be the same (10).

LESSON 7

RESOURCES	Paper; numeral cards 1–9 (from page 13); calculators (optional).
LEARNING OUTCOMES	**ORAL AND MENTAL STARTER** ● **Add mentally a 'near multiple of 10' to a two-digit number...** by adding 10, 20, 30... and adjusting. **MAIN TEACHING ACTIVITY** ● Extend understanding that more than two numbers can be added. ● Use knowledge that addition can be done in any order to do mental calculations more efficiently.
ORAL AND MENTAL STARTER	NEAR TENS 3: Ask each child to show a given two-digit starter number with numeral cards, then replace it with a number 11, 21, 31, 19, 29 or 39 more.
MAIN TEACHING ACTIVITY	ON TARGET: Draw a large square on the board and write a target total inside (eg 100). Ask children to volunteer some two-digit numbers to be written at the corners. The aim is to make these numbers total the target number. Practise addition skills, drawing on those taught in Lesson 6. Give the children blank sheets of paper and set appropriate targets (at two or three levels of difficulty).
DIFFERENTIATION	Less able: Use triangles, thus adding three numbers to make each total. More able: Make smaller totals, using fractions and/or negative numbers.
PLENARY	Discuss the activity. Try a couple of squares that make totals to 1000, using 'convenient' numbers at the corners, such as multiples of 50 or 25.

LESSON 8

RESOURCES

1–100 square (page 16).

PREPARATION

Make one copy per child of page 16, plus an enlarged version.

LEARNING OUTCOMES

ORAL AND MENTAL STARTER

● Repeat addition or multiplication in a different order.

MAIN TEACHING ACTIVITY
- Extend understanding of the operation of addition.
- Partition into tens and units, then recombine.
- Derive quickly all pairs of multiples of 5 with a total of 100.

ORAL AND MENTAL STARTER

CHECK IT OUT: Present a triple addition bond and brainstorm ways of adding the numbers. Reinforce that the order of addition has no effect on the answer, and is often guided by the numbers (eg there is often a 'convenient' pairing such as 7 + 3).

MAIN TEACHING ACTIVITY

PAIRS TO 100: Tell the class that you are going to show them how to use a 100 grid to find complements. Explain that when two numbers add up to a given target total, these numbers are called **complements** (eg 45 and 55 are complements of 100). Point to a multiple of 5 ending with a 5. Demonstrate how you can count on in tens and ones to 100 using either of two methods: counting down the column to 95, then along the row to 100; or counting along the row to a multiple of 10, then down that column in tens to 100. Write some pairs on the board; talk about how the tens digits have a total of 90, with the two 5s 'making up' the remaining 10.

Practise counting on from any two-digit number, using the 100 grid (eg 63 + □ = 100). Check the totals by teaching explicitly the skill of partitioning and then recombining: 63 + 37 = 60 + 30 + 3 + 7 = 90 + 10 = 100.

Write some number questions on the board similar to the one shown above (see also **Differentiation**) and give each child a 1–100 square. They should copy the questions on paper, leaving enough room to cut out and paste the correct numbers from the grid. Emphasise the idea of a 'missing number' in a puzzle.

DIFFERENTIATION

Less able: Answer questions involving a total of 20 rather than 100.
More able: Find complements of 500 or 1000.

PLENARY

Repeat the **Oral and mental starter** for multiplication triples. Use the idea of multiplication as 'repeated addition' to show that the order of multiplication does not affect the answer.

RESOURCES	One copy per child of photocopiable page 133, perhaps modified (see **Differentiation**); a large 8 × 8 grid; a dry-wipe marker.
LEARNING OUTCOMES	**ORAL AND MENTAL STARTER** • Use doubling or halving, starting from known facts, to multiply or divide. **MAIN TEACHING ACTIVITY** • Extend understanding of the operation of subtraction. • Say or write a subtraction statement corresponding to a given addition statement.
ORAL AND MENTAL STARTER	DOUBLE TROUBLE: Discuss ways of multiplying 8 × 8. Try strategies such as: double 8, double again and then again; double 4 × 8; double one 8 and halve the other. Use the same strategies to find other multiples of 8.
MAIN TEACHING ACTIVITY	MISSING NUMBERS: Write '□ + □ = 100' on the board. Ask: *What might the two numbers be?* Invite different answers, each time asking *How did you work that out?* Provide copies of page 133 and discuss a question or two from each column. You should distinguish those with only one possible correct solution (eg 22 – 15 = □) from those which are open (eg □ – □ = 7). Give support as required.
DIFFERENTIATION	Less able: Use a sheet cut into columns and/or modified (but with some questions still open). More able: Go on to explore solutions to □ + □ = 1000.
PLENARY	Return to the **Oral and mental starter**, modelling 8 × 8 as a large grid. Ask: *How could the grid be partitioned to find a total, if we did not immediately know the answer?* Mark the different ways suggested by the children (eg partition into four 4 × 4 grids, count the squares in one section, then mentally double and double again).

RESOURCES

Numeral cards 1–9 (page 13); coins; counting equipment; chocolate (optional).

PREPARATION

Prepare a visual stimulus for the lesson, perhaps displaying three different chocolate bars to advertise your 'shop'.

LEARNING OUTCOMES

ORAL AND MENTAL STARTER

● **Subtract mentally a 'near multiple of 10' from a two-digit number...** by subtracting 10, 20, 30... and adjusting.

MAIN TEACHING ACTIVITY

● Solve word problems involving money, including finding totals and giving change, and working out which coins to pay. Explain how the problem was solved.

VOCABULARY
Change; price; double; treble; count on/up; 100 pence; pound.

ORAL AND MENTAL STARTER

NEAR TENS 4: As for Lesson 7, but this time ask each child to show a number that is 11, 21, 31, 19, 29 or 39 less.

MAIN TEACHING ACTIVITY

THREE BARS: In role as 'shopkeeper', talk about how you maintain the shop and how you need to be quick with handling money. Invite two children to play the roles of shopkeeper and customer. The customer will buy three chocolate bars. Give prices for the three bars on display, either contrived to give easy calculations (eg 10p, 20p, 30p) or realistic (eg 32p, 29p, 25p). When the customer makes the request, which may be a multiple purchase of the same type of bar or a mixed purchase, ask the class to help the shopkeeper total the amount. Continue the role-play with an exchange of money (eg £1.00), with 'shopkeeper's addition' being used to calculate the change. Explain which coins would be used, and convey the rationale for this. Extend the range of coins/notes considered (eg to £2 or £5).

Ask the children to model this activity in pairs, swapping roles halfway through and recording each transaction.

DIFFERENTIATION

Contrive the prices as suggested above. For the least able children, take on the role of shopkeeper and work through the activity with a small group, using real coins to demonstrate.

PLENARY

Play a 'Double your money' quiz game with two teams, each starting with 1p. Ask the teams (in turn) some simple maths questions. Double their total after each correct answer. The winning team is the first to reach £1.00 (which takes only seven correct answers).

Place value cards (extension sheet for page 23)

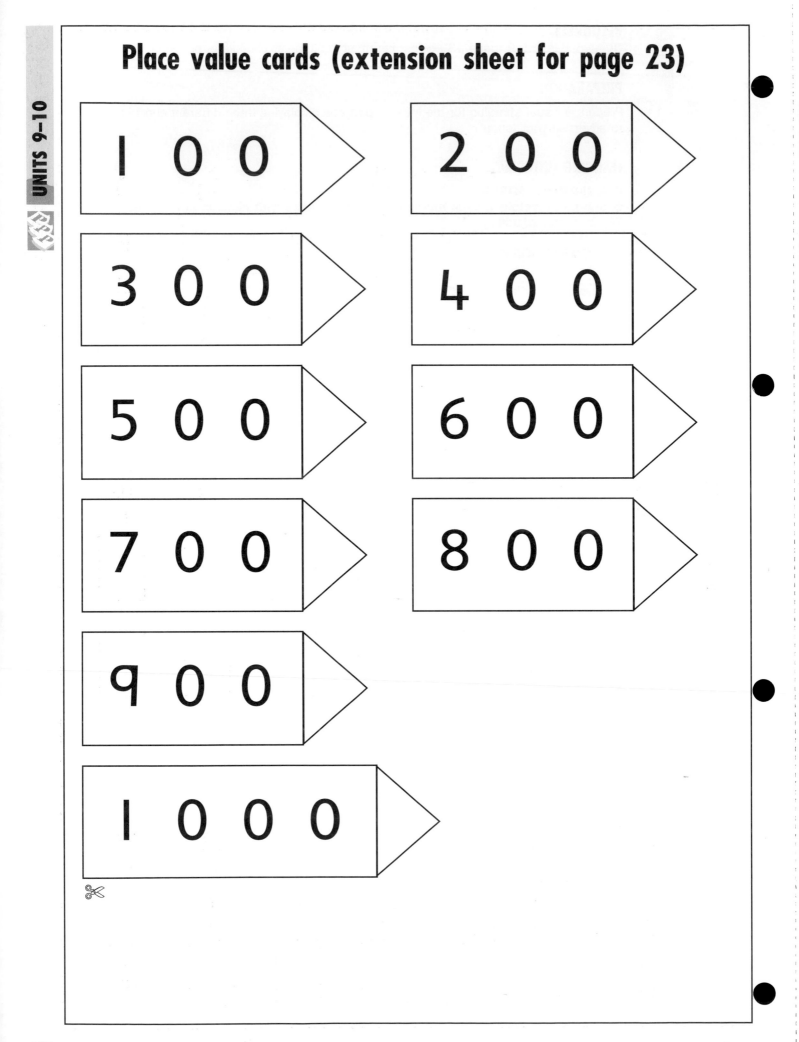

Missing numbers

☐ – 27 = ☐

41 – ☐ = 16

73 – ☐ = 54

☐ – 43 = 52

☐ – 29 = 51

98 – ☐ = 57

☐ – 39 = 46

☐ – ☐ = 7

☐ – ☐ = 26

☐ – ☐ = 19

☐ – ☐ = 37

☐ – ☐ = 24

☐ – ☐ = 52

☐ – ☐ = 87

17 – 9 = ☐

14 – ☐ = 9

22 – ☐ = 15

☐ – 7 = 4

☐ – 12 = 31

☐ – 9 = 23

24 – ☐ = 8

UNIT 11

ORGANISATION (5 LESSONS)

	LEARNING OUTCOMES	ORAL AND MENTAL STARTER	MAIN TEACHING ACTIVITY	PLENARY
LESSON 1 +2	• **Recognise unit fractions such as $^1/_2$ and $^1/_4$, and use them to find fractions of shapes and numbers.** • Estimate a simple fraction.	5× FACTS: Revise multiples of 5. PLACE VALUE: Use to add or subtract multiples of 10 or 100.	HALF TIME: Represent 'a half' in different ways. QUARTERS: Represent 'a quarter' in different ways.	Estimate simple fractions. Share and discuss work done.
LESSON 3	• Recognise that halving is the inverse of doubling. • **Recognise unit fractions such as $^1/_2$ and $^1/_4$, and use them to find fractions of shapes and numbers.** • Begin to recognise simple equivalent fractions. • Compare familiar fractions.	PLACE VALUE 2: Use to multiply by 10.	HALF AND HALF: Explore repeated halving of a square and a number.	Approximation activities involving fractional parts.
LESSON 4	• **Recognise unit fractions such as $^1/_2$ and $^1/_4$, and use them to find fractions of shapes.** • Begin to recognise simple fractions that are several parts of a whole, such as $^3/_4$. • Begin to recognise simple equivalent fractions. • Compare familiar fractions.	3× FACTS: Revise multiples of 3.	CUT AND PASTE: Arrange half and quarter shapes to make units in different ways.	Recap 3× FACTS as rapid question and answer session.
LESSON 5	• **Recognise unit fractions such as $^1/_2$ and $^1/_4$, and use them to find fractions of shapes.** • Derive quickly halves corresponding to doubles of all whole numbers to at least 20.	4× FACTS: Revise multiples of 4.	HALF AND HALF 2: Halve numbers twice over; look at pattern of results.	Recap 4× FACTS as rapid question and answer session.

ORAL AND MENTAL SKILLS **Know by heart multiplication facts for the 5 times table.** Say the number that is 1, 10 or 100 more or less than any given two-digit or three-digit number. To multiply by 10, shift the digits of a number one place to the left. **Recognise that division is the inverse of multiplication.** Begin to know the 3 and 4 times tables.

Lessons 1, 3 and 4 are given in full. Lessons 2 and 5 follow on from what has already been taught and are given in outline.

RESOURCES

Large sheets of A3 paper; some visual 'half' and 'quarter' prompts; numeral cards 1–9 (page 13).

PREPARATION

Provide some visual prompts to support the idea of 'half', eg a beaker half full of water, a geared clock showing 'half past the hour'.

LEARNING OUTCOMES

ORAL AND MENTAL STARTER
● **Know by heart multiplication facts for the 5 times table.**
● Say the number that is 1, 10 or 100 more or less than any given two- or three-digit number.

MAIN TEACHING ACTIVITY
● **Recognise unit fractions such as $^1/_2$ and $^1/_4$, and use them to find fractions of shapes and numbers.**
● Estimate a simple fraction.

VOCABULARY

Half; empty; full; half past; quarter; different ways; quarter to/ past; a quarter full.

ORAL AND MENTAL STARTER

5× FACTS: Chant the 5 times table forwards and backwards to and from 50. Ask questions out of sequence, encouraging children to derive unknown facts from known facts where necessary.

MAIN TEACHING ACTIVITY

HALF TIME: Talk to the class about when we use the term 'half' in mathematics and everyday life, eg time, shapes, food, money, capacity (half full), number lines, word problems, number sentences. Use some 'half' resources (see **Preparation**) to demonstrate and reinforce the idea.

Give individuals or pairs large sheets of paper. Ask them to make a poster about halves, using pictures, words, symbols and/or diagrams.

DIFFERENTIATION

Less able: Use the visual prompts provided as a starting point.
More able: Go on immediately to making a 'quarters' poster (as in Lesson 2).

PLENARY

Develop approximation involving fractional parts: *What is half of 395 approximately equal to? What is a quarter of 105 roughly equal to? Show where 72 is approximately using this unmarked 0–100 number line* (about $^3/_4$ of the way).

LESSON 2

For the **Oral and mental starter**, PLACE VALUE, use a set of numeral cards to show a two-digit number; ask the children what numbers are 10, 20, 30 etc more or less. Show three-digit numbers and ask the children what numbers are 100, 200, 300 etc more or less. For the **Main teaching activity**, QUARTERS, repeat from Lesson 1 but working on the idea of 'a quarter' (using time, money, food etc). Differentiate as before (more able children can make an 'eighths' poster). Use the **Plenary** to share and discuss the posters.

LESSON 3

RESOURCES

Coloured pencils; 8 × 8 grids of squared paper (ideally 2cm squares); a set of 0–9 numeral cards (page 13), Blu-tack.

PREPARATION

Each child will need an 8 × 8 grid.

LEARNING OUTCOMES

ORAL AND MENTAL STARTER
● To multiply by 10, shift the digits of a number one place to the left.
● **Recognise that division is the inverse of multiplication.**

MAIN TEACHING ACTIVITY
● Recognise that halving is the inverse of doubling.
● **Recognise unit fractions such as $^1/_2$ and $^1/_4$, and use them to find fractions of shapes and numbers.**
● Begin to recognise simple equivalent fractions.
● Compare familiar fractions.

ORAL AND MENTAL STARTER

PLACE VALUE 2: Write the headings H, T and U on the board. Place a single-digit numeral card in the U column and ask the children to multiply this number by 10. Move the card into the T column and add a 0 numeral card as a place holder. Repeat, to practise multiplying single- and two-digit numbers by 10.

MAIN TEACHING ACTIVITY

HALF AND HALF: Talk about repeated doubling, going from 1 to over 100 or 1000. Explain that today, the class will do the opposite: they will start at a large number and finish at 1.

Provide the 8 × 8 grids and ask the class to tell you how many small squares there are. Explain that the task is to colour in half of the 64 squares and count how many squares that is. They should then colour half of the remaining half in a different colour, and continue until they have reduced the uncoloured area to 1 square, then write down the number of squares in each colour.

DIFFERENTIATION

Less able: Work with a 4 × 4 grid.
More able: Label each colour with a statement such as 'red: an eighth of 64 is 8'.

PLENARY

Ask the children to write on their grids the number of squares in each block of colour. Ask individuals to make totals from given combinations of these numbers (8 + 4 or 4 + 2 + 1 etc). Explain that **any** number up to 64 can be made by adding some of these numbers.

LESSON 4

RESOURCES

Photocopiable page 138; scissors; adhesive; OHP (optional).

PREPARATION

Make a copy of page 138 for each child, and an enlarged or OHT copy.

LEARNING OUTCOMES

ORAL AND MENTAL STARTER
● Begin to know the 3 times table.

MAIN TEACHING ACTIVITY
● **Recognise unit fractions such as $1/2$ and $1/4$, and use them to find fractions of shapes.**
● Begin to recognise simple fractions that are several parts of a whole, such as $3/4$.
● Begin to recognise simple equivalent fractions.
● Compare familiar fractions.

ORAL AND MENTAL STARTER

3× FACTS: Repeat from Lesson 1, but with the 3 times table.

MAIN TEACHING ACTIVITY

CUT AND PASTE: Recap on the 'half' and 'quarter' work from the Autumn term (Lessons 1 and 2, Unit 11). Explain that today, the children will use cut-out halves and quarters to make unit shapes in as many different ways as possible. Use an enlarged or OHT copy of page 138 to demonstrate making fractional pieces and reassembling them.

Let the children work with copies of the sheet, overlaying fractional pieces on the shaded squares. Discuss whether, for example, two arrangements which differ only in the orientation of the pieces are really 'different'. Finally, the children should stick down three different arrangements on the shaded squares.

DIFFERENTIATION

Less able: Work with additional teacher support; use an enlarged version of the sheet.
More able: Label their arrangements (eg '$1/2$ and $1/4$ and $1/4$').

PLENARY

Recap on 3× FACTS through a rapid 'question and answer' session.

LESSON 5

RESOURCES	1–100 square (page 16); blank paper.
LEARNING OUTCOMES	**ORAL AND MENTAL STARTER** ● Begin to know the 4 times table. **MAIN TEACHING ACTIVITY** ● **Recognise unit fractions such as $1/2$ and $1/4$, and use them to find fractions of numbers.** ● Derive quickly halves corresponding to doubles of all whole numbers to at least 20.
ORAL AND MENTAL STARTER	4× FACTS: Repeat from Lesson 1, but with the 4 times table.
MAIN TEACHING ACTIVITY	HALF AND HALF 2: Ask the children to stand up, think of a number less than 100, halve it mentally, then sit down if their number does not halve to make a whole number. Ask those still standing to halve their answer mentally and remain standing if the new answer is whole. Ask those still standing to give their final answer, and ask the class to calculate the number they started with. Ask the children to work individually, looking for numbers which can be halved and halved again to make whole numbers. They should record each successful case using numbers cut and pasted from a 1–100 square, eg 24 ... halved ... 12 ... halved ... 6.
DIFFERENTIATION	If the initial whole-class activity is problematic, ask the children to repeat it in small groups. Less able: Work with numbers below 50 on the **Main teaching activity**. More able: Work using initial numbers over 100.
PLENARY	Recap on 4× FACTS through a rapid 'question and answer' session.

Make a unit square

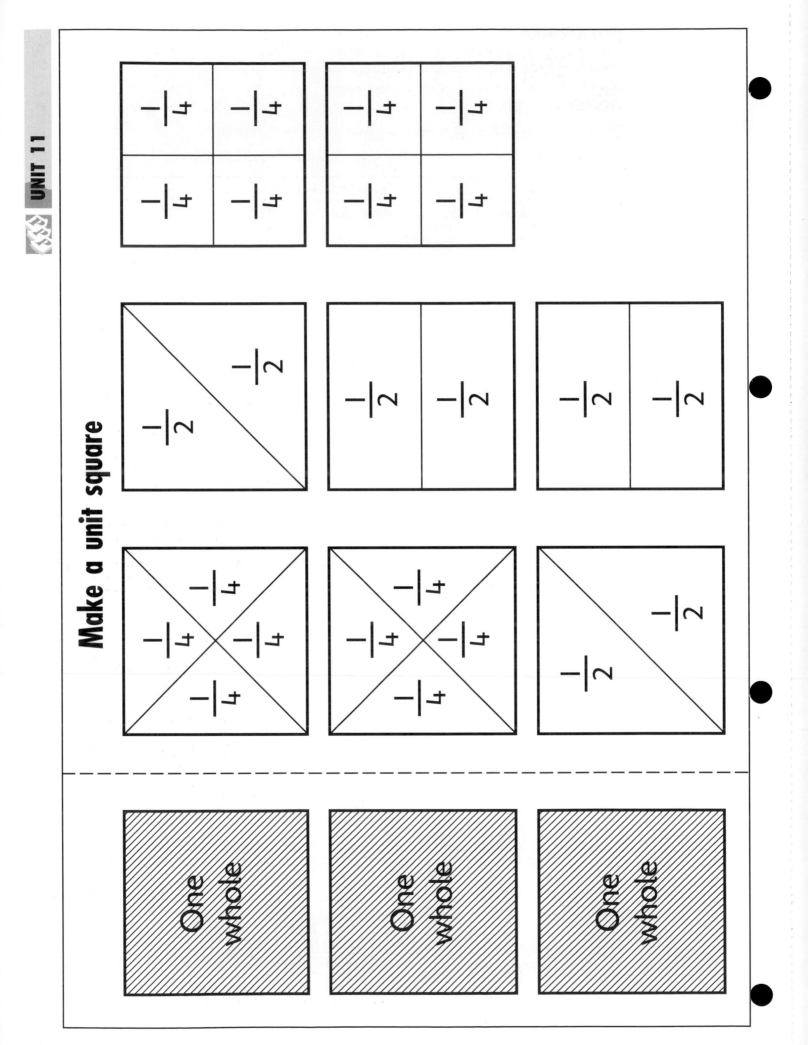

UNIT 12

ORGANISATION (5 LESSONS)

	LEARNING OUTCOMES	ORAL AND MENTAL STARTER	MAIN TEACHING ACTIVITY	PLENARY
LESSON 1	● **Solve a given problem by organising and interpreting numerical data in simple lists, tables and graphs,** for example: Carroll diagrams.	MOVING ON UP: Play a two-digit number ordering game.	CARROLL DIAGRAMS: Extend from Term 1. Collect and order data.	Play MOVING ON UP with two teams.
LESSON 2	● **Solve a given problem by organising and interpreting numerical data in simple lists, tables and graphs,** for example: Venn diagrams.	MOVING ON UP 2: Include subtraction.	VENN DIAGRAMS: Extend from Term 1.	Play MOVING ON UP 2 with two teams.
LESSON 3	● **Solve a given problem by organising and interpreting numerical data in simple lists, tables and graphs.**	MOVING ON UP 3: Include multiplication.	GRAPHS: Use ICT to generate a range of graphs from data.	Play MOVING ON UP 3 with two teams.
LESSON 4	● **Solve a given problem by organising and interpreting numerical data in simple lists, tables and graphs.**	MOVING ON UP 4: Make and order three-digit numbers.	GIANT PIE: Make an 'instant' pie chart.	Play MOVING ON UP 4 with two teams.
LESSON 5	● **Solve a given problem by organising and interpreting numerical data in simple lists, tables and graphs.**	MOVING ON OUT: Review place value and rounding.	Simple questionnaire.	Review of the unit.

ORAL AND MENTAL SKILLS   Understand and use the vocabulary of comparing and ordering numbers. Compare two given three-digit numbers, say which is more or less, and give a number which lies between them. Round any two-digit number to the nearest 10 and any three-digit number to the nearest 100.

Lessons 3–5 are given in full; Lessons 1 and 2 follow on from what was taught in Term 1.

RESOURCES	Photocopiable page 81 (one copy per child); numeral cards (different sets for different groups, depending on ability – see **Main teaching activity**); scissors; adhesive; a large dice.
LEARNING OUTCOMES	**ORAL AND MENTAL STARTER** ● Understand and use the vocabulary of comparing and ordering numbers. **MAIN TEACHING ACTIVITY** ● **Solve a given problem by organising and interpreting numerical data in simple lists, tables and graphs,** for example: Carroll diagrams.
ORAL AND MENTAL STARTER	MOVING ON UP: Gather the class around you. Draw spaces for three two-digit numbers on the board. Roll a dice; enter the number thrown in a space suggested by the class. The challenge is to finish with three numbers in ascending order. Play a few times and begin to gather strategies. (This is an extension of Year 2 work.)
MAIN TEACHING ACTIVITY	CARROLL DIAGRAMS: Review the previous term's work on Carroll diagrams (Lesson 2, Unit 13, Term 1). Provide a fresh challenge involving a double sort with number facts. It may be possible to select a new set of numbers which sample a multiplication table currently being studied, eg asking the children to sort a range of numbers as being multiples/not multiples of 3 and 4.
DIFFERENTIATION	Less able: Provide additional teacher support. More able: Sort a range of numbers as being factors/not factors of two given numbers, eg 24 and 60.
PLENARY	Repeat MOVING ON UP with two teams, each using its own playing board.

RESOURCES

Sets of place value cards (photocopiable pages 23 and 132); Tape recorder and cassette (optional).

PREPARATION

Consider how to organise the **Main teaching activity**.

LEARNING OUTCOMES

ORAL AND MENTAL STARTER

● Understand and use the vocabulary of comparing and ordering numbers.
● Round any two-digit number to the nearest 10 and any three-digit number to the nearest 100.

MAIN TEACHING ACTIVITY

● **Solve a given problem by organising and interpreting numerical data in simple lists, tables and graphs.**

VOCABULARY

Survey; Yes/No questions; questionnaire.

ORAL AND MENTAL STARTER

MOVING ON OUT: Use place value cards to review place value and rounding. Display numbers and ask questions (eg *What is 273 to the nearest 100? In the number 238, how much is the middle digit 'worth'?*), then exchange cards to confirm correct responses.

MAIN TEACHING ACTIVITY

QUESTIONS: Discuss questionnaires, in particular the idea of a 'Yes or No' response.
    Organise the class into large groups and select a theme (eg the popularity of different subjects in school) for the questions. Each child or pair should devise up to five questions, each requiring a 'Yes or No' answer, and use them to gather information from each member of their group. This activity may require a lot of management, and you may therefore wish to develop it with different groups across the day or week.

DIFFERENTIATION

Less able: Record their questions on cassette instead of writing them down.
More able: Collate the groups' outcomes to find class results.

PLENARY

Recap on the themes covered in this unit. Focus on any points which caused difficulty.

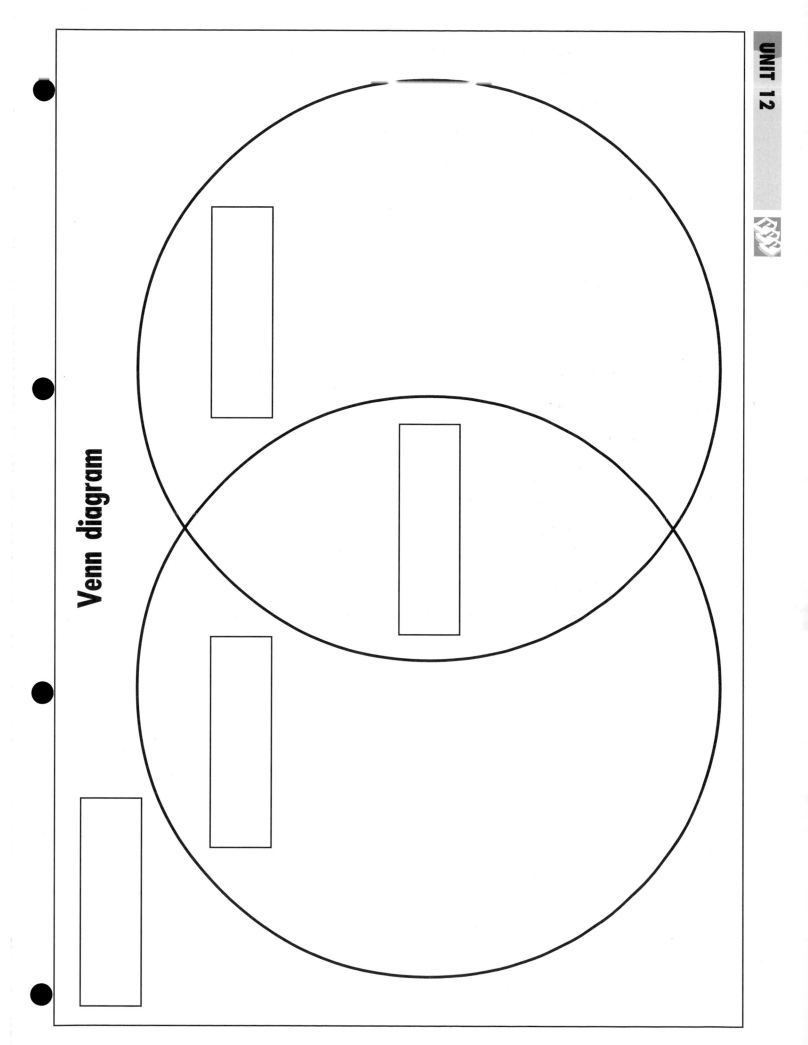

Venn diagram

UNIT 13: Assess & Review

Choose from the following activities. During the **Group activities**, some of the children can complete assessment sheets 4a and 4b, which assess their skills in manipulating 'near multiples of 10' and their understanding of division (including awareness that division is the inverse of multiplication).

RESOURCES

Assessment sheets 4a and 4b; squared paper; photocopiable page 138.

PREPARATION

Provide an enlarged version of this graph:

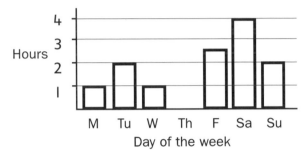

ORAL AND MENTAL STARTER

ASSESSMENT

Can the children:
● **Solve a given problem by organising and interpreting numerical data in simple lists, tables and graphs?**
● **Explain their methods and reasoning** (when solving problems)?
HANDLING DATA: Present a graph (see **Preparation**). Explain that it shows the amount of time that one boy spent watching TV over the course of one week. Ask a series of questions (of increasing complexity), for example:
● *On which day of the week did he watch no TV?*
● *When did he watch 2 hours?*
● *On which day did he watch most TV? Why do you think this was?*
● *How many hours did he watch over the weekend?*
EXPLAINING METHODS AND REASONING: Provide some questions relating to each of the four operations, similar to those on assessment sheet 3b, for example:
● *What is 25 × 8?*
● *What is the total cost of four items at £3.99 each?*
● *What is one eighth of 120?*

GROUP ACTIVITIES

ASSESSMENT

Do the children:
● **Count on or back in tens or hundreds, starting from any two- or three-digit number?**
● **Recognise unit fractions such as $1/2$ or $1/4$, and use them to find fractions of numbers?**
● **Solve a given problem by organising and interpreting numerical data in simple lists, tables and graphs?**
FRACTIONS: Repeat the **Main teaching activity** from Lesson 4, Unit 11, using copies of page 138. Use this to check the children's awareness of equivalence, eg *How many quarters would you need to make two whole shapes?*
HANDLING DATA: Refer back to the data handling data exercise above. Provide squared paper and ask the children to produce a similar graph for a suitable set of data (either fictitious or collected previously).

Name: Date:

Assessment sheet 4a

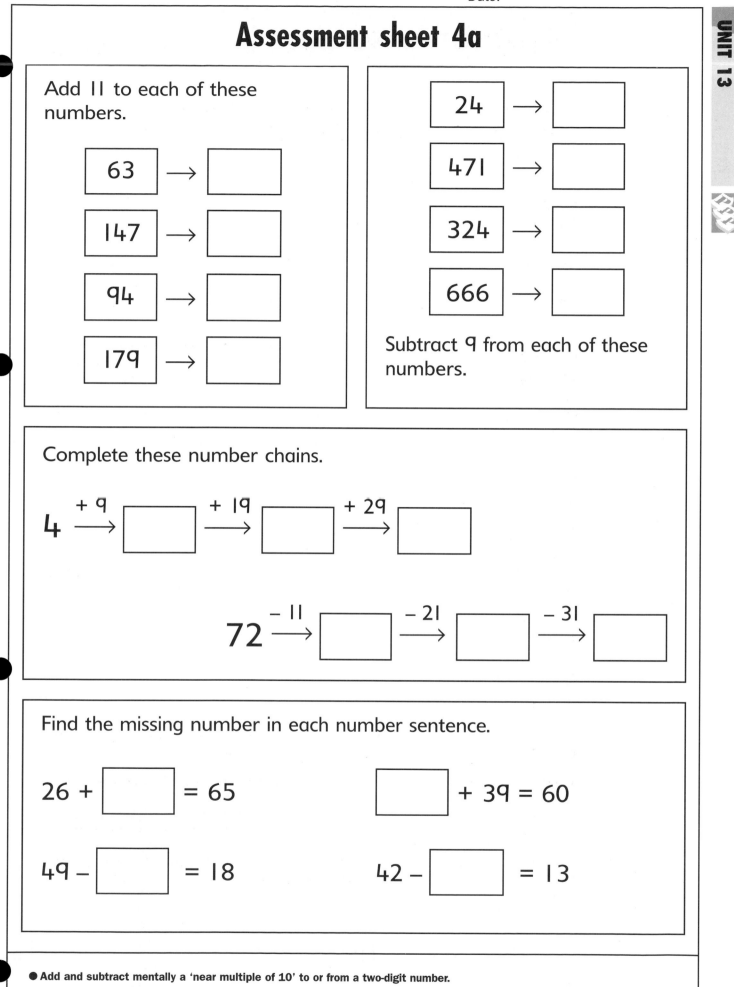

Add 11 to each of these numbers.

63 →

147 →

94 →

179 →

24 →

471 →

324 →

666 →

Subtract 9 from each of these numbers.

Complete these number chains.

4 →(+9) →(+19) →(+29)

72 →(−11) →(−21) →(−31)

Find the missing number in each number sentence.

26 + ☐ = 65   ☐ + 39 = 60

49 − ☐ = 18   42 − ☐ = 13

● Add and subtract mentally a 'near multiple of 10' to or from a two-digit number.

Assessment sheet 4b

Complete this table:

×	2	4	7	6	3	8	5	9
5								
2								

Use the results to help you answer the following:

$20 \div 5 = \boxed{}$

$45 \div 9 = \boxed{}$

$\boxed{} \div 8 = 5$

$18 \div \boxed{} = 2$

$14 \div \boxed{} = 7$

$\boxed{} \div \boxed{} = 2$

48 eggs are put into boxes that hold 6 eggs each. How many boxes are needed?

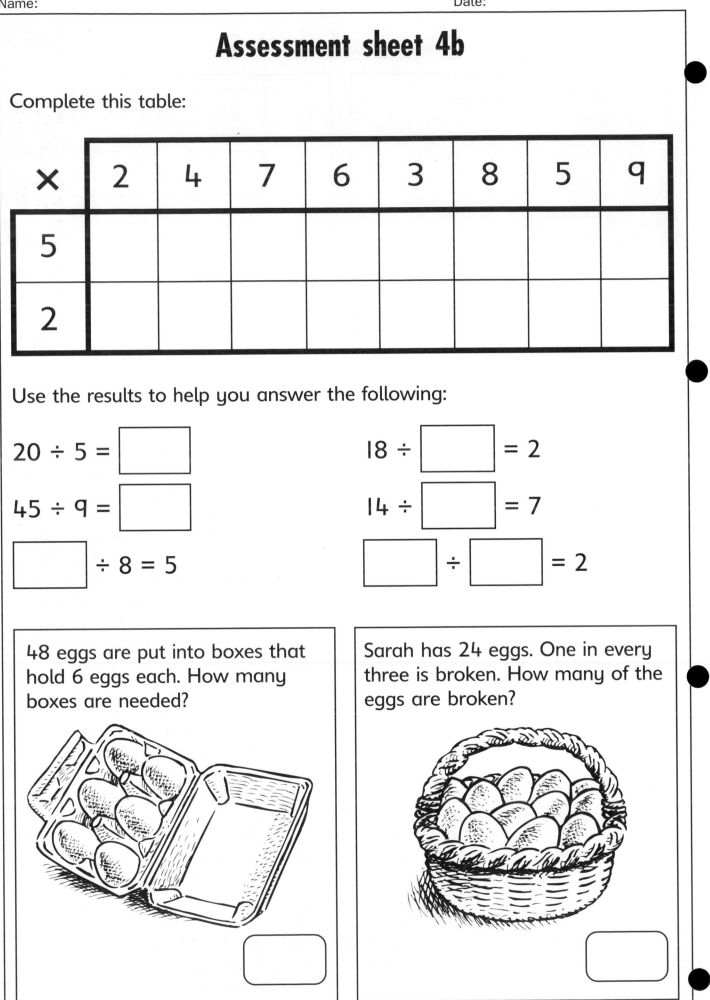

Sarah has 24 eggs. One in every three is broken. How many of the eggs are broken?

TERM 3

In this term, the expectations are raised to meet those presented in the *FfTM*. Work on mental calculation involves the manipulation of large numbers, such as finding a pair of multiples of 5 to total 100. Vertical addition is developed, building on the 'empty number line' approach. Recall of basic multiplication facts should be rapid for a growing proportion of the children. The concept of counting continues to be refined and extended, including counting in steps such as 50. Work on fractions includes showing fractional parts beyond 1 on a number linc. A growing emphasis is given to the use of precise shape vocabulary such as the words **edge**, **face** and **vertex**. Right angles are explored as a measure of turn. The links between the standard metric units of length, capacity and weight are made overt. Pictograms are introduced in data handling. The use of a computer database places further emphasis on the application of ICT within mathematics.

ENLARGE THIS SHEET TO A3 AND USE IT AS YOUR MEDIUM-TERM PLANNING GRID.

ORAL AND MENTAL SKILLS   Count on in steps of 3 or 4 from any small number to at least 50, then back again. Begin to know the 3 and 4 times tables. Extend understanding of the operations of addition and subtraction, and continue to recognise that addition can be done in any order. Use patterns of similar calculations. Derive quickly: doubles of all whole numbers to at least 20; doubles of multiples of 50 to 500. Identify near doubles, using doubles already known (eg 80 + 81). Recognise three-digit multiples of 50 and 100. Recognise two-digit and three-digit multiples of 5. Derive quickly: all pairs of multiples of 5 with a total of 100; division facts corresponding to the 2, 5 and 10 times tables. **Know by heart: all addition and subtraction facts for each number to 20; multiplication facts for the 2, 5 and 10 times tables.** Shift the digits one place to the left to multiply by 10. **Recognise that division is the inverse of multiplication.** Use doubling or halving, starting from known facts.

Unit	Topic	Objectives: children will be taught to...
1	Place value, ordering, estimating, rounding. Reading numbers from scales.	● Understand and use the vocabulary of estimation and approximation. ● Round any two-digit number to the nearest 10 and any three-digit number to the nearest 100. ● Suggest suitable units and measuring equipment to estimate or measure length or capacity. ● Read scales to the nearest division (labelled or unlabelled).
2–3	Understanding + and –. Mental calculation strategies (+ and –). Money and 'real life' problems. Making decisions and checking results. Pencil and paper procedures.	● Extend understanding of the operations of addition and subtraction, and recognise that addition can be done in any order; read and begin to write the related vocabulary. ● Use patterns of similar calculations. ● Use informal pencil and paper methods to support, record or explain HTU +/– HTU. ● **Understand and use £.p notation** (for example, know that £3.06 is £3 and 6p). ● Extend understanding that subtraction is the inverse of addition. ● Begin to use column addition for HTU + TU where the calculation cannot easily be done mentally. ● Recognise all coins and notes. ● Solve word problems involving numbers in 'real life' and money. Explain how the problem was solved.
4–6	Measures, including problems. Shape and space. Reasoning about shapes.	● Classify and describe 3-D shapes (including prisms), referring to their properties. ● Classify and describe 2-D shapes (including quadrilaterals), referring to their properties. ● Solve mathematical problems or puzzles, recognise simple patterns and relationships, generalise and predict. Suggest extensions by asking 'What if...?' ● **Identify** and sketch **lines of symmetry in simple shapes, and recognise shapes with no lines of symmetry.** ● Sketch the reflection of a simple shape in a mirror line along one edge. ● Read and begin to write the vocabulary related to position, direction and movement. ● **Identify right angles** in 2-D shapes and the environment. ● Compare angles with a right angle. ● Measure and compare using standard units (m, cm, kg, g, l, ml). ● Make and describe right angled turns, including turns between the four compass points. ● Recognise that a straight line is equivalent to two right angles. ● Suggest suitable units and measuring equipment to estimate or measure length, mass or capacity.
7	Assess and review	

ORAL AND MENTAL SKILLS   Use doubling or halving, starting from known facts. Shift the digits one/two places to the left to multiply by 10/100. **Recognise that division is the inverse of multiplication.** Begin to know the 3 and 4 times tables. Know by heart doubles of all whole numbers to at least 20. Read and begin to write the vocabulary of comparing and ordering numbers. Understand that more than two numbers can be added together. Use knowledge that addition can be done in any order to do mental calculations more efficiently, for example: put the larger number first and count on; add three or four small numbers by putting the larger number first and/or by finding pairs totalling 9, 10 or 11; partition into '5 and a bit' when adding 6, 7, 8 or 9. **Know by heart multiplication facts for the 2, 5 and 10 times tables.** Understand and use the vocabulary related to time. **Use units of time (minute, hour) and know the relationships between them.** Read the time to 5 minutes on an analogue clock. Solve word problems involving measures. Explain how the problem was solved. Use known number facts and place value to multiply and divide mentally.

Unit	Topic	Objectives: children will be taught to...
8	Counting and properties of numbers. Reasoning about numbers.	● Count on in steps of 3, 4 or 5 from any small number to at least 50, then back again. ● Recognise two-digit and three-digit multiples of 2, 5 or 10. ● **Explain methods and reasoning** orally and, where appropriate, in writing. ● Investigate a general statement about familiar numbers by finding examples that satisfy it. ● Solve mathematical problems or puzzles, recognise simple patterns or relationships, generalise and predict.
9–10	Understanding × and ÷. Mental calculation strategies (× and ÷). Money and 'real life' problems. Making decisions and checking results.	● **Choose and use appropriate operations** and ways of calculating **to solve word problems.** ● Solve word problems involving money, including finding totals. Explain how the problem was solved. ● **Understand and use £.p notation.** ● **Know what each digit represents,** and partition three-digit numbers into a multiple of 100, a multiple of ten and ones (HTU). ● **Understand and use £.p notation.** ● Recognise all coins. ● **Understand division** as grouping (repeated subtraction) or sharing. Read and begin to write the related vocabulary. ● Say or write a division statement corresponding to a given multiplication statement. ● Begin to find remainders after simple division. ● Round up or down after division, depending on the context. ● Recognise that division is the inverse of multiplication. ● Begin to recognise simple equivalent fractions.
11	Fractions.	● Recognise unit fractions (eg $\frac{1}{2}$, $\frac{1}{4}$) and use them to find fractions of shapes. ● Begin to recognise simple fractions (eg $\frac{3}{4}$) that are several parts of a whole. ● Compare familiar fractions. ● Estimate a simple fraction.
12	Understanding + and –. Mental calculation strategies (+ and –). Pencil and paper procedures. Time, including problems. Making decisions and checking results.	● Use knowledge that addition can be done in any order to do mental calculations more efficiently. For example: put the larger number first and count on; find pairs totalling 9, 10 or 11; partition into tens and units, then recombine. ● Repeat addition in a different order. ● Use informal pencil and paper methods to support, record or explain HTU + TU, HTU + HTU. ● Read and begin to write the vocabulary related to time. ● **Use units of time (minute, hour, day, week, month, year) and know the relationships between them.** ● Use a calendar. Read the time to 5 minutes on an analogue clock and a 12-hour digital clock, and use the notation 9:40.
13	Handling data.	● **Solve a given problem by organising and interpreting numerical data in simple lists, tables and graphs,** eg pictograms, frequency tables, bar charts.
14	Assess and review.	

UNIT 1

ORGANISATION (3 LESSONS)

	LEARNING OUTCOMES	ORAL AND MENTAL STARTER	MAIN TEACHING ACTIVITY	PLENARY
LESSON 1	• Understand and use the vocabulary of estimation and approximation. • Round any two-digit number to the nearest 10 and any three-digit number to the nearest 100.	STEPS OF 3: Count on and back in threes.	ROUND ABOUT: Round numbers (to the nearest 10) in a game.	Round numbers (to the nearest 100) in a game.
LESSON 2	• Understand and use the vocabulary of estimation and approximation. • Round any two-digit number to the nearest 10 and any three-digit number to the nearest 100.	STEPS OF 4: Count on and back in fours.	ROUGH TALK: Use approximation to judge when an answer is reasonable.	Estimate to the nearest 100.
LESSON 3	• Suggest suitable units and measuring equipment to estimate or measure length or capacity. • Read scales to the nearest division (labelled or unlabelled).	3S AND 4S: Chant the 3 and 4 times tables. Explore divisibility by 3.	SCALES 2: Read from scales; record measurements of length and capacity.	Compare the children's findings, using appropriate units and recording.

ORAL AND MENTAL SKILLS Count on in steps of 3 or 4 from any small number to at least 50, then back again. Begin to know the 3 and 4 times tables.

Lessons 1 and 2 are given in full. Lesson 3 follows on from what was taught in Term 2 and is given in outline.

RESOURCES

A counting stick; dice; counters; paper.

PREPARATION

Draw a 'Bingo card' on the board as shown on page 150. Each group of 2–4 children will need a pair of standard dice. Each child will need a piece of paper and seven counters.

LEARNING OUTCOMES

ORAL AND MENTAL STARTER
● Count on in steps of 3 from any small number to at least 50, then back again.
● Begin to know the 3 times table.

MAIN TEACHING ACTIVITY
● Understand and use the vocabulary of estimation and approximation.
● Round any two-digit number to the nearest 10.

ORAL AND MENTAL STARTER

STEPS OF 3: Starting at 0, count in threes up to at least 48 and back down to 0. Repeat with other starting numbers below 10.

MAIN TEACHING ACTIVITY

ROUND ABOUT: Discuss when we may need to round numbers up or down mentally (eg

---

VOCABULARY

Approximately; nearest (round to the nearest...); round up/down; just over/under; nearly; roughly; close to; between; halfway between.

when shopping). Clarify that the convention of rounding to the nearest 10 is rounding down with units values of 1–4 and up for units values of 5–9. Discuss rounding to the nearest 50 or 100. Consider contexts when this might be appropriate, eg the approximate attendance of a concert.

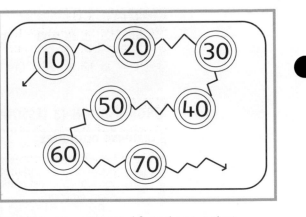

Give each child a sheet of paper and seven counters. Ask the children to copy the 'Bingo card' from the board (see figure). Give each group of 2–4 children a pair of dice. Explain the rules: *Take turns to roll both dice. Use the numbers rolled to make a number, eg 3 and 1 can make 13 or 31. Round it to the nearest 10 and cover that number on your card with a counter (in this example, it will be either 10 or 30). The winner is the first player to cover all of his or her multiples of 10.*

DIFFERENTIATION

Less able: Work with peer and/or additional adult support.
More able: Use three dice and cover multiples of 50 from 100–700.

PLENARY

Play a rounding game where each child draws a grid to accommodate three digits. Roll a dice and call out the outcome. The children must commit that number to one of their three cells (representing H, T and U). Repeat twice more. The aim is to make a total which, when rounded to the nearest hundred, is 500. Note that this will sometimes be impossible (eg with dice throws of 2, 4 and 3).

LESSON 2

RESOURCES

Objects for counting (see **Differentiation**).

PREPARATION

Prepare some questions at two or three levels of difficulty (see **Differentiation**).

LEARNING OUTCOMES

ORAL AND MENTAL STARTER
● Count on in steps of 4 from any small number to at least 50, then back again.
● Begin to know the 4 times table.

MAIN TEACHING ACTIVITY
● Understand and use the vocabulary of estimation and approximation.
● Round any two-digit number to the nearest 10 and any three-digit number to the nearest 100.

VOCABULARY

Approximate; calculate; difference (between); rounding up/down; nearest.

ORAL AND MENTAL STARTER

STEPS OF 4: As for Lesson 1, but counting in fours from 0 (and then other numbers) to at least 48.

MAIN TEACHING ACTIVITY

ROUGH TALK: Talk about approximation and when it can be useful, eg three tins of sardines at 39p each is approximately 3 × 40p = £1.20. Discuss an example, eg 9 × 11 is approximately 10 × 10.

Provide groups with questions that can be approximated by rounding one or both numbers up/down, eg 19 + 42 or 6 × 17. Ask the children to find an approximate answer to each question, calculate the actual answer, and then compare the two.

DIFFERENTIATION

Set questions to match the abilities of your teaching groups at two or three levels.
Less able: Use addition and/or subtraction only.
More able: Use all four operations, finding three-digit answers.

PLENARY

Present a range of contextual questions to encourage estimation to the nearest 100, eg
How much money, to the nearest pound, would I need to buy eight giant bars of chocolate at £1.29 each? Encourage quick answers based on the use of estimation and approximation (eg rounding the cost of one item to the nearest multiple of 10p).

LESSON 3

RESOURCES	Photocopiable page 90.
LEARNING OUTCOMES	**ORAL AND MENTAL STARTER** ● Begin to know the 3 and 4 times tables. **MAIN TEACHING ACTIVITY** ● Suggest suitable units and measuring equipment to estimate or measure length or capacity. ● Read scales to the nearest division (labelled or unlabelled).
ORAL AND MENTAL STARTER	3S AND 4S: Engage the class in chanting the 3 and 4 times tables in the conventional way (ie '1 times 3 is 3...'). At this stage, some of the children should recognise multiples of 3 or 4 when presented out of sequence. Use this opportunity to show the class that any multiple of 3 'reduces' to 3, 6 or 9, eg $54 \rightarrow 5 + 4 = 9$ (and is therefore a multiple of 3); $99 \rightarrow 9 + 9 = 18 \rightarrow 1 + 8 = 9$ (a multiple of 3); $38 \rightarrow 3 + 8 = 11 \rightarrow 1 + 1 = 2$ (therefore not a multiple of 3).
MAIN TEACHING ACTIVITY	SCALES 2: Refer back to Lesson 3, Unit 1, Term 2 to adapt copies of page 90. Build on past attainment by moving up a level of complexity, using the guidance notes for that lesson.
DIFFERENTIATION	See above.
PLENARY	Review and record the units used for each of the measurements. Elaborate further on how the compound measure of speed is generated, ie the distance covered over a length of time. Identify the use of 'per' to mean 'for every'. Allow time for the children to record the units after each answer, if they have not already done so.

UNITS 2-3

ORGANISATION (10 LESSONS)

	LEARNING OUTCOMES	ORAL AND MENTAL STARTER	MAIN TEACHING ACTIVITY	PLENARY
LESSON 1	• Extend understanding of the operations of addition and subtraction, and recognise that addition can be done in any order. • Use patterns of similar calculations.	3× AND 4×: Practise 3 and 4 times tables using numeral cards.	STAGING POSTS: Use a number line to count on to a given total.	Count on in tens beyond a given number, then count back to compensate.
LESSON 2 +3	• Use informal pencil and paper methods to support, record or explain HTU ± HTU. • **Understand and use £.p notation** (for example, know that £3.06 is £3 and 6p).	STAGING POSTS 2: Count on from a TU number along a number line. STAGING POSTS 3: As above, with compensation.	BUDGET: Select items to spend money within a given total.	Review the work done. Discuss methods of pricing in sales.
LESSON 4	• Extend understanding that subtraction is the inverse of addition.	STAGING POSTS 4: Count on from an HTU number along a number line.	OPEN UP: Find unknown numbers in open questions.	Share strategies.
LESSON 5	• Extend understanding of the operations of addition and subtraction; read and begin to write the related vocabulary.	STAGING POSTS 5: As above, with compensation.	ON THE TAKE: Solve subtraction problems and explain strategies used.	Share strategies for subtraction.
LESSON 6	• Use informal pencil and paper methods to support, record or explain HTU + TU, HTU + HTU. • Begin to use column addition for HTU + TU where the calculation cannot easily be done mentally.	DOUBLE UP: Practise recall or quick calculation of doubles (totals to 20).	VERTICAL ADDITION: Use vertical computation involving addition of digits in each column.	Extend to HTU + TU and HTU + HTU.
LESSON 7	• Use informal pencil and paper methods to support, record or explain HTU – TU, HTU – HTU.	DOUBLE UP: Practise recall or quick calculation of doubles (totals to 40).	GOING DOWN: Use empty number line for TU – TU by counting up from smaller number.	Extend to HTU – TU and HTU – HTU.
LESSON 8	• Recognise all coins and notes. • **Understand and use £.p notation** (eg know that £3.06 is £3 and 6p).	NEAR DOUBLES: Practise recall of near doubles.	GIVING CHANGE: Practise with money (in role).	Set money doubling problem.
LESSON 9	• Solve word problems involving numbers in 'real life'. Explain how the problem was solved.	COUNT IN 50S: Practise multiples of 50 and 100.	PIGS AND DUCKS: Explore an open addition problem.	Try a similar, but closed, problem.
LESSON 10	• Solve word problems involving money. Explain how the problem was solved. • **Understand and use £.p notation** (eg know that £3.06 is £3 and 6p).	NEAR DOUBLES 2: Practise calculating near doubles with a three-digit total.	STEPS: Explore two-step problems involving money.	Discuss solution to problem from **Plenary** of Lesson 8.

ORAL AND MENTAL SKILLS   Begin to know the 3 and 4 times tables. Extend understanding of the operations of addition and subtraction, and continue to recognise that addition can be done in any order. Use patterns of similar calculations. Derive quickly: doubles of all whole numbers to at least 20; doubles of multiples of 50 to 500. Identify near doubles, using doubles already known (eg 80 + 81). Recognise three-digit multiples of 50 and 100.

Lessons 1, 2, 4–8 and 10 are given in full. Lessons 3 and 9 follow on from what has already been taught and are given in outline.

RESOURCES

A large teaching number line and dry-wipe marker pen; individual number lines; numeral cards; dice (optional); calculators (optional).

PREPARATION

All the children will need access to a large number line.

LEARNING OUTCOMES

ORAL AND MENTAL STARTER

● Begin to know the 3 and 4 times tables.

MAIN TEACHING ACTIVITY

● Extend understanding of the operations of addition and subtraction, and continue to recognise that addition can be done in any order.
● Use patterns of similar calculations.

VOCABULARY

Count to/on/ from; start from/at; carry on; continue; answer; check; work out; estimate.

ORAL AND MENTAL STARTER

3× AND 4×: Encourage recall or quick derivation of 3 and 4 times table facts by generating random numbers with a 1–10 pack of numeral cards, then asking children to multiply them by 3 or 4.

MAIN TEACHING ACTIVITY

STAGING POSTS: Explain that this lesson is about subtracting. Use a large number line to demonstrate counting on from various numbers to a fixed larger number. Make the latter a key 'staging post' such as 20, 50 or 100. Discuss strategies used for counting from, say, 26 to 50: *Do you count up to 30 first? Do you count in tens from 26 to 46 and then count on? Are there other possible strategies? Do we always use the same strategy? Which strategy do you like best? Why?*

Ask the children, working individually or in pairs, to generate a start number and find the complementary number which is needed to 'make it up' to a given staging post. The start numbers could be provided by yourself, chosen by the child, or generated by throwing two dice (and either multiplying the two digits or simply placing them side by side). You may like to give the children their own number lines, and/or a calculator to help them check their answers.

DIFFERENTIATION

Less able: Work with a 0–20 number line.
More able: Count on to 100 (or more).

PLENARY

Introduce the idea of counting on in tens along an unstructured number line, going beyond a staging post and then counting back to compensate (eg counting on from 32 to 100 by counting in tens to 102 and then counting back 2 units). This approach may have arisen in the **Main teaching activity**.

RESOURCES

Toy and games catalogues or leaflets; calculators (optional); scissors and glue (optional).

PREPARATION

All the children will need access to a catalogue or leaflet. You may wish to give some children simpler lists (see **Differentiation**).

LEARNING OUTCOMES

ORAL AND MENTAL STARTER

● Extend understanding of the operations of addition and subtraction, and continue to recognise that addition can be done in any order.
● Use patterns of similar calculations.

MAIN TEACHING ACTIVITY

● Use informal pencil and paper methods to support, record or explain HTU ± HTU.
● **Understand and use £.p notation** (for example, know that £3.06 is £3 and 6p).

VOCABULARY

Buy; bought; more/most expensive; less/least expensive; cheap; costs less; cheaper; record; pick out.

ORAL AND MENTAL STARTER

STAGING POSTS 2: Use the board to revise counting on from two-digit numbers along an unstructured number line (see Lesson 1).

MAIN TEACHING ACTIVITY

BUDGET: Explain that this lesson is about spending money. Look at some of the catalogues and leaflets together. Talk through the main features of the presentation (eg numbering items) and pricing. Emphasise the recording of amounts of money, eg £3.99 means £3 and 99p.

Ask the children to imagine they have a set amount of money (say £20) to spend on items of their choice. They can spend up to the limit, but must not go over it. They should record the amounts spent and sketch the items chosen. If the source materials are disposable, the pictures can be cut and pasted alongside the calculations.

Monitor how the children work, and encourage a range of calculation methods. Depending on your main objectives, you may or may not prefer to offer calculators. This activity continues in Lesson 3.

DIFFERENTIATION

Less able: Use a simplified list with a limited number of items and/or lower prices. Work with a lower target total. More able: Present their work, perhaps as a table (with teacher guidance).

PLENARY

Review the work done. Set targets for the follow-up (Lesson 3).

LESSON 3

For the **Oral and mental starter**, STAGING POSTS 3, revisit counting on and compensating with two-digit numbers as covered in the **Plenary** of Lesson 1. Continue the **Main teaching activity** from Lesson 2 – use your introduction to recap. Differentiate as for Lesson 2. In the **Plenary**, talk about why prices are often 'nearly' whole numbers of pounds (eg £2.99). Introduce some of the language of sales: discount, 50% off, two for the price of one, etc.

LESSON 4

RESOURCES

Paper; pens or pencils; counting equipment (optional).

PREPARATION

Some pupils may need access to counting equipment.

LEARNING OUTCOMES

ORAL AND MENTAL STARTER
● Extend understanding of the operations of addition and subtraction, and continue to recognise that addition can be done in any order.

MAIN TEACHING ACTIVITY
● Extend understanding that subtraction is the inverse of addition.

VOCABULARY

Is the same as...; equals; find; different; investigate.

ORAL AND MENTAL STARTER

STAGING POSTS 4: As for Lesson 2, but count on from three-digit numbers with no compensation.

MAIN TEACHING ACTIVITY

OPEN UP: Discuss the open-ended question □ – △ = 10. Invite examples of solutions (eg 21 – 11, 13 – 3). Now present a 'double-sided' statement such as 10 + □ = 30 – △. This is more challenging. Using the relevant vocabulary (see **Vocabulary**), identify one or two possible solutions. Emphasise that the = sign indicates the equality of the left and right sides of the equation, rather than just meaning 'do the operation'.

Give the children suitable open-ended questions (see **Differentiation**) and ask them to find as many different solutions as possible. Organise them according to prior attainment, perhaps setting the task as a collaborative exercise for pairs or threes (recording on large sheets of paper).

DIFFERENTIATION

Less able: Work on the first type of example (□ – △ = 10).
More able: Find solutions for the statement 100 + □ = 500 – △.

PLENARY

Review as a class some of the solutions found by each group. Talk about how they were found, reinforcing the idea that one solution can be used to generate further solutions.

LESSON 5

RESOURCES

Photocopiable page 160.

PREPARATION

Make one copy per child of page 160, modified for different abilities (see **Differentiation**).

LEARNING OUTCOMES

ORAL AND MENTAL STARTER
● Extend understanding of the operation of addition and the related vocabulary, and continue to recognise that addition can be done in any order.
● Use patterns of similar calculations.

MAIN TEACHING ACTIVITY
● Extend understanding of the operations of addition and subtraction; read and begin to write the related vocabulary.

ORAL AND MENTAL STARTER

STAGING POSTS 5: As for Lesson 3, but count on from three-digit numbers and use compensation. (**NB** The idea of compensating 'near multiples of 10' was introduced in Year 2.)

MAIN TEACHING ACTIVITY

ON THE TAKE: Ask some rapid recall questions involving subtraction. You might reuse the flashcards from Lesson 4, Unit 2, Term 2. Make sure that some of the questions involve 'gaps' in places other than immediately after the = sign (eg □ – 6 = 12).

Provide copies of page 160. Ask the children (working individually or in pairs) to calculate the answer to each question and to explain (in writing) how they did it. Affirm that there is no single 'correct' method.

DIFFERENTIATION

Less able: Use a modified version of page 160, with fewer examples and smaller numbers; work with teacher support to help them evaluate their calculation strategies.
More able: Use a version of page 160 amended to give similar questions with larger numbers, eg '171 take away 89'.

PLENARY

Gather the class together to share their different strategies. Include in the discussion the use of strategies such as counting on to calculate differences, rounding up or down and then compensating or using addition as the inverse of subtraction.

LESSON 6

RESOURCES

Numeral cards (page 13), a '+' operation card.

LEARNING OUTCOMES

ORAL AND MENTAL STARTER
● Derive quickly doubles of all whole numbers to at least 20.

MAIN TEACHING ACTIVITY
● Use informal pencil and paper methods to support, record or explain HTU + TU, HTU + HTU.
● Begin to use column addition for HTU + TU where the calculation cannot easily be done mentally.

ORAL AND MENTAL STARTER

DOUBLE UP: Use a quickfire question and answer session to practise recall or quick calculation of doubles to a maximum total of 20.

MAIN TEACHING ACTIVITY

VERTICAL ADDITION: Remind the class of the **Oral and mental starters** in Unit 1 that involved the use of an unstructured number line for calculation. Explain that this lesson is about developing and extending their calculation methods. Represent a two-digit addition problem vertically, using the key methods identified in the *FfTM* (see figure). Both of these methods should be explored. The first involves dealing with the most significant digits first; as such, it is more similar to mental methods. The second method relates more closely to traditional approaches, but avoids the use of 'carrying'. Stress that, because addition is commutative, it can be done in either way.

Give each child five numeral cards (see **Differentiation**) and a '+' symbol. For most of the children, use numerals 2, 3, 5, 6 and 7. This will give some units totals greater than 9, and some overall totals exceeding 100. Ask them to make some two-digit addition problems, using any four cards each time. For each combination, they should write down the sum on plain paper, using both of the methods exemplified above.

```
   57            57
  +36           +36
  ___           ___
   80    and    13
   13           80
  ___           ___
   93           93
```

DIFFERENTIATION

Less able: Use numerals 1–5. This will keep the totals within 100 and limit the sub-totals. More able: Move on to HTU + TU in advance of the **Plenary**.

PLENARY

Show how the activity would work with HTU + TU and HTU + HTU, or even with four-digit numbers. Ask the class to evaluate which of the two methods they liked best.

RESOURCES

Blank paper; pencils; empty number lines (optional).

LEARNING OUTCOMES

ORAL AND MENTAL STARTER

● Derive quickly doubles of all whole numbers to at least 20.

MAIN TEACHING ACTIVITY

● Use informal pencil and paper methods to support, record or explain HTU – TU, HTU – HTU.

VOCABULARY
How many more to make...?; more; subtract; take away; minus; draw; sketch; present; represent.

ORAL AND MENTAL STARTER

DOUBLE UP: Use a quickfire question and answer session to practise recall or quick calculation of doubles to a maximum total of 40.

MAIN TEACHING ACTIVITY

GOING DOWN: Remind the class of the **Main teaching activity** from Lesson 1, involving the use of an unstructured ('empty') number line for calculation. Explain that this lesson is about developing and extending other calculation methods for subtraction (finding the difference). Demonstrate some examples of written subtraction, using approaches from the *FfTM* related to counting on from the smaller number. As you write down the subtractions, show them on an empty number line (see figure).

Provide some calculations involving two-digit numbers for the class to complete. Support as required.

$$32 \xrightarrow{+8} 40 \xrightarrow{+20} 60 \xrightarrow{+3} 63$$

$32 + 8 + 20 + 3 = 63$
so $63 - 32 = 31$

DIFFERENTIATION

Less able: Use the number line to find answers, without writing out calculation.
More able: Find differences between three digit numbers in advance of the **Plenary**.

PLENARY

Demonstrate counting on to 1000, starting with a number below 100 and then with a number below 300. Repeat for a calculation such as 432 – 279. Ask the class whether this is significantly harder than with two-digit numbers. Introduce vertical subtraction, using approaches given in the *FfTM*.

RESOURCES

Real coins (or photocopiable page 100); simple hand-drawn £5, £10 and £20 banknotes.

PREPARATION

Each child or pair will need 1p, two 2ps, 5p and 10p coins for working to 20p, an additional 20p and 10p coin if working to 50p, and a 50p coin if working to £1.00. (See **Differentiation**.) These coins could be cut from an enlarged version of page 100. Some children will also need to use £2 coins and banknotes.

LEARNING OUTCOMES

ORAL AND MENTAL STARTER
● Identify near doubles, using doubles already known (eg 80 + 81).

MAIN TEACHING ACTIVITY
● Recognise all coins and notes.
● **Understand and use £.p notation** (eg know that £3.06 is £3 and 6p).

ORAL AND MENTAL STARTER

NEAR DOUBLES: Use a quickfire question and answer session to practise recall of near doubles involving two-digit addition (eg 80 + 81).

MAIN TEACHING ACTIVITY

GIVING CHANGE: This activity follows on from Lesson 7, since the 'shopkeeper's addition' method of giving change is a practical application of counting on from the smaller number. Explain how traditional shopkeeping often involves counting on as an efficient way of calculating and giving the correct change. (Modern tills calculate the change required automatically.) Engage in a role-play with one or two children to simulate a purchase. Use real coins or giant coin replicas (from page 100).

Ask the children, in pairs, to take turns at creating an amount within the given total, and to use counting on to calculate the appropriate change. After each turn, they should record the cost and change (as evidence for assessment). They should be using as full a range of coins and notes as possible.

DIFFERENTIATION

Less able: Work within a total of 20p or 50p.
More able: Use the £1 and £2 coins, and pictures of £5, £10 and £20 notes.

PLENARY

Introduce a puzzle: *Would you rather be given £30 as a one-off payment or have 1p in January, double that in February, double that in March and so on through to December?* This can be left for thinking about (perhaps at home), and will be revisited in Lesson 10. Note that this problem builds on the 'double your money' idea in Term 2. Use this context to record amounts of money in the conventional way, eg £30.00, £0.01.

RESOURCES	Pencil; paper; models or pictures of pigs and ducks (see **Differentiation**).
LEARNING OUTCOMES	**ORAL AND MENTAL STARTER** ● Recognise three-digit multiples of 50 and 100. **MAIN TEACHING ACTIVITY** ● Solve word problems involving numbers in 'real life'. Explain how the problem was solved.
ORAL AND MENTAL STARTER	COUNT IN 50S: Practise counting in 50s to 500. Relate to counting in fives to 50. Consider why even multiples of 50 give multiples of 100. Count in 100s to 1000.
MAIN TEACHING ACTIVITY	PIGS AND DUCKS: Begin with some word problems involving multiples of 2 and 4, eg *20 legs – how many people is that? How many wheels will six cars have?* Set a problem: *A farmer gathers all his pigs and ducks into one pen. They have a total of 20 legs between them. How many pigs and how many ducks are there?* Start by identifying 'ducks only' and 'pigs only' sets, and representing these on the board in ways suggested by the class. Ask the children to find mixed combinations of animals that meet these criteria, and to represent them in any way they feel is appropriate. You might expect some children to find all the possible combinations, others to find only one or two.
DIFFERENTIATION	Less able: Work with models or pictures. Find combinations for a total of 8 legs. More able: Work systematically, perhaps finding all possible combinations.
PLENARY	Ask a related question: *There are 22 legs in a field, belonging to 6 animals that are either pigs or ducks. How many of each animal are there?* This extends the **Main teaching activity** as there is only one answer: 5 pigs and 1 duck.

RESOURCES

A selection of coins (see **Differentiation**).

PREPARATION

Prepare written tasks for the Main teaching activity (see below). Group work may allow the use of portable display boards for this.

LEARNING OUTCOMES

ORAL AND MENTAL STARTER
● Identify near doubles, using doubles already known (eg 80 + 81).

MAIN TEACHING ACTIVITY
● Solve word problems involving money. Explain how the problem was solved.
● **Understand and use £.p notation** (eg know that £3.06 is £3 and 6p).

VOCABULARY
What could we try next?; best way; another way.

ORAL AND MENTAL STARTER

NEAR DOUBLES 2: Use a question and answer session to practise calculating near doubles with totals greater than 100. Compare strategies for calculation.

MAIN TEACHING ACTIVITY

STEPS: Explain that this lesson is about working out problems logically. Introduce some closed questions involving money, eg *A pencil costs 22p and a pen 34p. How much for both?* or *How much are 3 pencil sharpeners at 33p each?*

Set the children working individually on the two written problems below. Explain that they are likely to be harder than the previous ones, because the solution involves more than one step: **A.** *Two rulers cost 86p. A pen costs 10p more than a ruler. How much do pens and rulers cost?* **B.** *Three pencils cost 48p. Two pencils and a pen cost 56p. How much do pencils and pens cost?*

DIFFERENTIATION

Less able: Work with additional support and/or one-step problems. In the latter case, use real coins.
More able: Solve problems of a similar type to **A** and **B**, but involving amounts of money up to and beyond £10.00. Consider different strategies for finding answers.

PLENARY

Follow up the **Plenary** from Lesson 8. Demonstrate that it is better to go for the doubling option, as this generates more than £30 over 12 instalments (a total of £40.95). Record each stage using £.p notation.

Subtraction strategies

Question	Answer	How I did it
16 take away 9		
24 subtract 17		
10 less than 39		
What is the difference between 40 and 27?		
How many less than 26 is 14?		
14 is taken away from a number. The answer is 27. What is the number?		
What must I take from 32 to leave 18?		
100 less than 364 is …?		

UNITS 4-6

ORGANISATION (13 LESSONS)

	LEARNING OUTCOMES	ORAL AND MENTAL STARTER	MAIN TEACHING ACTIVITY	PLENARY
LESSON 1	• Classify and describe 3-D shapes (including prisms), referring to their properties.	5×: Test recall of 5 times table facts.	SOLID SHAPES: Record properties of some common 3-D shapes.	PLENARY Discuss names and properties of other solid shapes.
LESSON 2	• Classify and describe 2-D shapes (including quadrilaterals), referring to their properties.	PAIRS OF 5S: Derive pairs of even multiples of 5 totalling 100.	2-D SHAPES: Use a two-piece tangram to make various shapes.	Look at commercial shape posters.
LESSON 3	• Solve mathematical problems or puzzles, recognise simple patterns and relationships, generalise and predict. Suggest extensions by asking 'What if...?' • **Identify** and sketch **lines of symmetry in simple shapes, and recognise shapes with no lines of symmetry.** • Sketch the reflection of a simple shape in a mirror line along one edge.	MORE PAIRS: Derive pairs of odd multiples of 5 totalling 100.	HALF PICTURES: Use a set of interlocking cubes to create patterns with line symmetry.	Consider a chessboard shape problem.
LESSON 4 +5	• Solve mathematical problems or puzzles, recognise simple patterns and relationships, generalise and predict. Suggest extensions by asking 'What if...?'	ADD UP: Practise recall of addition bonds to 20 and beyond. TAKE AWAY: Practise recall of subtraction bonds within 20.	SQUARES: Use pegboards to make different squares. PENTAGONS: Extend to making different pentagons.	Discuss solutions to chessboard problem from Lesson 3. Revisit the shape posters used in Lesson 2.
LESSON 6	• Read and begin to write the vocabulary related to position, direction and movement. • **Identify right angles** in 2-D shapes and the environment. • Compare angles with a right angle.	PLACE VALUE: Use to multiply by 10.	ALL RIGHT NOW: Sort 2-D shapes according to their angle properties.	Discuss angle properties of shapes in maths and in the environment.
LESSON 7 +8	• Measure and compare using standard units (m, cm).	PLACE VALUE: Use to multiply by 100. Use to divide by 10 or 100.	I SHRUNK THE KIDS: Create a half size drawing, using a suitable approach to measurement.	Review the progress made. Display the pictures.
LESSON 9 +10	• Read and begin to write the vocabulary related to position, direction and movement. • Make and describe right angled turns, including turns between the four compass points. • Recognise that a straight line is equivalent to two right angles.	TWICE AS MUCH: Use doubling as a strategy for multiplying. DOUBLE AND HALVE: Use as a strategy for multiplying.	ROUTES: Draw pathways on a grid network. Record pathways using compass directions and co-ordinates.	Introducing co-ordinates and directions Discuss which way of recording directions is best.
LESSON 11	• Read and begin to write the vocabulary related to position, direction and movement.	2× AND 5×: Practise recall of times table facts.	SPINNERS: Use a pegboard to generate 'rotating patterns'.	Relate angles within a shape to angles of turn.

cont...

LEARNING OUTCOMES	ORAL AND MENTAL STARTER	MAIN TEACHING ACTIVITY	PLENARY
LESSON 12 + 13 ● Suggest suitable units and measuring equipment to estimate or measure length, mass or capacity. ● Measure and compare using standard units (m, cm, kg, g, l, ml). ● Read scales to the nearest division (labelled or unlabelled).	÷2 AND ÷10: Derive division facts from 2× and 10× tables. ÷5: Derive division facts from 5× table.	MEASURING UP: Measure and record masses, lengths and capacities of various items.	Overview of units of measurement. Review of measurement tasks and clarification.

ORAL AND MENTAL SKILLS Recognise two-digit and three-digit multiples of 5. Derive quickly: all pairs of multiples of 5 with a total of 100; division facts corresponding to the 2, 5 and 10 times tables. **Know by heart: all addition and subtraction facts for each number to 20; multiplication facts for the 2, 5 and 10 times tables.** Shift the digits one place to the left to multiply by 10. **Recognise that division is the inverse of multiplication.** Use doubling or halving, starting from known facts.

Lessons 1–4, 6, 7, 9, 11 and 12 are given in full. Lessons 5, 8, 10 and 13 follow on from what has already been taught and are given in outline.

LESSON 1

RESOURCES

Numeral cards (page 13); solid shapes; photocopiable page 171.

PREPARATION

Make one copy per child of page 171. Provide a set of solid shapes (including those listed on page 171) for each table.

LEARNING OUTCOMES

ORAL AND MENTAL STARTER
● Recognise two-digit and three-digit multiples of 5.
● **Know by heart multiplication facts for the 5 times table.**

MAIN TEACHING ACTIVITY
● Classify and describe 3-D shapes (including prisms), referring to their properties.

VOCABULARY

Cube; cuboid; triangular-based pyramid; square-based pyramid; triangular prism.

ORAL AND MENTAL STARTER

5×: Test the childrens' quick recall of 5 times table facts, generated at random using a set of numeral cards 1–10. You should expect some children to possess rapid recall when these multiples are presented out of sequence.

MAIN TEACHING ACTIVITY

SOLID SHAPES: Explain that this lesson is about looking at 3-D shapes. Look at an example of each of the solid shapes listed on page 171. Discuss what is meant by the words **face**, **vertex** (plural **vertices**) and **edge**. Look at the number of faces, edges and vertices on one particular shape.

Provide sets of shapes and copies of page 171. Ask the children to complete the sheet by working with the shapes. They can then add details of further shapes in the empty rows.

DIFFERENTIATION

Less able: Focus on the number of faces on each shape.
More able: Look for patterns. For example, in a cube, the total number of faces (6) and vertices (8) is 2 **more** than the number of edges (12). Is this true of other shapes?

PLENARY

Use other solid shapes (eg a pentagonal prism) to discuss shape names and properties. At this stage, you might talk about the end faces of prisms being the same shape and size (congruent). A cube is a special prism in which **all** the faces are congruent.

LESSON 2

RESOURCES
Card; paper; pencils; rulers; commercial shape posters (from educational suppliers).

PREPARATION
Make one two-piece tangram (see **Main teaching activity**) per child or pair.

LEARNING OUTCOMES

ORAL AND MENTAL STARTER
● Derive quickly all pairs of multiples of 5 with a total of 100.

MAIN TEACHING ACTIVITY
● Classify and describe 2-D shapes (including quadrilaterals), referring to their properties.

ORAL AND MENTAL STARTER

VOCABULARY
Circle; triangle; square; rectangle; pentagon; hexagon; octagon.

PAIRS OF 5S: Return to multiples of 5 and confirm that, given 4 × 5, the children can both calculate the answer (20) and give the complementary number taking the answer up to 100 (ie 80). Practise with even multiples of 5 only.

MAIN TEACHING ACTIVITY

2-D SHAPES: Revise the names of common 2-D shapes – circle, triangle, square, rectangle, pentagon, hexagon, octagon – and discuss their properties. Introduce the **trapezium** and **parallelogram**, and explain their properties. **NB** This can be a complex matter since, for example, a square is a special kind of rectangle, which in turn is a special kind of parallelogram.

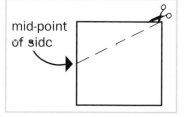

mid-point of side

Give each child or pair a two-piece tangram, made from a square piece of card (see figure, left). Ask the children to place the two pieces of card edge to edge to make different plane shapes. Draw their attention to the fact that **any** five-sided shape is a pentagon, and so on. They should sketch their shapes (freehand) on paper and label them with the appropriate shape names.

DIFFERENTIATION

Less able: Work with shape outlines (or cut-out windows) within which the different arrangements can be manipulated.
More able: Align sides of different length to make irregular shapes and label them (see figure below).

PLENARY

Use commercial shape posters as a stimulus for further discussion of 2-D shapes.

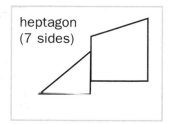

heptagon (7 sides)

LESSON 3

RESOURCES

Interlocking cubes; safety mirrors; plain paper; squared paper; a chessboard.

PREPARATION

Each child or pair will need a mirror and six cubes. More cubes and other resources may be needed (see **Differentiation**).

LEARNING OUTCOMES

ORAL AND MENTAL STARTER
● Derive quickly all pairs of multiples of 5 with a total of 100.

MAIN TEACHING ACTIVITY

● Solve mathematical problems or puzzles, recognise simple patterns and relationships, generalise and predict. Suggest extensions by asking 'What if...?'
● **Identify** and sketch **lines of symmetry in simple shapes, and recognise shapes with no lines of symmetry.**
● Sketch the reflection of a simple shape in a mirror line along one edge.

ORAL AND MENTAL STARTER

MORE PAIRS: Continue with multiples of 5 and confirm that, given 5 × 5, the children can calculate the answer (25) and give the complementary number taking it up to 100 (ie 75). Practise with odd multiples of 5 only.

MAIN TEACHING ACTIVITY

HALF PICTURES: Explain that this lesson is about symmetry. Draw some 'half pictures' with a line of symmetry at the edge where reflection is to occur. It will be helpful to consider both freeform shapes and shapes created on a squared grid; the latter format encourages accuracy in mapping the reflection to exactly the same shape and size as the original.

Ask the children to arrange their six cubes as shown below, then use the mirror to create as many symmetrical patterns as possible. They should record their solutions on plain paper. Monitor the work done. Children may encounter perceptual difficulties in mapping the reflection to the appropriate positions, or they may dispense with the mirror prematurely, leading to errors.

DIFFERENTIATION

Less able: Record on squared paper – perhaps using cubes, cube stamps or gummed squares.
More able: Try to make symmetrical patterns without the mirror, then use the mirror to check.

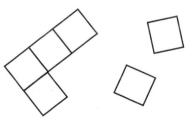

PLENARY

Show the class a chessboard and ask them to think about the number of squares. They are likely to recognise the 8 × 8 arrangement quickly. Ask them what squares they can find on the board, other than 8 × 8 (the perimeter) and 1 × 1 (a single square). What about 2 × 2, 3 × 3 etc? Leave them to think about it. This problem will be revisited in Lesson 5.

RESOURCES

Dice; pegboards; pegs; elastic bands; dotted paper; squared paper.

PREPARATION

All the children will need access to a selection of pegboards (9-pin, 16-pin and 25-pin).

LEARNING OUTCOMES

ORAL AND MENTAL STARTER
● **Know by heart all addition and subtraction facts for each number to 20.**

MAIN TEACHING ACTIVITY
● Solve mathematical problems or puzzles, recognise simple patterns or relationships, generalise and predict. Suggest extensions by asking 'What if...?'

ORAL AND MENTAL STARTER

ADD UP: Consolidate instant recall of addition bonds to 20 by rolling two standard dice and calling out the numbers. The children have to add these quickly and record the **complement** that makes the total up to 20.

VOCABULARY

Symmetry; symmetrical; line of symmetry; mirror line; reflection; match; grid; horizontal; vertical.

LESSON 4 +5

VOCABULARY

Shape; square; predict; show me; copy; pegs; pegboard; same way; different way; pentagon; acute angle; right angle.

MAIN TEACHING ACTIVITY

SQUARES: Recap on the properties of squares, emphasising that a square is a square regardless of its orientation in space.

Share different pegboards between groups. Ask the children to make some different squares on the pegboard, using pegs and elastic bands. The squares can be different in size or in position, and the children should record their squares accurately on dotted paper. Each group should have a turn using each type of board.

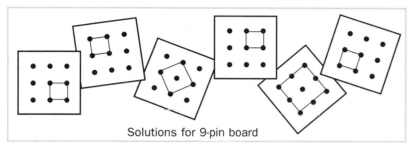

Solutions for 9-pin board

DIFFERENTIATION

Less able: Use a provided outline drawing of the pegboard for recording. Work with one type of pegboard only. More able: Try to find all the possible solutions for a given size of board. There are six different squares for a 9-pin board (see figure).

PLENARY

Consider the chessboard problem from Lesson 3. Some able children may have found all the possible squares, but it is not necessary for the class to do this; what is more important is that they appreciate the pattern. Identify the 64 1 × 1 squares. Demonstrate (perhaps with a card window) how it is possible to move across and down the board to show the 2 × 2 squares etc, up to the single 8 × 8 square. The children should realise that we are talking about a **lot** of squares!

LESSON 5

For the **Oral and mental starter**, TAKE AWAY, practise recall of subtraction facts within 20. For the **Main teaching activity**, PENTAGONS, draw some different pentagons on the board. Discuss them, working towards a definition of a pentagon: a closed shape with five straight sides. Distinguish between regular and irregular pentagons. Discuss the angles and develop related vocabulary (**acute angle, right angle**). Ask the children to create different-shaped pentagons on pegboards. Each group should stick to one size of pegboard. Less able children could use a 9-pin board, which has the lowest potential number of shapes. More able children could investigate the areas of their pentagons. In the **Plenary**, revisit some of the posters used in Lesson 2.

LESSON 6

RESOURCES

A large set square or angle measurer, photocopiable page 172; a blank chart (see **Preparation**); a maths dictionary.

PREPARATION

Prepare a large, blank version of the chart on page 89 of the *FfTM*.

LEARNING OUTCOMES

ORAL AND MENTAL STARTER
● Shift the digits one place to the left to multiply by 10.

MAIN TEACHING ACTIVITY
● Read and begin to write the vocabulary related to position, direction and movement.
● **Identify right angles** in 2-D shapes and the environment.
● Compare angles with a right angle.

ORAL AND MENTAL STARTER

PLACE VALUE: Provide a single-digit number and write it in the units column of a hundreds,

VOCABULARY
Boundary; right angle; triangle; square; rectangle; pentagon; parallelogram.

tens and units grid. Ask the class to calculate the number that is ten times larger. Write the digit you started with in the grid beneath your last entry, but this time in the tens column. Explain that this is what happens when we multiply by 10. Add a 0 to it, showing how 0 acts as a **place holder**. Use the term **boundary** to explain how the digit crosses into the tens: *It moves across the boundary from the units to the tens.*

MAIN TEACHING ACTIVITY

ALL RIGHT NOW: Recap on how to measure a right angle, using a large teaching set square, an angle measurer (see page 172) or the corner of a sheet of card. Investigate whether a regular pentagon (drawn or projected) has any right angles.

Provide copies of page 172 and alert the children to the regular pentagon shape. Ask them to copy the chart shown below onto a sheet of A4 paper (landscape). Show how the regular pentagon would be cut and pasted in the right hand column of the chart. Now ask them to cut and paste all the shapes into the correct columns of their chart. They should use the angle measurer to check for right angles.

'no right angles'	'all right angles'	'some right angles'

DIFFERENTIATION

Less able: Work with peer support in pairs or threes.
More able: Try to identify the shapes and label them by name.

PLENARY

Use a maths dictionary to talk about how angle properties help to define a shape. Encourage the children to relate this work to shapes in the environment (food, roads, buildings etc).

RESOURCES

A printed map; a photograph of an image from a microscope; large sheets of paper; large pens; length measuring equipment (rulers and tape measures); strips of paper (optional); calculators (optional); numeral cards 0–9 (page 13).

PREPARATION

The **Main teaching activity** is resource-intensive, and is carried over two lessons. A large sheet of paper will be needed for each group of three or four pupils.

LEARNING OUTCOMES

ORAL AND MENTAL STARTER
● Shift the digits two places to the left to multiply by 100.
● **Recognise that division is the inverse of multiplication.**

VOCABULARY

Compare; half; size; nearly; roughly; measure.

MAIN TEACHING ACTIVITY
● Measure and compare using standard units (m, cm).

ORAL AND MENTAL STARTER

PLACE VALUE: As for Lesson 6, this time multiplying a single-digit number by 100.

MAIN TEACHING ACTIVITY

I SHRUNK THE KIDS: Discuss the idea of scaling up and down, using examples such as microscopic images (scaling up) and maps (scaling down). Talk about how and when a range of items of length measuring equipment are used.

Explain that the task is for one child in each group of three or four to be drawn to half size. Clarify what this means: not only should the image's height be half the child's height, but all other measurements (eg head size, shoulder width) must be reduced in proportion. Allow the children to choose their methods and equipment, or suggest methods for each group to match ability levels (see **Differentiation**). When they have drawn an accurate image, they should add details such as clothes and facial features. Explain that this activity will continue into the next lesson, allowing for careful completion and/or redrawing.

DIFFERENTIATION

Less able: Work with additional adult support. Use informal units of measure (such as cubes), or use strips of paper folded in half and translated directly onto the paper. Most of the class should measure accurately in metres and centimetres, using mental methods and/or calculators to ascertain half sizes.
More able: Expect multiple measures to be made with accuracy, mental calculation for halving, and recording in m, cm and mm.

PLENARY

Review progress and set targets for the next session.

LESSON 8

Develop the **Oral and mental starter** from Lessons 6 and 7 by showing how dividing a number by 10 or 100 reverses the effect of multiplying by 10 or 100. Avoid saying that division 'makes numbers smaller', as this can lead to confusion in the future (eg division of negative numbers). Present several numeral cards at random and ask the children to make each number ten times larger, then ten times larger again, then ten times smaller, then ten times smaller again. Continue the **Main teaching activity** from Lesson 7. In the **Plenary**, have a 'show and tell' session to share measurement and drawing methods. Display the results around the room.

LESSON 9 + 10

RESOURCES

Photocopiable page 173; a giant version of one grid from page 173; bold pens; a programmable floor vehicle such as 'Pixie', 'Pip' or 'Roamer' (optional).

PREPARATION

Make one copy per child of page 173. The giant grid should be large enough to be walked along, or of a suitable size to match a unit length of a programmable vehicle.

VOCABULARY

Beside; next to; direction; left; right; up; down; forwards; sideways; backwards; across; along; to; from; away from; towards; movement; quarter turn; North (N); East (E); South (S); West (W); compass point; co-ordinate.

LEARNING OUTCOMES

ORAL AND MENTAL STARTER
● Use doubling or halving, starting from known facts.

MAIN TEACHING ACTIVITY
● Read and begin to write the vocabulary related to position, direction and movement.
● Make and describe right angled turns, including turns between the four compass points.
● Recognise that a straight line is equivalent to two right angles.

ORAL AND MENTAL STARTER

TWICE AS MUCH: Ask the question $6 \times 7 = \square$. Demonstrate that one strategy is to calculate 3×7 and then double the answer. Ask similar questions, eg $8 \times 4 = \square$.

MAIN TEACHING ACTIVITY

ROUTES: Gather the children around the giant grid and ask for volunteers to walk from the house to the car. They may only walk in the directions shown by the two arrows. Try two or three different routes without recording them. Alternatively, use a programmable floor vehicle to trace two or three routes.

Provide copies of page 173 and challenge the children to find all six different pathways, recording them on the sheet with a bold pen.

DIFFERENTIATION

Less able: Use a 2 × 1 grid with four solutions only.
More able: Start investigating routes on a 2 × 3 grid and recording attempts as informal jottings. Alternatively, record how they know they have found all the possible routes.

PLENARY

Look at the giant grid with the class, referring to the labelled axes. Explain how these help us to locate points on the grid (co-ordinates). Introduce the idea of using the four compass points for directions. Use turns on the grid, and/or an angle measure on the board, to demonstrate that two right angles are equivalent to a straight line.

LESSON 10

In the **Oral and mental starter**, DOUBLE AND HALVE, show the class how to use a 'double and halve' technique for problems such as 6 × 4: 12 (double 6) × 2 (halve 4) = 24. Explain how this can sometimes be helpful if the numbers are convenient. Work through a few examples together, eg 5 × 18 (10 × 9), or 20 × 6 (10 × 12). Extend the **Main teaching activity** from Lesson 9: repeat the giant grid demonstration (with children or a programmable vehicle), but this time refer to compass directions and co-ordinates. Show how a successful route can be drawn and then coded as follows: N, E, E, N or (0,1), (1,1), (2,1), (2,2). Ask the children to complete their copies of page 173 from Lesson 9 by writing a set of directions (both as compass directions and as co-ordinates) underneath each route they have drawn. Differentiate as for Lesson 9. Use the **Plenary** to consolidate the children's understanding and use of co-ordinates and compass directions. Ask the children which method of giving directions was easier to record.

RESOURCES

A set of numeral cards (page 13); pegboards (a selection of 9-pin, 16-pin and 25-pin); an OHP (optional); pegs; elastic bands; dotted paper; large cut-out shapes (see **Plenary**).

PREPARATION

All the children will need access to at least one pegboard.

LEARNING OUTCOMES

ORAL AND MENTAL STARTER
● **Know by heart multiplication facts for the 2 and 5 times tables.**

MAIN TEACHING ACTIVITY
● Read and begin to write the vocabulary related to position, direction and movement.

ORAL AND MENTAL STARTER

2× AND 5×: Use a shuffled set of numeral cards 1–10 to practise recall of 2 times table facts. Follow this with recall of multiples of 5. By this point, you should expect most children to have a secure grasp of these facts (particularly the 2× sequence).

MAIN TEACHING ACTIVITY

SPINNERS: Remind the children of the work they have done using pegboards in Unit 4. Explain that in this lesson they are going to investigate rotation and use it to create 'never-ending' patterns. Discuss rotation by referring to wheels, skaters etc. Show a triangle and/ or a non-square quadrilateral using a pegboard, an OHP or a transparent pegboard which can be projected. Show how it is possible to record the shape on dotted paper, rotate it clockwise around its centre through a quarter turn, record that position and so on. Demonstrate how the shape returns to its initial orientation on the fourth turn (or the second turn if it is an oblong).

Provide resources and ask the children to create rotating patterns of their own, based on triangles or quadrilaterals. They should use dotted paper for recording.

DIFFERENTIATION

Less able: Use foam shapes or shape stamps for recording the shapes.
More able: Use four or more pegboards to create an image on a digital camera.

PLENARY

Use large cut-out shapes (eg square, rectangle, equilateral triangle) to explore how many times these shapes fit within their own outlines. Reinforce the idea that a right-angled turn is a quarter of a full turn. Begin to explore what amount of turn is involved in other shapes, referring either to angles (eg 60°) or to fractions of a full turn.

NB Lessons 12 and 13 are particularly intensive on resources, and may require additional teacher support. You might also consider spreading these lessons across other, less intensive sessions to reduce the number of groups engaged in measurement at any one time.

LESSON 12 +13

RESOURCES

Equipment (see **Preparation**); paper.

PREPARATION

Prepare three tables as follows:
1. A selection of containers of different shapes and sizes, measuring cylinders, funnels, a water source (eg a tub or large bowl).
2. A selection of items to weigh, a balance scales, a spring balance, weights.
3. A selection of items to measure (length), rulers, tape measures (also calipers, micrometers and feeler gauges if available).

LEARNING OUTCOMES

ORAL AND MENTAL STARTER
● Recognise that division is the inverse of multiplication.
● Derive quickly division facts corresponding to the 2, 5 and 10 times tables.

MAIN TEACHING ACTIVITY
● Suggest suitable units and measuring equipment to estimate or measure length, mass or capacity.
● Measure and compare using standard units (m, cm, kg, g, l, ml).
● Read scales to the nearest division (labelled or unlabelled).

ORAL AND MENTAL STARTER

÷2 AND ÷10: Draw attention to the inverse nature of division and multiplication. Practise division by 2 and then by 10 (eg *18 divided by 2 is...?*).

VOCABULARY

Unit; measure; length; mass; capacity; litre; millilitre; metre; centimetre; gram; kilogram; more/less; longer/ shorter; longest/ shortest.

MAIN TEACHING ACTIVITY

MEASURING UP: Ask the class questions involving length, mass and capacity. These should focus on the common units for each of these three measures, sensible estimates of familiar objects, and the appropriate equipment for measurement in specific instances. The *FfTM* provides some helpful examples. Explain the equipment you have set out (see **Preparation**), demonstrating the accurate and appropriate use of each item.

Set the children working (in three groups) at the three tables. They should measure all the items provided, and record their findings in whatever way they choose. It may be appropriate, given that this is designed as a double session, to focus on the collection of 'field notes' for later re-presentation. Rotate the groups as they finish the measurement tasks on each table.

DIFFERENTIATION

Set up mixed-ability groups and encourage collaborative work, providing less able children with peer support. Alternatively, make the less able children a focus group with additional teacher support. More able children could record with appropriate units and begin to convert from/to larger units (eg 1m and 63cm = 1.63m).

PLENARY

Provide an overview of measure. Write the different kinds of measure (length, mass, capacity, time) as headings on the board, with the appropriate units (including imperial units) listed under each heading. Practise conversion between metric units, and make links across the table (eg 1ml of water weighs 1g).

LESSON 13

For the **Oral and mental starter**, ÷5, draw attention to the inverse nature of division and multiplication. Practise division by 5 (eg *35 divided by 5 is...?*). In the **Main teaching activity**, follow on from Lesson 12 to allow completion of work on all three aspects of measure and to give some time for the re-presenting of 'field notes'. The method of recording can be left open-ended, and may involve drawing items of measuring equipment as well as detailing the measurements taken. The latter could be listed in ascending order for each category of measurement. Use the **Plenary** to recap on the past two lessons' findings and discuss any errors or misunderstandings that have arisen.

3-D shapes

	Faces	Vertices	Edges		
Cube					
Cuboid					
Triangular-based pyramid					
Square-based pyramid					
Triangular prism					

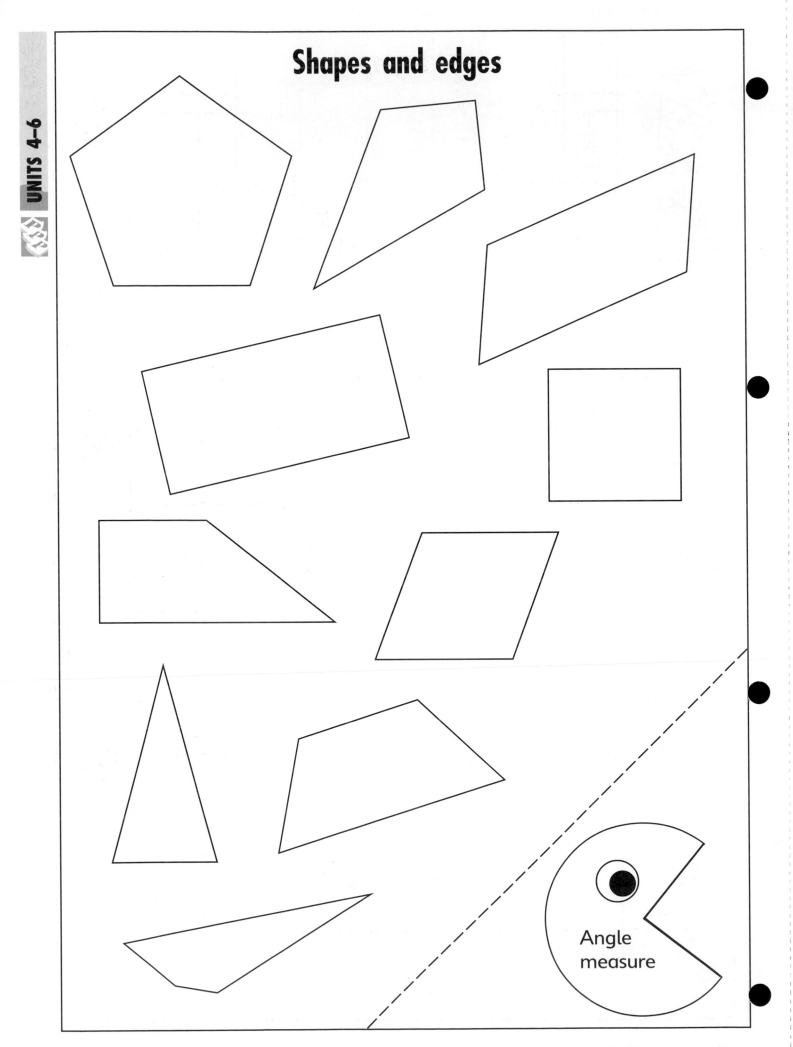

Shapes and edges

Angle measure

Parking spaces

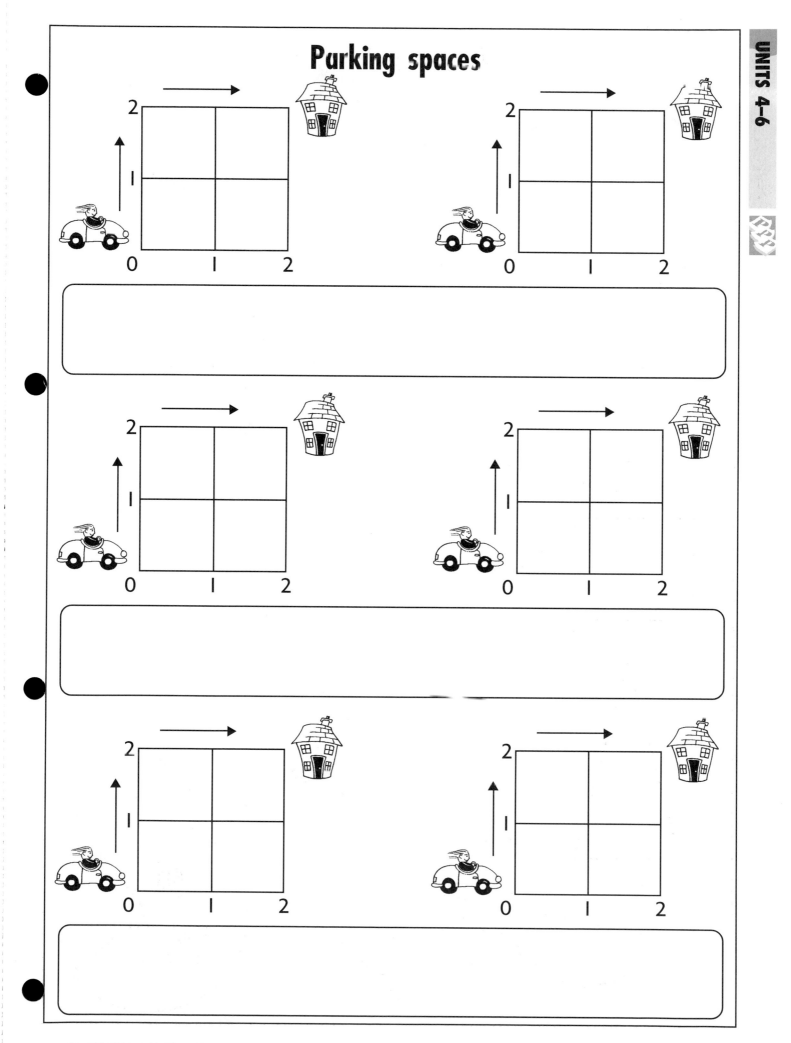

UNIT 7: Assess & Review

Choose from the following activities. During the **Group activities**, some children can complete assessment sheets 5a and 5b, which assess their skills in understanding and using £.p notation and their knowledge of subtraction facts for numbers to 20.

RESOURCES

Number sentence flashcards (see **Preparation**), assessment sheets 5a and 5b, 0–10 numeral cards, irregular shape templates (see figure, right).

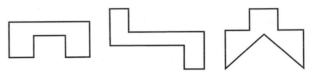

PREPARATION

Prepare a set of flashcards for the **Oral and mental starter** and a set of triangles similar to those used in Unit 14 of Term 1. This time, the triangles should involve multiplying by 2, 5 and 10 (see figure, right). Make a set of irregular shape templates with different numbers of lines of symmetry (see figure above right).

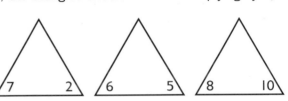

ORAL AND MENTAL STARTER

ASSESSMENT

Do the children:
● **Know by heart all addition facts for each number to 20?**
● **Know by heart multiplication facts for the 2, 5 and 10 times tables?**

ADDITION: Show flashcards featuring a range of statements (eg $9 + 8 = \Box$), in increasing order of difficulty. Read each sentence aloud, and allow the children a few seconds to work out and write down each answer. Collect in the recorded attempts and discuss methods.
MULTIPLICATION: Present each of the numeral cards 0–10 in random order. The children should multiply each number by 2, 5 or 10. Allow a few seconds for calculation and recording. Repeat.

GROUP ACTIVITIES

ASSESSMENT

Can the children:
● **Identify and sketch lines of symmetry in simple shapes, and recognise shapes with no lines of symmetry?**
● **Identify right angles** in 2-D shapes?
● **Recognise that division is the inverse of multiplication?**

MULTIPLICATION AND DIVISION: Provide a set of cut-out triangles. As before, the children should complete each triangle by multiplying the two given numbers, then write four related facts about these numbers underneath the triangle.
SYMMETRY AND SHAPE: Provide a set of irregular shapes. Ask the group to identify right angles and find the lines of symmetry. They could draw round the shape templates and mark the lines of symmetry on their copies.

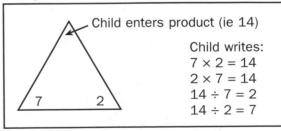

Child enters product (ie 14)

Child writes:
$7 \times 2 = 14$
$2 \times 7 = 14$
$14 \div 7 = 2$
$14 \div 2 = 7$

Assessment sheet 5a

Calculate the total price of these three items:

Answer in pence:

[   ]

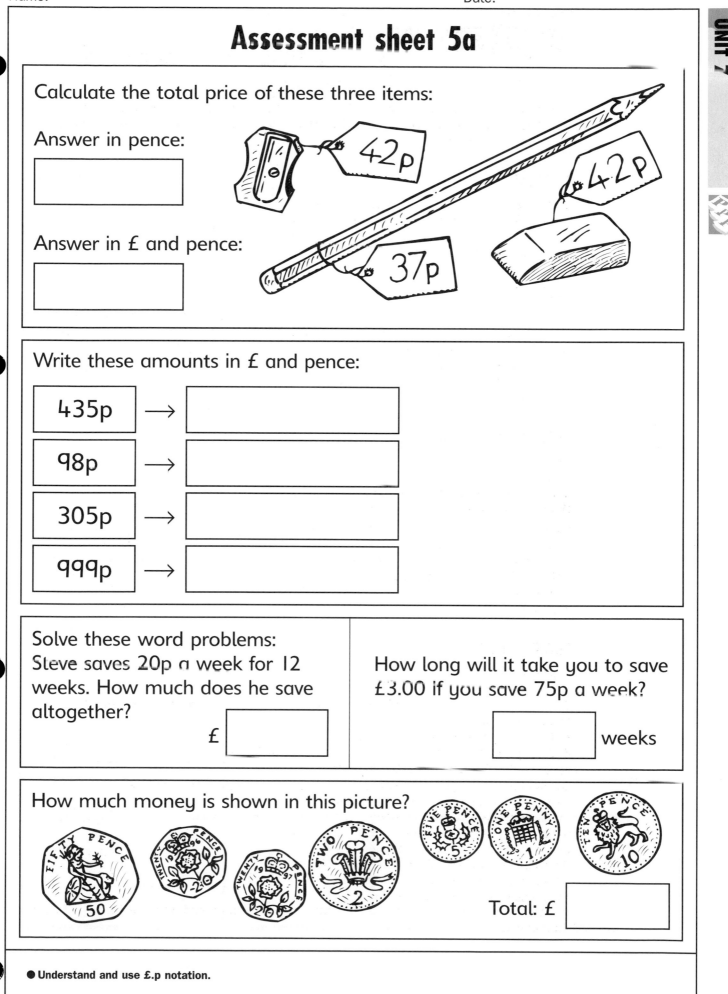

Answer in £ and pence:

[   ]

Write these amounts in £ and pence:

435p	→	
98p	→	
305p	→	
999p	→	

Solve these word problems:
Steve saves 20p a week for 12 weeks. How much does he save altogether?

£ [   ]

How long will it take you to save £3.00 if you save 75p a week?

[   ] weeks

How much money is shown in this picture?

Total: £ [   ]

● **Understand and use £.p notation.**

Assessment sheet 5b

Complete this table of differences. One has already been done for you.

Difference	12	6	14	7	3	18
19						
12		6				
20						
15						

Fill in the missing numbers to make each statement correct:

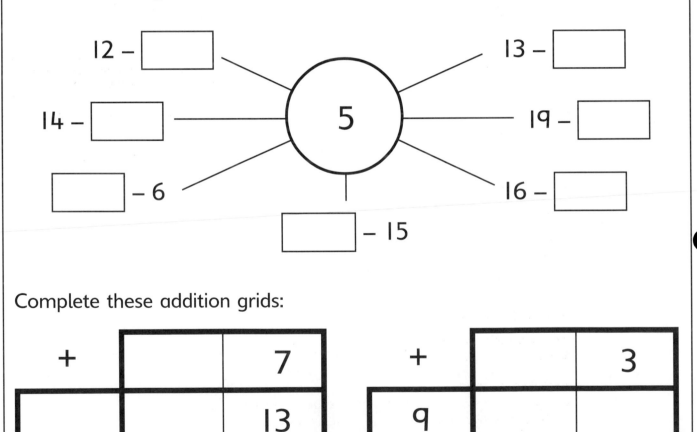

Complete these addition grids:

Know by heart all subtraction facts for each number to 20.

ORGANISATION (5 LESSONS)

LEARNING OUTCOMES		ORAL AND MENTAL STARTER	MAIN TEACHING ACTIVITY	PLENARY
LESSON 1	• Count on in steps of 3, 4 or 5 from any small number to at least 50, then back again. • Recognise two-digit and three-digit multiples of 2, 5 or 10.	HALF OF HALF: Find a quarter of a number by repeated halving.	TABLE PATTERNS: Investigate units digits patterns for multiples of numbers 2–9.	Share and compare findings.
LESSON 2	• **Explain methods and reasoning** orally and, where appropriate, in writing.	HALF OF HALF 2: Extend to three-digit numbers.	WORK IT OUT: Do calculations and explain methods.	Find various methods of doing a calculation.
LESSON 3 +4	• Investigate a general statement about familiar numbers by finding examples that satisfy it.	SHIFT THE DIGIT 1 and 2: Use place value to multiply by 10 and 100.	DIGITAL ROOTS: Find the digital roots of multiples of different numbers.	Share and compare findings.
LESSON 5	• Solve mathematical problems or puzzles, recognise simple patterns or relationships, generalise and predict. • **Explain methods and reasoning** orally and, where appropriate, in writing.	SHIFT THE DIGIT 3: Use place value to divide by 10 and 100.	MAGIC SQUARE: Use trial and improvement to solve an addition problem.	Attempt another square puzzle and discuss results.

ORAL AND MENTAL SKILLS Use doubling or halving, starting from known facts. Shift the digits one/two places to the left to multiply by 10/100. **Recognise that division is the inverse of multiplication.**

Lessons 1–3 and 5 are given in full. Lesson 4 follows on from what has already been taught and are given in outline.

RESOURCES

Paper; calculators (optional).

PREPARATION

Provide examples of earlier work (see below).

LEARNING OUTCOMES

ORAL AND MENTAL STARTER

● Use doubling or halving, starting from known facts.

MAIN TEACHING ACTIVITY

● Count on in steps of 3, 4 or 5 to at least 50, then back again.
● Recognise two-digit and three-digit multiples of 2, 5 or 10.

VOCABULARY
Repeated addition; in order; repeat; pattern.

ORAL AND MENTAL STARTER

HALF OF HALF: Building on the ideas of doubling and halving from the previous two terms, rehearse finding a quarter of a two-digit number by 'halving twice'. For example: *One quarter of 64 is half of 64 (32) and half again (16).* Only some numbers give rise to whole-number answers. Ask: *What are the numbers in this set?* (Multiples of 4.)

MAIN TEACHING ACTIVITY

TABLE PATTERNS: Explain that this lesson is about finding patterns in times tables. From earlier work, the children should be familiar with patterns arising from multiples of 2, 5 and 10. They will also recognise the idea of developing multiples of numbers by repeated addition from 0. Develop the 4× table pattern on the board, underlining the units digits. Chant the units sequence in order with the class; a pattern of repetition should be observed. Challenge the class to extend patterns of multiples into larger numbers (eg continue the pattern of multiples of 5 from 100 to 150).

Set the task: to develop a sequence of multiples of a single-digit number from 0 and investigate whether a repetition occurs in the units digits. (Every sequence repeats the units, but you have to be patient with some tables, such as 7 times.) Try to distribute the task so that, across the groups, each of the multiples from 2 to 9 is covered. Encourage the children to extend sequences beyond 50, or even beyond 100.

DIFFERENTIATION

Less able: Investigate the patterns in the 2, 4 and 5 times tables, where repetition is relatively frequent.
More able: Investigate patterns of 'near multiples', eg adding on 4 repeatedly from 1.

PLENARY

Compare the groups' findings. Why, for example, does the pattern of 5s repeat so quickly?

LESSON 2

RESOURCES

Photocopiable page 181; paper.

PREPARATION

Make one copy per child of page 181, perhaps modified for different groups (see **Differentiation**).

LEARNING OUTCOMES

ORAL AND MENTAL STARTER
● Use doubling or halving, starting from known facts.

MAIN TEACHING ACTIVITY
● **Explain methods and reasoning** orally and, where appropriate, in writing.

VOCABULARY
Explain; units; ones; digit.

ORAL AND MENTAL STARTER

HALF OF HALF 2: Repeat from Lesson 1, this time finding a quarter of three-digit numbers which are multiples of 4 (eg 112, 120, 180).

MAIN TEACHING ACTIVITY

WORK IT OUT: Ask some oral questions of the following type and scale: *What is 23 + 19? What is half of 36? How many more is 45 than 37?* After each question, ask: *How did you work it out?* Accept several methods, but try not to comment on their relative efficiency.

Explain that in this session you will be interested in both the answer and the method. You might refer back to the word problems activity in Lesson 7, Unit 10, Term 1. Provide copies of page 181, modified for different groups if necessary.

DIFFERENTIATION

Less able: Work with smaller numbers or fewer operations. Work in pairs, with each child acting as scribe for the other, or think through and record answers with teacher support.
More able: Work with three-digit numbers in the questions and (sometimes) the answers, using creative strategies.

PLENARY

Select one problem and brainstorm as many different ways as you can of solving it. Encourage the children to think of various ways, no matter how inefficient or protracted they may be. For example, 12 × 6 could be worked out as 12 + 12 + 12 +..., or as twice 12 × 3, or as (10 × 6) + (2 × 6), or twice 6 × 6 etc. This will help the children to see why certain methods are usually chosen over others.

LESSON 3 + 4

RESOURCES

Place value cards (from pages 23 and 132); base 10 materials; paper; calculators (optional).

PREPARATION

Provide examples of work from Lesson 1.

LEARNING OUTCOMES

ORAL AND MENTAL STARTER
● Shift the digits one/two places to the left to multiply by 10/100.

MAIN TEACHING ACTIVITY
● Investigate a general statement about familiar numbers by finding examples that satisfy it.

VOCABULARY
Tens; ones; place value; stands for; represents.

ORAL AND MENTAL STARTER

SHIFT THE DIGIT: This activity builds on previous work on place value and counting in tens. Provide a single-digit number (eg 6) and ask the class to make it 10 times larger, then 100 times larger. Write the outcomes as follows:

```
  6
 60
600
```

Use place value cards to reinforce this, emphasising the use of the 0 digits to replace the digits that have 'shifted to the left'. Repeat with other single-digit numbers.

MAIN TEACHING ACTIVITY

DIGITAL ROOTS: Explain that this lesson is about finding the 'digital root' of a number. Show an example: *The digital root of 27 is 2 + 7 = 9.* Point out that this 'bends the rules' by allowing the tens and units digits to be added as two single-digit numbers, with no regard for place value. Look at an example where the number does not reduce to a single-digit number: 48 becomes 4 + 8 = 12. In this case, you repeat the process: 12 becomes 1 + 2 = 3, so the digital root of 48 is 3.

Refer the children back to TABLE PATTERNS in Lesson 1. Set the task of revisiting one or more of these sequences, looking for repetition in the digital root.

DIFFERENTIATION

Less able: Look at multiples of 6 and 9, which have a shorter repeating pattern in the digital roots.
More able: Look at multiples of 7 and 8. Compare findings with those of Lesson 1.

PLENARY

Share findings as in Lesson 1. Note that some sequences which are relatively easy to generate (such as the 2× table) have long repeating patterns in the digital roots. By contrast, the 9× sequence has 'instant' repetition (the same number each time).

LESSON 4

For the **Oral and mental starter**, SHIFT THE DIGIT 2, use base 10 materials to show how multiplying a number such as 6 by 10 gives 6 tens, then 6 hundreds etc. For the **Main teaching activity**, recap on Lesson 3 and share thoughts on the task. The children should continue with one of the following tasks based on your judgement of their progress and learning need: either repeat the activity with different multiples, or investigate for repeated addition where the starting point is not 0. Encourage groups trying the latter to predict whether this will show a repeating digital root pattern, and to tell you why. Less able children could contrast the digital roots of odd and even number sequences. More able children could explore patterns for multiples of 11, and perhaps beyond. In the **Plenary**, compare findings as before.

RESOURCES

Numeral cards 1–9 (page 13); a blank 3 × 3 grid (to accommodate numeral cards); enlarged or OHT acetate numerals (optional); OHP (optional).

PREPARATION

Give each child a grid and a set of numeral cards, or give larger sets to pairs or groups.

LEARNING OUTCOMES

ORAL AND MENTAL STARTER
● **Recognise that division is the inverse of multiplication.**

MAIN TEACHING ACTIVITY
● Solve mathematical problems or puzzles, recognise simple patterns or relationships, generalise and predict. Suggest extensions by asking 'What if...?'
● **Explain methods and reasoning** orally and, where appropriate, in writing.

ORAL AND MENTAL STARTER

SHIFT THE DIGIT 3: Write a multiple of 100 or 1000 on the board, then write subsequent divisions by 10 in the appropriate columns underneath the original number. If necessary, provide column headings to reinforce the base 10 nature of the number system.

MAIN TEACHING ACTIVITY

MAGIC SQUARE: Explain that this lesson is a problem-solving activity which involves using the strategy of trial and improvement. Set the task: *Can you arrange the digits 1–9 in a 3 × 3 grid so that each row, column and diagonal totals 15?* Demonstrate the early stages of trial and improvement on the board, perhaps using large numerals or an OHP.
   Organise the class into pairs or groups of three for collaborative work.

DIFFERENTIATION

Less able: Use a prepared grid with 5 in the centre. If further support is needed, two more digits could be placed (see figure). More able: Try to find more than one solution. Do a similar exercise with the numbers 2–10 and the target number 18.

PLENARY

Use a large empty 3 × 3 grid to attempt a similar puzzle, working through the trialling process with the whole class: *Can you put the digits 1–9 in the cells so that the difference between any two horizontally or vertically next-door numbers is odd?* A solution is shown, right. Discuss any general findings, especially the distribution of the five odd numbers.

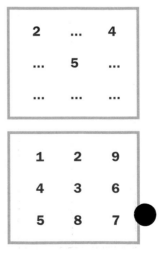

2	...	4
...	5	...
...	...	...

1	2	9
4	3	6
5	8	7

Calculation strategies

	How I worked it out	Answer
16 × 2		
39 + 46		
42 ÷ 7		
101 – 67		
12 × 6		

UNITS 9-10

ORGANISATION (10 LESSONS)

	LEARNING OUTCOMES	ORAL AND MENTAL STARTER	MAIN TEACHING ACTIVITY	PLENARY
LESSON 1 +2	● **Choose and use appropriate operations** and ways of calculating **to solve word problems.**	100 FACTS: Find numbers on a 1–100 square that meet particular criteria.	NUMBERS TO WORDS: Turn number sentences into word problems using + and –, then using × and ÷.	Solve word problems involving mixed operations, then involving remainders.
LESSON 3	● Solve word problems involving money, including finding totals. ● **Understand and use £.p notation.** ● **Know what each digit represents,** and partition three-digit numbers into a multiple of 100, a multiple of ten and ones (HTU).	100 FACTS: Continue from Lessons 1 and 2.	THREE GIFTS: Mix and match items to make total prices within a given limit.	Record amounts of money, using place value.
LESSON 4	● Solve word problems involving money, including finding totals. Explain how the problem was solved. ● **Understand and use £.p notation.**	100 FACTS: Continue from Lesson 3.	A LA CARTE: Mix and match items to make total prices within a given range. Show workings.	Share results and methods.
LESSON 5	● Solve word problems involving money, including finding totals. Explain how the problem was solved. ● **Understand and use £.p notation.** ● Recognise all coins.	100 FACTS: Continue from Lesson 4.	CASH IN HAND: Use a range of coins to make different totals.	Answer questions about money addition and how amounts are recorded.
LESSON 6	● **Understand division** as grouping (repeated subtraction) or sharing. Read and begin to write the related vocabulary. ● Say or write a division statement corresponding to a given multiplication statement.	÷ 3: Explore division facts of 3, referring to 3 times table facts.	DIVISION FACTS: Use a multiplication grid to derive division facts for a given number.	Discuss the language of division.
LESSON 7	● **Understand division** as grouping (repeated subtraction) or sharing. ● Begin to find remainders after simple division.	÷ 10: Use place value to reinforce division facts of 10.	REMAINDERS: Explore remainders in context of sharing objects.	Record division with remainders in a formal way.
LESSON 8	● Solve word problems involving numbers in 'real life'. Explain how the problem was solved. ● Round up or down after division, depending on the context. ● Begin to find remainders after simple division.	÷ 4: Explore division facts of 4, referring to 4 times table facts.	WORD PROBLEMS: Solve contextual division problems involving remainders.	Discuss methods used.
LESSON 9	● **Understand division** as grouping (repeated subtraction) or sharing. Read and begin to write the related vocabulary. ● Recognise that division is the inverse of multiplication. ● Begin to recognise simple equivalent fractions.	DOUBLE UP: Use repeated doubling to multiply by 8.	SPIDER DIAGRAM: Find division facts for a given number and record them as improper fractions.	Answer oral questions on division facts, using knowledge of multiplication facts.

LEARNING OUTCOMES	ORAL AND MENTAL STARTER	MAIN TEACHING ACTIVITY	PLENARY
● Begin to find remainders after simple division.	QUARTER: Find a quarter of a number by repeated halving.	ACCOUNTS: Carry out and record a division investigation.	Discuss the idea of a remainder as a fraction.

LESSON 10

ORAL AND MENTAL SKILLS   Begin to know the 3 and 4 times tables. Know by heart doubles of all whole numbers to at least 20. Read and begin to write the vocabulary of comparing and ordering numbers. **Recognise that division is the inverse of multiplication.** Use doubling and halving, starting from known facts.

Lessons 1, 5–7 and 9 are given in full. Lessons 2–4, 8 and 10 follow on from what has already been taught and are given in outline.

Note that the **Oral and mental starters** in Unit 9 focus on revising and confirming knowledge of multiplication facts, order, place value and doubles. This work is cumulative, and becomes increasingly difficult. The Initial **Preparation** for this is given in Lesson 1.

LESSON 1 +2

RESOURCES

Enlarged or OHT copies of a 1–100 square (page 16) with removable numbers, over-writeable sheets, or a dry-mark board; OHP (optional).

PREPARATION

Prepare eight copies of the 1–100 square, one with each of the following headings: multiples of 3; multiples of 4; multiples of 6; doubles; greater than 50; 50 or fewer; odd numbers; even numbers.

LEARNING OUTCOMES

ORAL AND MENTAL STARTER
● Begin to know the 3 and 4 times tables.
● Know by heart doubles of all whole numbers to at least 20.
● Read and begin to write the vocabulary of comparing and ordering numbers.

MAIN TEACHING ACTIVITY
● **Choose and use appropriate operations** and ways of calculating **to solve problems.**

VOCABULARY
Number sentence; sign; operation; subtraction; multiplication; division.

ORAL AND MENTAL STARTER

100 FACTS: Take each of the prepared 1–100 squares (see **Preparation**) in turn and ask the class to identify one number, or a pair of numbers for 'doubles', that satisfies that requirement. Cross it out or remove it from the 100 square. Talk to the children about their selections and observations. Retain the work, explaining that the same questions will be asked at the beginning of the next four lessons. As the smaller numbers will tend to be selected first, the task should become progressively more difficult.

MAIN TEACHING ACTIVITY

NUMBERS TO WORDS: Review the introduction to the **Main teaching activity** in Lesson 2, Unit 8. Explain that this time, you are going to start with a symbolic calculation and turn it into a word problem. Provide an example: *For 23 + 19, we could say 'I have 23p and my friend has 19p. How much do we have to spend altogether?'* Provide two more examples of number sentences (addition or subtraction only) and ask the class for suitable word problems.

Write some challenges on the board for the class (or provide differentiated tasks for groups). Ask the children to convert each number sentence into a word problem, then find the answer. Suitable challenges might include: 39 + 96 = ☐ ; 32 – ☐ = 17; 17 + 27 + 19 = ☐.

DIFFERENTIATION

Less able: Work with smaller numbers and/or simpler number sentences (ones with the missing number at the end are easier to interpret).
More able: Solve problems involving units such as £ and p.

PLENARY

Work together through some more complex word problems (with some involving mixed operations) written on the board, eg *My friend and I spent £9.50 altogether, but I spent £1.30 more than her. How much did we each spend?* or *If three people share £8.40 fairly between them, how much does each get?* or *If I double a number and add 32, I get 66. What number did I start with?* or *I am 8 years old. In 3 years' time my brother will be twice my age. How old is my brother now?*

LESSON 2

Continue the **Oral and mental starter** from Lesson 1. For the **Main teaching activity**, recap on the previous **Main teaching activity** and **Plenary**. Explain that this lesson will focus on multiplication and division. Start by asking the children to convert 55 × 6 into a word problem (eg six cakes at 55p each). Try one or two more examples, using only multiplication and division. Offer some challenges as before, eg 32 × 8 = ☐; 12 × ☐ = 108; 84 ÷ 4 = ☐. The children should show any informal jottings they have made for calculation, providing further evidence of their understanding. Less able children could work only with multiplication (as repeated addition). More able children could work with larger numbers and both operations. In the **Plenary**, pursue ideas from the previous lesson about identifying the right operation for a given word problem. Give some examples which leave 'untidy' solutions, with remainders which need to be interpreted according to the context, eg: *A coach carries 55 passengers. How many coaches would be needed for 300 people? How many 24p stamps could you buy with £5.00?*

LESSON 3

RESOURCES	As Lesson 1 for **Oral and mental starter**; wrapped gifts with detachable price labels (see **Main teaching activity**); real coins and notes (as appropriate).
LEARNING OUTCOMES	**ORAL AND MENTAL STARTER** ● Begin to know the 3 and 4 times tables. ● Know by heart doubles of all whole numbers to at least 20. ● Read and begin to write the vocabulary of comparing and ordering numbers. **MAIN TEACHING ACTIVITY** ● Solve word problems involving money, including finding totals. Explain how the problem was solved. ● Understand and use £.p notation. ● **Know what each digit represents,** and partition three-digit numbers into a multiple of 100, a multiple of ten and ones (HTU).
ORAL AND MENTAL STARTER	Continue from Lesson 2.
MAIN TEACHING ACTIVITY	THREE GIFTS: Present two wrapped gifts with detachable labels giving their price. Demonstrate how to add the prices using an informal written method, eg £2.40 + £3.25 = £2.00 + £3.00 + 40p + 25p = £5.65. Reinforce the correct use of £.p notation. Change one or both of the labels to try more examples. Create a shopping scenario involving several gifts with a range of different prices, eg £2.40, £3.20, £4.40, £5.40, £3.60 and £2.80. Label each gift with a price tag. Set the challenge, which is to find as many different combinations of three gifts as possible within an overall limit of £10.00.
DIFFERENTIATION	Less able: Work with lower prices and/or find combinations of any two gifts. More able: Try to find the closest total to £10.00. (Is it possible to spend exactly £10.00?)
PLENARY	Focus on the place value aspects of the amounts (eg *What is the middle digit worth in £3.26?*). Consider how, for example, the middle digit 0 is used as a 'place holder' in writing £3.06.

RESOURCES	As Lesson 1 for **Oral and mental starter**; photocopiable page 190; an enlarged or OHT version of page 190; paper; coins (optional); OHP (optional).
LEARNING OUTCOMES	**ORAL AND MENTAL STARTER** ● Begin to know the 3 and 4 times tables. ● Know by heart doubles of all whole numbers to at least 20. ● Read and begin to write the vocabulary of comparing and ordering numbers. **MAIN TEACHING ACTIVITY** ● Solve word problems involving money, including finding totals. Explain how the problem was solved. ● **Understand and use £.p notation.**
ORAL AND MENTAL STARTER	Continue from Lesson 3.
MAIN TEACHING ACTIVITY	A LA CARTE: Display an enlarged or OHT version of page 190. Discuss its layout and content, clarifying the idea of a three-course meal. Combine the prices of any two items, recording as in Lesson 3. Give each child a copy of page 190. The task is given on the sheet: to create some four-course meals costing between £10.00 and £15.00. The calculations should be made on a separate piece of paper and kept as evidence of the children's calculation techniques.
DIFFERENTIATION	Less able: Work with lower, more 'convenient' prices (eg multiples of 25p and 50p), placing the appropriate coins beside each item and then combining them into one pile. More able: Calculate the change from £20, or even £50, when the bill is paid.
PLENARY	Share outcomes and approaches to recording and calculation.

RESOURCES

As Lesson 1 for **Oral and mental starter**; paper; coins (real or plastic).

PREPARATION

Each group will need a full set of coins or replicas (all values).

LEARNING OUTCOMES

ORAL AND MENTAL STARTER

● Begin to know the 3 and 4 times tables.
● Know by heart doubles of all whole numbers to at least 20.
● Read and begin to write the vocabulary of comparing and ordering numbers.

MAIN TEACHING ACTIVITY

● Solve word problems involving money, including finding totals. Explain how the problem was solved.
● **Understand and use £.p notation.**
● Recognise all coins.

VOCABULARY

Change;
change over;
in order;
exchange.

ORAL AND MENTAL STARTER

Continue from Lesson 4.

MAIN TEACHING ACTIVITY

CASH IN HAND: This is a simple activity to set up, but is potentially quite challenging. Tell the children that you are holding two coins tightly in your hand, and ask them to say how much money they think you are holding. Accept a range of possible answers. You may want to imply the beginnings of a strategy to consider many or all of the potential totals methodically.

   Give each group a full set of coins. Ask them to investigate the different totals they could make with three coins. Circulate around the groups, providing encouragement and/or coins to support their learning.

DIFFERENTIATION

Less able: Work with lower-value coins only (say to 20p) and/or make totals with two coins.
More able: Use a systematic strategy to find all possible solutions. Record using £.p notation.

PLENARY

Ask questions involving the use of any three coins: *What is the largest possible total if all the coins are the same? What is the largest possible total if all the coins are different? How are these amounts recorded in pounds and pence notation? What change would we get from this* [given] *amount?*

LESSON 6

RESOURCES

Photocopiable page 62; paper; OHP (optional).

PREPARATION

Provide one copy of page 62 per child or pair. An OHT version will also be useful.

LEARNING OUTCOMES

ORAL AND MENTAL STARTER
● Begin to know the 3 times table.
● **Recognise that division is the inverse of multiplication.**

MAIN TEACHING ACTIVITY
● **Understand division** as grouping (repeated subtraction) or sharing. Read and begin to write the related vocabulary.
● Say or write a division statement corresponding to a given multiplication statement.

VOCABULARY

Share; equal groups of; divided by/into; once, twice, three times... etc.

ORAL AND MENTAL STARTER

÷3: Develop the children's awareness of division facts for the 3 times table by asking *What do we get if we divide 27, 18, 12* (etc) *by 3?* Make overt links between multiplication and division.

MAIN TEACHING ACTIVITY

DIVISION FACTS: Start this topic by asking some contextual questions involving division (eg *How many tandems would you need for 8 people?)* Stress the inverse nature of multiplication and division. Provide copies of page 62 and remind the class how it was used to find multiplication facts, then demonstrate, perhaps using an OHP, how it was also used to find division facts (refer back to Lesson 1, Unit 9, Term 1).

Set groups a target number (see **Differentiation**) and ask them to find and record division facts with that number as the answer. If the number is 4, for example, the grid can be used to find facts such as 24 ÷ 6 = 4 and 36 ÷ 9 = 4.

DIFFERENTIATION

Set a target number for each group of a magnitude to suit their growing knowledge and recall of specific multiplication tables.
Less able: Work on division statements giving an answer of 2.
More able: Work without the grid to generate division facts with answers greater than 100.

PLENARY

Talk about the language of division with the class, using the vocabulary listed above and referring to both sharing and repeated subtraction.

RESOURCES

Numeral cards 0–9 (page 13); Blu-Tack; counters; PE hoops (optional); structural apparatus (optional).

PREPARATION

Access to a large space (hall or playground) will be useful. Each group will need enough counters for a handful.

LEARNING OUTCOMES

ORAL AND MENTAL STARTER
● **Recognise that division is the inverse of multiplication.**

MAIN TEACHING ACTIVITY
● **Understand division** as grouping (repeated subtraction) or sharing.
● Begin to find remainders after simple division.

VOCABULARY

Remainder; one each, two each...; how many left over?

ORAL AND MENTAL STARTER

÷ 10: Write H, T and U in the conventional arrangement on the board. Use numeral cards and Blu-Tack to attach the digits of a multiple of 10 (eg 90) in the appropriate columns. Ask the children how many tens make that number. Use this to show the effect of dividing by 10. Remove the 0 card and shift the 9 into the units column. Repeat for other multiples of 10, extending beyond 100.

MAIN TEACHING ACTIVITY

REMAINDERS: Remind the class of earlier work which introduced the idea of a remainder as 'what is left over after sharing'. Demonstrate how it is possible to divide up a large group of children (or even the whole class) in different ways. If possible, scatter PE hoops in a large space and call out a number between 2 and 6. The children should form groups of that number, each group standing inside a hoop. After each attempt, talk about the remainder and relate the groupings to repeated addition and/or multiplication.

Set a table-based task for groups of up to five children: *Take a handful of counters and count them. Share them equally within your group, record how many you have each and how many are left over. Then put the counters back. Repeat until each of you has taken a handful.*

DIFFERENTIATION

Less able: Work in pairs, using larger objects to reduce the number in a handful.
More able: Use structural apparatus featuring a mixture of tens and units in each handful, so that equal sharing requires exchange.

PLENARY

Review the work done and demonstrate how it can be recorded more formally:
21 ÷ 4 = 5 remainder 1 or 5 r 1.

LESSON 8

RESOURCES	Photocopiable page 191; counting apparatus (optional).
LEARNING OUTCOMES	**ORAL AND MENTAL STARTER** ● Begin to know the 4 times table. **MAIN TEACHING ACTIVITY** ● Solve word problems involving numbers in 'real life'. Explain how the problem was solved. ● Round up or down after division, depending on the context. ● Begin to find remainders after simple division.
ORAL AND MENTAL STARTER	÷4: Develop the children's awareness of division facts for the 4 times table by asking how many fours make 16, 24, 36 etc. Make overt links between multiplication and division.
MAIN TEACHING ACTIVITY	WORD PROBLEMS: Present some word problems similar to those on page 191. You may like to use visual models to make them more 'real'. Work through them together, stressing the key words that indicate which operation is needed. Give out copies of page 191 and talk through how to interpret and solve the first two questions. Ask the children to complete the sheet, working individually or in pairs. Remind them to show their working.
DIFFERENTIATION	Less able: Work with a modified sheet containing lower or simpler numbers, eg *How many 2s make 28?* Work with individual guidance and/or counting apparatus. More able: Extend the scale of the numbers to 100 and beyond. Solve similar problems in the context of money, eg *If you share £1.36 equally between three people, how much money will be left over?*
PLENARY	Talk about the different methods by which individuals or pairs completed each task.

LESSON 9

RESOURCES

Paper; objects for counting.

PREPARATION

Provide a large supply of counting objects.

LEARNING OUTCOMES

ORAL AND MENTAL STARTER
● Use doubling, starting from known facts.

MAIN TEACHING ACTIVITY
● **Understand division** as grouping (repeated subtraction) or sharing. Read and begin to write the related vocabulary.
● **Recognise that division is the inverse of multiplication.**
● Begin to recognise simple equivalent fractions.

VOCABULARY

Different ways; what could we try next?

ORAL AND MENTAL STARTER

DOUBLE UP: Build on earlier work with doubling by writing 8 × 15 on the board. Demonstrate how the answer can be found through 'doubling up', asking the children to help you at each stage:

	1 × 15	= 15
so	2 × 15	= 30
so	4 × 15	= 60
so	8 × 15	= 120

MAIN TEACHING ACTIVITY

SPIDER DIAGRAM: Recap on work from Lesson 6 involving the multiplication grid. Now write a number (eg 2) in the centre of the board and say: *I am doing a division problem in my head and the answer is 2. What is the problem?* Take a range of possible questions and write them as $\frac{4}{2}$, $\frac{16}{8}$ etc. Radiate lines from the number to the various solutions, making a 'spider diagram'.

UNIT 11

ORGANISATION (5 LESSONS)

	LEARNING OUTCOMES	ORAL AND MENTAL STARTER	MAIN TEACHING ACTIVITY	PLENARY
LESSON 1 +2	● **Recognise unit fractions (eg ¹/₂, ¹/₄) and use them to find fractions of shapes.** ● Begin to recognise simple fractions (eg ³/₄) that are several parts of a whole. ● Begin to recognise simple equivalent fractions. ● Compare familar fractions.	TARGET TOTALS: Make a given total by adding numbers (first one-digit, then two-digit) from a set.	FRACTION PIECES: Make a whole shape in different ways using ¹/₂ and ¹/₄ pieces, then also using ¹/₈.	Repeat TARGET TOTALS with different numbers.
LESSON 3	● **Recognise unit fractions and use them to find fractions of shapes.** ● Begin to recognise simple equivalent fractions. ● Compare familar fractions.	TARGET PRODUCTS: As above, but multiplying numbers.	FRACTION DICE: Make a whole shape using ¹/₂, ¹/₄ and ¹/₈ pieces (after dice throws).	Repeat TARGET PRODUCTS with different numbers.
LESSON 4	● **Recognise unit fractions and use them to find fractions of shapes.** ● Begin to recognise simple equivalent fractions. ● Compare familar fractions. ● Estimate a simple fraction.	TARGET PRODUCTS 2: As above, but focusing on multiplication of three numbers.	FRACTION WALL: Use a 'brick wall' image to look at equivalent fractions.	Estimate fractions on a number line or counting stick.
LESSON 5	● **Recognise unit fractions and use them to find fractions of shapes.** ● Begin to recognise simple equivalent fractions. ● Compare familar fractions.	TARGETS: Make target numbers by combining operations.	FRACTION LINE: Use a number line to count on in fractions past 1.	Repeat TARGETS with different numbers.

ORAL AND MENTAL SKILLS Understand that more than two numbers can be added together. Use knowledge that addition can be done in any order to do mental calculations more efficiently, for example: put the larger number first and count on; add three or four small numbers by putting the larger number first and/or by finding pairs totalling 9, 10 or 11; partition into '5 and a bit' when adding 6, 7, 8 or 9. **Know by heart multiplication facts for the 2, 5 and 10 times tables.** Begin to know the 3 and 4 times tables.

Lessons 1 and 3–5 are given in full. Lesson 2 follows on from what has already been taught and are given in outline.

RESOURCES

Large numeral cards; photocopiable page 196; scissors.

PREPARATION

Make two copies per child of page 196, cut into two parts. Keep the '¹/₈s wheel' for Lesson 2 (also see **Differentiation**).

LEARNING OUTCOMES

ORAL AND MENTAL STARTER

Understand that more than two numbers can be added together. Understand that addition can be done in any order to do mental calculations more efficiently, for example: put the larger number first and count on; add three or four small numbers by putting the larger number first and/or by finding pairs totalling 9, 10 or 11; partition into '5 and a bit' when adding 6, 7, 8 or 9.

Set a number (see **Differentiation**). Provide paper for individuals or pairs and support as required.

DIFFERENTIATION

Less able: Work with small target numbers. Use counting objects to make or check divisions.
More able: Work with larger target numbers, or write questions involving fractions (eg '2¹/₂ divided by 1¹/₄').

PLENARY

Test the children's knowledge and understanding of the work covered over Lessons 6–9. You may need to test groups at staggered times across this lesson. Alternatively, you could give each group a chosen number (appropriate to their ability level) and then ask the whole class questions such as *How many times does your number go into 30? Is there anything left over?* Focus on whether the children can use multiplication facts to support division when asked oral questions. With more able pupils, you should expect rapid recall of facts.

LESSON 10

RESOURCES	Counters (or other suitable counting objects); small set rings; an OHP (optional).
LEARNING OUTCOMES	**ORAL AND MENTAL STARTER** ● Use halving, starting from known facts. **MAIN TEACHING ACTIVITY** ● Begin to find remainders after simple division.
ORAL AND MENTAL STARTER	QUARTER: Ask the class to calculate what half of 12 is mentally. Share strategies. Ask: *What is a quarter of 12?* Extend their understanding of a quarter as 'half of a half', and try with numbers such as 24, 28 and 36. This links with previous and later work on fractions.
MAIN TEACHING ACTIVITY	ACCOUNTS: Review the **Plenary** from Lesson 7, involving the formal recording of division with remainders. Explain that in this lesson, they will divide up a number of counters. Demonstrate (perhaps using small set rings and an OHP) how to share 16 counters into groups of 1, 2, 3, 4 etc. For each grouping, identify the number in each set and whether there is a remainder. Give each group a set number of counters (see **Differentiation**) and ask them to share them out between 1, 2, 3, 4, 5 and 6. You may want to offer this as an individual task. After each sharing, the children should record the result formally.
DIFFERENTIATION	Less able: Work with 12 counters, as this number is manageable in size and has several factors. More able: Work with a prime number (eg 29) which is comparatively large and always leaves a remainder. Try to predict the results from their knowledge of multiplication facts.
PLENARY	Talk about the sizes of the remainders in the **Main teaching activity**. Clarify that the remainder can never be greater than the number of subsets. Introduce the idea that a remainder can be seen as a fraction, eg a remainder of 1 between four subsets is equal to a quarter each.

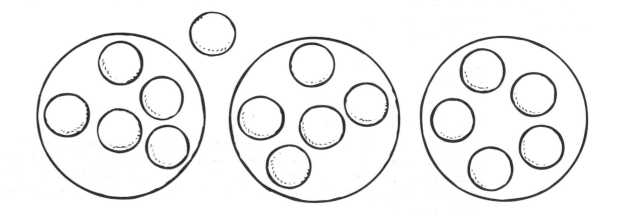

Breakfast bar

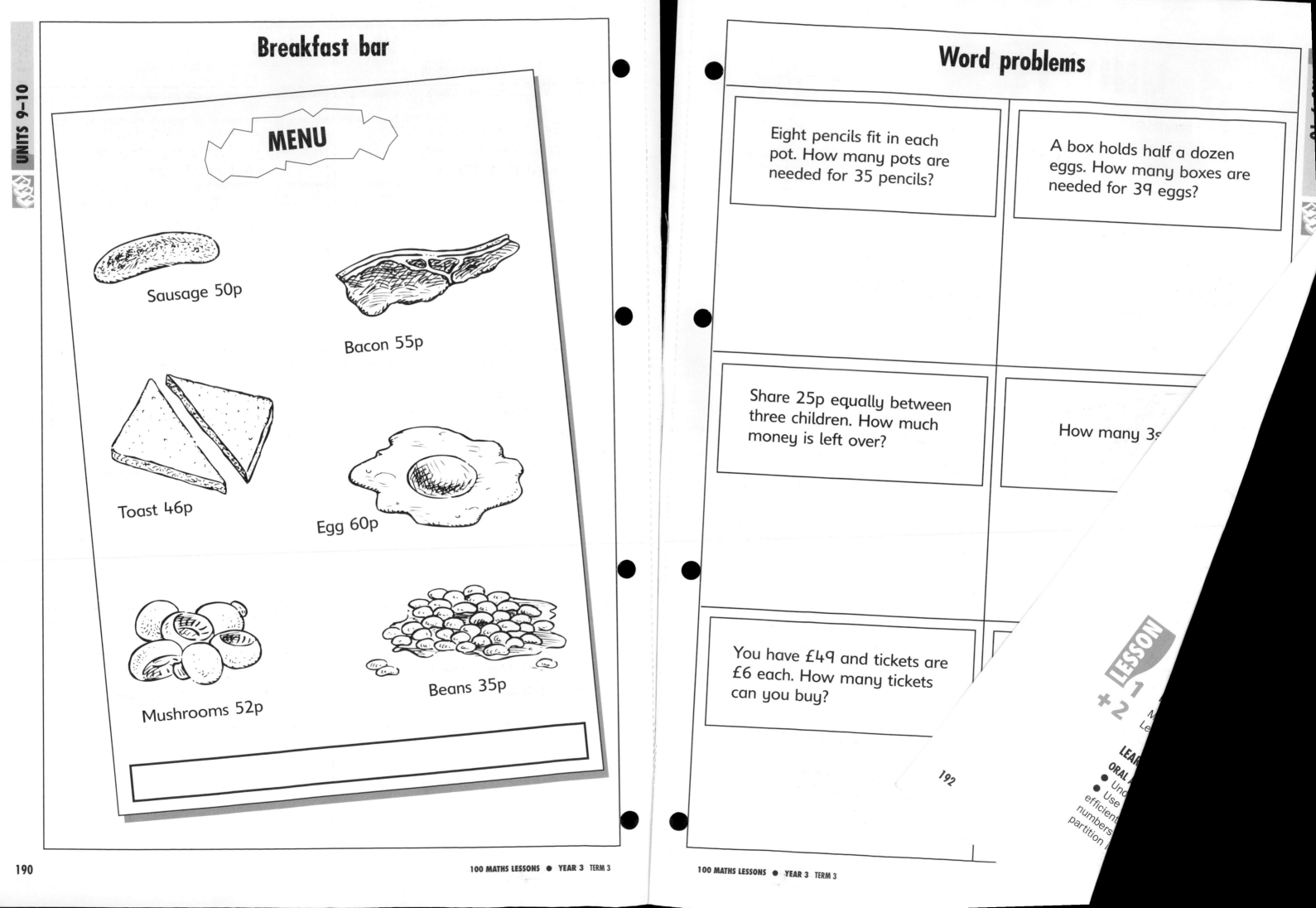

MENU

Sausage 50p

Bacon 55p

Toast 46p

Egg 60p

Mushrooms 52p

Beans 35p

Word problems

Eight pencils fit in each pot. How many pots are needed for 35 pencils?

A box holds half a dozen eggs. How many boxes are needed for 39 eggs?

Share 25p equally between three children. How much money is left over?

How many 3s

You have £49 and tickets are £6 each. How many tickets can you buy?

192

Set a number (see **Differentiation**). Provide paper for individuals or pairs and support as required.

DIFFERENTIATION

Less able: Work with small target numbers. Use counting objects to make or check divisions.
More able: Work with larger target numbers, or write questions involving fractions (eg '$2\frac{1}{2}$ divided by $1\frac{1}{4}$').

PLENARY

Test the children's knowledge and understanding of the work covered over Lessons 6–9. You may need to test groups at staggered times across this lesson. Alternatively, you could give each group a chosen number (appropriate to their ability level) and then ask the whole class questions such as *How many times does your number go into 30? Is there anything left over?* Focus on whether the children can use multiplication facts to support division when asked oral questions. With more able pupils, you should expect rapid recall of facts.

LESSON 10

RESOURCES	Counters (or other suitable counting objects); small set rings; an OHP (optional).
LEARNING OUTCOMES	**ORAL AND MENTAL STARTER** ● Use halving, starting from known facts. **MAIN TEACHING ACTIVITY** ● Begin to find remainders after simple division.
ORAL AND MENTAL STARTER	QUARTER: Ask the class to calculate what half of 12 is mentally. Share strategies. Ask: *What is a quarter of 12?* Extend their understanding of a quarter as 'half of a half', and try with numbers such as 24, 28 and 36. This links with previous and later work on fractions.
MAIN TEACHING ACTIVITY	ACCOUNTS: Review the **Plenary** from Lesson 7, involving the formal recording of division with remainders. Explain that in this lesson, they will divide up a number of counters. Demonstrate (perhaps using small set rings and an OHP) how to share 16 counters into groups of 1, 2, 3, 4 etc. For each grouping, identify the number in each set and whether there is a remainder. Give each group a set number of counters (see **Differentiation**) and ask them to share them out between 1, 2, 3, 4, 5 and 6. You may want to offer this as an individual task. After each sharing, the children should record the result formally.
DIFFERENTIATION	Less able: Work with 12 counters, as this number is manageable in size and has several factors. More able: Work with a prime number (eg 29) which is comparatively large and always leaves a remainder. Try to predict the results from their knowledge of multiplication facts.
PLENARY	Talk about the sizes of the remainders in the **Main teaching activity**. Clarify that the remainder can never be greater than the number of subsets. Introduce the idea that a remainder can be seen as a fraction, eg a remainder of 1 between four subsets is equal to a quarter each.

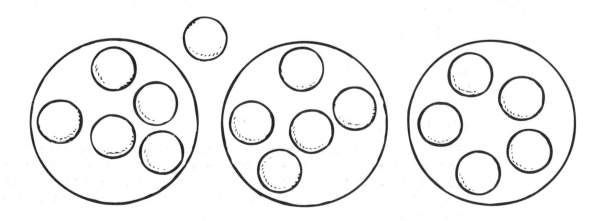

Breakfast bar

MENU

Sausage 50p

Bacon 55p

Toast 46p

Egg 60p

Mushrooms 52p

Beans 35p

Word problems

Eight pencils fit in each pot. How many pots are needed for 35 pencils?

A box holds half a dozen eggs. How many boxes are needed for 39 eggs?

Share 25p equally between three children. How much money is left over?

How many 3s in 53?

You have £49 and tickets are £6 each. How many tickets can you buy?

There are 34 children. If they sit at tables in fours, how many tables are needed?

UNIT 11

ORGANISATION (5 LESSONS)

LEARNING OUTCOMES	ORAL AND MENTAL STARTER	MAIN TEACHING ACTIVITY	PLENARY
LESSON 1 +2 • **Recognise unit fractions (eg $1/2$, $1/4$) and use them to find fractions of shapes.** • Begin to recognise simple fractions (eg $3/4$) that are several parts of a whole. • Begin to recognise simple equivalent fractions. • Compare familar fractions.	TARGET TOTALS: Make a given total by adding numbers (first one-digit, then two-digit) from a set.	FRACTION PIECES: Make a whole shape in different ways using $1/2$ and $1/4$ pieces, then also using $1/8$.	Repeat TARGET TOTALS with different numbers.
LESSON 3 • **Recognise unit fractions and use them to find fractions of shapes.** • Begin to recognise simple equivalent fractions. • Compare familar fractions.	TARGET PRODUCTS: As above, but multiplying numbers.	FRACTION DICE: Make a whole shape using $1/2$, $1/4$ and $1/8$ pieces (after dice throws).	Repeat TARGET PRODUCTS with different numbers.
LESSON 4 • **Recognise unit fractions and use them to find fractions of shapes.** • Begin to recognise simple equivalent fractions. • Compare familar fractions. • Estimate a simple fraction.	TARGET PRODUCTS 2: As above, but focusing on multiplication of three numbers.	FRACTION WALL: Use a 'brick wall' image to look at equivalent fractions.	Estimate fractions on a number line or counting stick.
LESSON 5 • **Recognise unit fractions and use them to find fractions of shapes.** • Begin to recognise simple equivalent fractions. • Compare familar fractions.	TARGETS: Make target numbers by combining operations.	FRACTION LINE: Use a number line to count on in fractions past 1.	Repeat TARGETS with different numbers.

ORAL AND MENTAL SKILLS   Understand that more than two numbers can be added together. Use knowledge that addition can be done in any order to do mental calculations more efficiently, for example: put the larger number first and count on; add three or four small numbers by putting the larger number first and/or by finding pairs totalling 9, 10 or 11; partition into '5 and a bit' when adding 6, 7, 8 or 9. **Know by heart multiplication facts for the 2, 5 and 10 times tables.** Begin to know the 3 and 4 times tables.

Lessons 1 and 3–5 are given in full. Lesson 2 follows on from what has already been taught and are given in outline.

RESOURCES

Large numeral cards; photocopiable page 196; scissors.

PREPARATION

Make two copies per child of page 196, cut into two parts. Keep the '$1/8$s wheel' for Lesson 2 (also see **Differentiation**).

LEARNING OUTCOMES

ORAL AND MENTAL STARTER

● Understand that more than two numbers can be added together.
● Use knowledge that addition can be done in any order to do mental calculations more efficiently, for example: put the larger number first and count on; add three or four small numbers by putting the larger number first and/or by finding pairs totalling 9, 10 or 11; partition into '5 and a bit' when adding 6, 7, 8 or 9.

MAIN TEACHING ACTIVITY
- **Recognise unit fractions (eg $^1/_2$, $^1/_4$) and use them to find fractions of shapes.**
- Begin to recognise simple fractions (eg $^3/_4$) that are several parts of a whole.
- Begin to recognise simple equivalent fractions.
- Compare familar fractions.

VOCABULARY

Part; equal; halves; quarters; eighths; equivalent.

ORAL AND MENTAL STARTER

TARGET TOTALS: Present the numbers 3, 4, 7 and 9 using large numeral cards. Ask the children (as a class, in pairs or individually) to make a given addition total using two or more cards (eg 14 is made by adding 3, 4 and 7). Encourage use of the strategies developed in the **Main teaching activities** in Unit 10, Term 2. (Refer to this, and to the objectives above, for guidance.)

MAIN TEACHING ACTIVITY

FRACTION PIECES: Recap on earlier units involving fractions. Talk about how other work has involved making 'number stories' for a given total, eg $^1/_2 + ^1/_2 = 1$. Explain that this lesson is about making number stories for a total of 2, using halves and quarters.

Give out scissors and copies of the upper part of page 196. The children should make sets of fraction pieces, so that each child has four half sections and eight quarter sections. Ask them to use the two solid circles to overlay halves and quarters in different combinations (eg $^1/_2 + ^1/_2 + ^1/_2 + ^1/_4 + ^1/_4 = 2$), then record by sticking down the pieces. The children as a group could record different solutions to give a wider range.

DIFFERENTIATION

Less able: Make combinations for a total of 1 unit only and stick them down.
More able: Move straight on to FRACTION PIECES 2.

PLENARY

Repeat the **Oral and mental starter**, changing the numerals.

LESSON 2

Repeat the **Oral and mental starter** from Lesson 1, this time using 11, 13, 14 and 18. Start by asking for addition totals of a pair of numbers, then extend to larger target totals with three numbers. Extend the **Main teaching activity** from Lesson 1 by asking the children to investigate ways of covering a single circle with halves, quarters and eights (using the rest of page 196). By discussion, underline the children's awareness of non-unit fractions, equivalence and comparison. Less able children could attempt the core task from Lesson 1: making combinations to occupy two units. More able children could write a range of equivalence statements such as: $\frac{1}{2} + \frac{1}{4} = \frac{1}{4} + \frac{1}{4} + \frac{1}{4}$. For the **Plenary**, repeat the **Oral and mental starter** with different numerals as in Lesson 1.

RESOURCES

Large numeral cards; photocopiable page 196; fraction dice.

PREPARATION

Make two copies of page 196 for each small group, and an enlarged copy for demonstration. Make fraction dice (one per small group) by marking blank dice with stickers saying: $\frac{1}{2}, \frac{1}{4}, \frac{1}{4}, \frac{1}{8}, \frac{1}{8}$, 0.

LEARNING OUTCOMES

ORAL AND MENTAL STARTER
- **Know by heart multiplication facts for the 2 and 5 times tables.**
- Begin to know the 3 and 4 times tables.

MAIN TEACHING ACTIVITY

● **Recognise unit fractions (eg $^1/_2$, $^1/_4$) and use them to find fractions of shapes.**
● Begin to recognise simple equivalent fractions.
● Compare familar fractions.

VOCABULARY

One half, two halves etc; one quarter, two quarters etc; one eighth, two eighths etc; dice.

ORAL AND MENTAL STARTER

TARGET PRODUCTS: Present large numeral cards showing 2, 3, 4, 5 and 6. Ask the children to multiply two or more of the numbers to make a given target number. Note when a target can be 'hit' in more than one way, eg $12 = 6 \times 2$ or 3×4.

MAIN TEACHING ACTIVITY

FRACTION DICE: Demonstrate the following game, then ask the children to play it in groups of two to four. Each player has three complete circles (from page 196). The players take turns to roll the dice and place the appropriate fraction piece on any of the three circles. The aim is to continue filling up the circles until all three are fully covered. Once pieces are laid on a circle, they cannot be moved. The final piece must fill the last space exactly.

DIFFERENTIATION

The children should work in mixed-ability groups, providing peer support (with additional teacher input if necessary).

PLENARY

Repeat the **Oral and mental starter** as in Lessons 1 and 2.

LESSON 4

RESOURCES

Squared paper; an 'empty' counting stick or number line.

PREPARATION

Each child will need a sheet of squared paper, pre-cut in some cases (see **Differentiation**).

LEARNING OUTCOMES

ORAL AND MENTAL STARTER
● **Know by heart multiplication facts for the 2 and 5 times tables.**
● Begin to know the 3 and 4 times tables.

MAIN TEACHING ACTIVITY
● **Recognise unit fractions (eg $^1/_2$, $^1/_3$, $^1/_4$, $^1/_5$, $^1/_{10}$) and use them to find fractions of shapes.**
● Begin to recognise simple fractions that are several parts of a whole, eg $^3/_4$.
● Begin to recognise simple equivalent fractions.
● Compare familar fractions.
● Estimate a simple fraction.

ORAL AND MENTAL STARTER

TARGET PRODUCTS 2: Repeat from Lesson 3, but this time ask the class to find products involving two and then three numbers (eg $40 = 2 \times 4 \times 5$).

MAIN TEACHING ACTIVITY

FRACTION WALL: Draw a large blank grid (see figure) on the board. In the top section write 'one whole'. Ask the children what fractions the lengths are in the next row; add '$^1/_2$' in each of the two sections. Continue down the next two rows. Use this to talk about **equivalent** fractions, eg *How many eighths make three quarters?* Rub out the fraction wall.

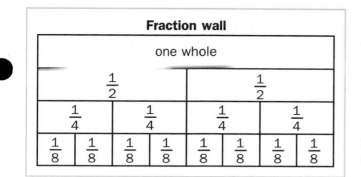

Fraction wall

one whole							
$\frac{1}{2}$				$\frac{1}{2}$			
$\frac{1}{4}$		$\frac{1}{4}$		$\frac{1}{4}$		$\frac{1}{4}$	
$\frac{1}{8}$	$\frac{1}{8}$	$\frac{1}{8}$	$\frac{1}{8}$	$\frac{1}{8}$	$\frac{1}{8}$	$\frac{1}{8}$	$\frac{1}{8}$

Provide squared paper. Ask the children to make their own fraction wall with total dimensions of 16×4. Ask the children to write some equivalence sums of their own.

DIFFERENTIATION

Less able: Use squared paper pre-cut to 16×4.
More able: Develop more complex fraction sentences, eg $\frac{1}{4} + \frac{1}{4} = \frac{1}{4} + \frac{1}{8} + \frac{1}{8}$.

PLENARY

Draw a new fraction wall on the board to demonstrate $\frac{1}{3}$ and $\frac{1}{6}$. To consolidate and challenge further, provide an 'empty' number line and say that the scale runs from 0 to 1, then ask children to estimate where various fractions lie. End with some relatively small fractions (eg $\frac{1}{5}$, $\frac{1}{10}$) to reinforce the idea that such quantities have an infinite range.

RESOURCES

Numeral cards; squared paper; rulers.

PREPARATION

Draw an empty number line on the board with 12 equally spaced points marked ready for labelling. Some copies of this on paper may be needed (see **Main teaching activity**).

LEARNING OUTCOMES

ORAL AND MENTAL STARTER
● Understand that more than two numbers can be added together.
● Use knowledge that addition can be done in any order to do mental calculations more efficiently.
● **Know by heart multiplication facts for the 2, 5 and 10 times tables.**
● Begin to know the 3 and 4 times tables.

MAIN TEACHING ACTIVITY
● Begin to recognise simple fractions that are several parts of a whole, eg $\frac{3}{4}$, $\frac{2}{3}$ or $\frac{3}{10}$.
● Begin to recognise simple equivalent fractions.
● Compare familar fractions.

VOCABULARY
Decimal; one tenth, two tenths, three tenths etc.

ORAL AND MENTAL STARTER

TARGETS: Show numeral cards 2, 3, 4 and 6. Ask the class to 'hit' various target numbers using one addition and one multiplication each time, eg $20 = (2 + 3) \times 4$.

MAIN TEACHING ACTIVITY

FRACTION LINE: Use the empty number line to remind the children of work with number lines and whole numbers. Demonstrate how a sequence of fractions can extend beyond 1, counting on in (say) halves from 0 to 6. Ask the children to use a ruler to mark up a number line with 12 divisions on squared paper, then count on in steps of a given fraction.

DIFFERENTIATION

Less able: Use prepared empty number lines. Count in steps of half up to (say) 6.
Average/more able: Count in tenths and consider their decimal equivalents, adapting the number line as necessary.

PLENARY

Repeat the **Oral and mental starter** as in Lessons 1–3.

Fraction wheels

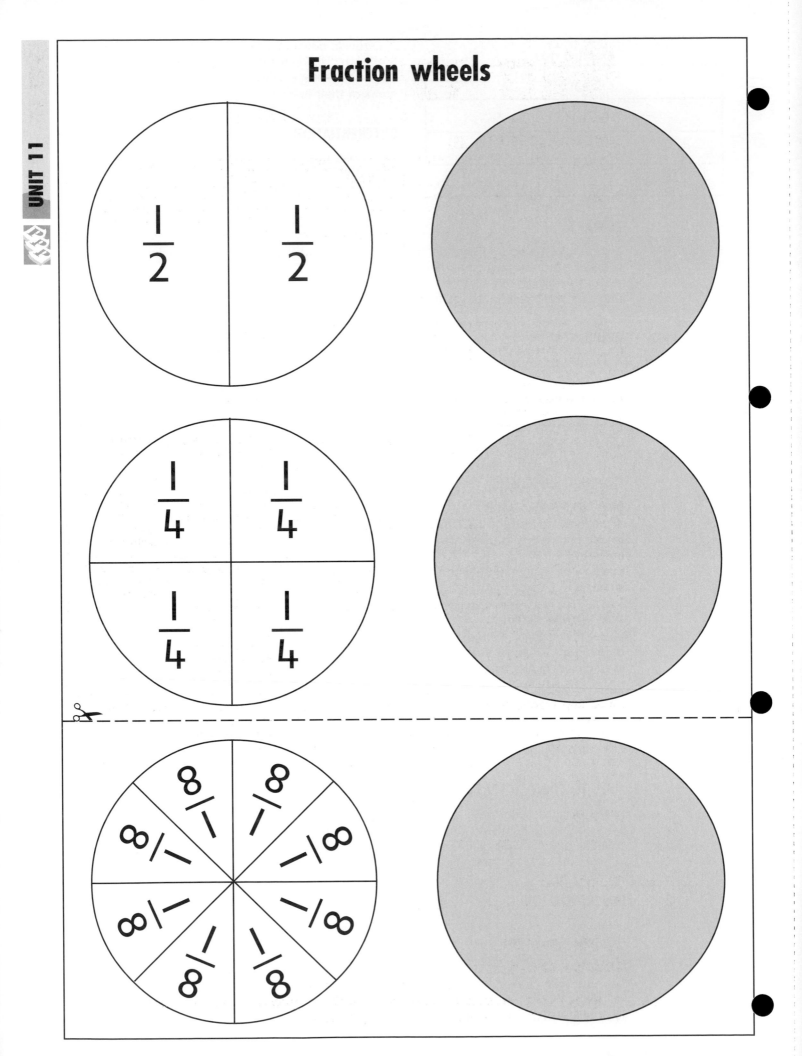

UNIT 12

ORGANISATION (5 LESSONS)

LEARNING OUTCOMES		ORAL AND MENTAL STARTER	MAIN TEACHING ACTIVITY	PLENARY
LESSON 1	● Use knowledge that addition can be done in any order to do mental calculations more efficiently. For example: put the larger number first and count on; find pairs totalling 9, 10 or 11; partition into tens and units, then recombine. ● Repeat addition in a different order.	TAKE FIVE: Count in fives on a clock face, stating the corresponding times.	TARGET 100: Solve a problem involving addition of several numbers.	Find triple bonds of 200 using a number line.
LESSON 2	● Use knowledge that addition can be done in any order to do mental calculations more efficiently. For example: put the larger number first and count on; partition into tens and units, then recombine.	HALF AN HOUR: Use a clock face to add half an hour to a time.	ON TARGET 2: Extend from Lesson 7, Unit 10, Term 2 by using more or larger numbers.	Groups present their solutions.
LESSON 3	● Use informal pencil and paper methods to support, record or explain HTU + TU, HTU + HTU.	QUARTER HOUR: Use a clock face to add $1/4$ or $3/4$ hour to a time.	HTU + HTU: Use a vertical addition method.	Reinforce conventions of column addition.
LESSON 4	● Use informal pencil and paper methods to support, record or explain HTU − TU, HTU − HTU.	ANY TIME: Use a clock face to add any multiple of 5 minutes to a time.	HTU − HTU: Use a vertical subtraction method.	Reinforce conventions of column subtraction.
LESSON 5	● Read and begin to write the vocabulary related to time. ● **Use units of time (minute, hour, day, week, month, year) and know the relationships between them.** ● Use a calendar. Read the time to 5 minutes on an analogue clock and a 12-hour digital clock, and use the notation 9:40.	BACK LATER: Solve oral word problems involving time differences.	AS TIME GOES BY: Explore time by looking at a calendar. Order different times of day; record them using analogue and digital clock conventions.	Discuss the 24-hour day, am. and pm.

ORAL AND MENTAL SKILLS   Understand and use the vocabulary related to time. **Use units of time (minute, hour) and know the relationships between them.** Read the time to 5 minutes on an analogue clock. Solve word problems involving measures. Explain how the problem was solved.

Lessons 1, 4 and 5 are given in full; Lessons 2 and 3 follow on from what has already been taught and are given in outline.

LESSON 1

RESOURCES

A geared clock; paper.

PREPARATION

Refer to earlier class work (see below).

LEARNING OUTCOMES

ORAL AND MENTAL STARTER
● Understand and use the vocabulary related to time.
● **Use units of time (minute, hour) and know the relationships between them.**
● Read the time to 5 minutes on an analogue clock.

MAIN TEACHING ACTIVITY

● Use knowledge that addition can be done in any order to do mental calculations more efficiently. For example: put the larger number first and count on; find pairs totalling 9, 10 or 11; partition into tens and units, then recombine.
● Repeat addition in a different order.

VOCABULARY

More; fewer; larger; smaller; greater; less; last; last but one; first, second etc; about the same as; too many; not enough; exact.

ORAL AND MENTAL STARTER.

TAKE FIVE: Link counting in fives to the passage of time in 5-minute intervals. Demonstrate with a geared clock, giving the time every 5 minutes as it passes through one hour.

MAIN TEACHING ACTIVITY

TARGET 100: Recap on the work of Unit 10, Term 2, involving addition of three numbers. Remind the class that addition can be done in any order. Write the numerals 1–9 on the board and explain the task: to punctuate this chain of numbers with + signs, without changing the order, so as to make a total as near as possible to 100. Demonstrate an attempt, eg 12 + 34 + 56 + 7 + 8 + 9 gives a total of 126. Let the children work individually to find the best solution.

Collect solutions and identify the closest one to 100. Emphasise that, for example, 96 and 104 are the same distance from 100. Discuss and reinforce the mental addition strategies used: putting the largest numbers together first; looking for pairs which give multiples or 'near multiples' of 10; partitioning into tens and units, then recombining.

DIFFERENTIATION

Less able: Try to make a target total near 60 using 1, 2, 3, 4 and 5 only.
More able: Focusing on working systematically, trial and improvement and recording.

PLENARY

Practise making number sentences of the type $\square + \square + \square = 200$ using an empty number line on the board (mark the extremes 0 and 200). Ask for a suitable start number and mark this in its approximate position. Ask for another number to take the total towards 200. Use the line to count on to 200, bridging through multiples of 10 as necessary. Check the total by adding the numbers in reverse order.

RESOURCES	Large sheets of paper; large marker pens; a geared clock.
LEARNING OUTCOMES	**ORAL AND MENTAL STARTER** ● Solve word problems involving measures. ● Understand and use the vocabulary related to time. ● **Use units of time (minute, hour) and know the relationships between them.** ● Read the time to 5 minutes on an analogue clock. **MAIN TEACHING ACTIVITY** ● Use knowledge that addition can be done in any order to do mental calculations more efficiently.
ORAL AND MENTAL STARTER	HALF AN HOUR: Set the clock to show 'quarter past 3'. Without moving the hands, ask the children to visualise the time in half an hour. Discuss strategies such as counting on to each clock numeral or mentally dividing the clock in half with a line passing through '3' and '9'. Practise with other times.
MAIN TEACHING ACTIVITY	ON TARGET 2: Revise some useful strategies for adding a chain of numbers (see **Learning outcomes**). Revisit ON TARGET from Lesson 7, Unit 10, Term 2: increase the magnitude of the numbers and/or upgrade to a pentagon or hexagon to add more numbers. Ask the children to work in small groups to present one of their favourite solutions on a large (A3) sheet of paper.
DIFFERENTIATION	Less able: Work with triangles, the corner numbers giving a total of 10, 20, 50 or 100 (as appropriate). More able: Find combinations of four or more numbers (depending on the chosen shape) to make totals up to 1000.
PLENARY	Share recorded solutions in a 'show and tell' session. Look at some examples where the numbers on all the corners are the same. Consider useful strategies for finding more examples (eg compensating, finding convenient pairings).

LESSON 3

RESOURCES	Six numeral cards per child (page 13); paper; a geared clock.
LEARNING OUTCOMES	**ORAL AND MENTAL STARTER** ● Understand and use the vocabulary related to time. ● **Use units of time (minute, hour) and know the relationships between them.** ● Read the time to 5 minutes on an analogue clock. **MAIN TEACHING ACTIVITY** ● Use informal pencil and paper methods to support, record or explain HTU + HTU.
ORAL AND MENTAL STARTER	QUARTER HOUR: Repeat the **Oral and mental starter** from Lesson 2, this time advancing a quarter or three quarters of an hour.
MAIN TEACHING ACTIVITY	HTU + HTU: Recap on the addition methods introduced in Lesson 6, Unit 3. Give each child six different numeral cards. Ask the children to use their cards to make two three-digit numbers, then add them together on paper. They should try various combinations. *What is the largest total you can make? What is the smallest total? Can you make a total near to 500?*
DIFFERENTIATION	Less able: Add TU + TU only. More able: Work systematically. Arrange solutions in numerical order.
PLENARY	Demonstrate three-digit column addition for the whole class, confirming the importance of accurate layout to conserve place value.

LESSON 4

RESOURCES

Paper; a geared clock.

PREPARATION

Refer to previous class work (see **Main teaching activity**).

LEARNING OUTCOMES

ORAL AND MENTAL STARTER
● Understand and use the vocabulary related to time.
● **Use units of time (minute, hour) and know the relationships between them.**
● Read the time to 5 minutes on an analogue clock.
● Count on in steps of 5.

MAIN TEACHING ACTIVITY
● Use informal pencil and paper methods to support, record or explain HTU – HTU.

VOCABULARY

Count on;
count up;
difference;
strategy.

ORAL AND MENTAL STARTER

ANY TIME: Build on the previous two **Oral and mental starters** by asking the class to advance a clock by any multiple of 5 minutes within the hour. Encourage them to visualise the hands moving before testing their answers on the geared clock.

MAIN TEACHING ACTIVITY

HTU – HTU: Refer back to Lesson 7, Unit 3, and recap on the main ideas. Work through the idea of subtraction of one three-digit number from another by counting on from the smaller number, using a vertical subtraction algorithm as well as 'counting' along an empty number line on the board (see figure).

Write some more three-digit subtraction (HTU – HTU) problems on the board in a vertical format. Ask the children to work them out, using the vertical method to support their mental visualisation of a number line.

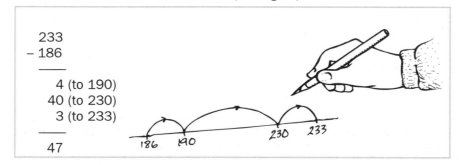

```
  233
– 186
 ────
    4 (to 190)
   40 (to 230)
    3 (to 233)
 ────
   47
```

DIFFERENTIATION

Less able: Work on large squared paper (to help with place value). Make the larger number a multiple of 10. Work within 100 if necessary.
More able: Extend the larger number to 1000, then beyond.

PLENARY

Demonstrate three-digit column subtraction for the whole class, confirming the importance of accurate layout to conserve place value.

RESOURCES

A clock stamp; a geared clock.

PREPARATION

Use a clock stamp to print 12 blank clocks on an A4 sheet.

LEARNING OUTCOMES

ORAL AND MENTAL STARTER
● Solve word problems involving measures. Explain how the problem was solved.
● Understand and use the vocabulary related to time.
● **Use units of time (minute, hour) and know the relationships between them.**

MAIN TEACHING ACTIVITY
● Read and begin to write the vocabulary related to time.
● **Use units of time (minute, hour, day, week, month, year) and know the relationships between them.**
● Use a calendar. Read the time to 5 minutes on an analogue clock and a 12-hour digital clock, and use the notation 9:40.

<table>
<tr><td>VOCABULARY</td></tr>
<tr><td>Clock face; am; pm; interval.</td></tr>
</table>

ORAL AND MENTAL STARTER

BACK LATER: Ask time questions about going on a trip that takes several hours. Give the departure time and duration of the trip and ask for the return time, or give the departure and return times and ask for the duration. Use a geared clock to check answers.

MAIN TEACHING ACTIVITY

AS TIME GOES BY: This session has two distinct activities. Gather the children around a wall calendar and show them how it is organised: months in chronological sequence, with a predictable number of days in each month; each date organised to show the day of the week on which it falls; the first day of each month following on from the last of the month before; months often starting on different days of the week. Practise related skills by asking questions, eg *On what day does the 8th of August fall this year? What is the date two weeks from now? How many days are there from Christmas Day to New Year's Day?*

Give each child a sheet of blank clock faces. Recap on the work of Lesson 5, Unit 12, Term 1. Present a series of times to the nearest five minutes (out of sequence), eg *twenty-five to six, ten past three.* Ask the children to show each time on a clock face by drawing in the hands, then write the digital time (eg 9:40) underneath.

DIFFERENTIATION

Less able: Work with times in half-hour or 15-minute intervals.
More able: Work with times to the minute, eg *twelve minutes to four.*

PLENARY

Talk about the 24-hour day, and how each 12-hour time occurs twice. Explain the use of am and pm to denote which half of the day it is. (This will be developed in Year 4.)

UNIT 13

ORGANISATION (5 LESSONS)

	LEARNING OUTCOMES	ORAL AND MENTAL STARTER	MAIN TEACHING ACTIVITY	PLENARY
LESSON 1	● **Solve a given problem by organising and interpreting numerical data in simple lists, tables and graphs,** eg pictograms.	TENS: Multiply by multiples of 10.	PICTOGRAM: Present data as a one-to-one pictogram.	Use pictogram to answer questions about the data.
LESSON 2	● **Solve a given problem by organising and interpreting numerical data in simple lists, tables and graphs,** eg simple frequency tables.	TENS 2: As for Lesson 1, but with unknown number not at end of number sentence.	TRAFFIC SURVEY: Collect data in a survey, using tallying. Present the data using a frequency table.	Collect and begin to analyse the data.
LESSON 3	● **Solve a given problem by organising and interpreting numerical data in simple lists, tables and graphs,** eg bar charts.	TENS 3: Divide multiples of 100 by 10 or 100.	TRAFFIC SURVEY 2: Represent the data using a bar chart.	Share and interpret the bar charts.
LESSON 4	● **Solve a given problem by organising and interpreting numerical data in simple lists, tables and graphs,** eg simple pictograms (symbol representing two units).	TENS 4: As for TENS 3, but with unknown number not at end of number sentence.	PICTOGRAM 2: Present data as a one-to-many pictogram.	Share and evaluate the pictograms.
LESSON 5	● **Solve a given problem by organising and interpreting numerical data in simple lists, tables and graphs.**	TENS 5: Revise TENS 1–4. Discuss strategies used.	DATABASE: Enter data on a computer database. Use this to answer questions and create graphs.	Compare graphs: which way is best for the purpose?

ORAL AND MENTAL SKILLS   Use known number facts and place value to multiply and divide mentally. **Recognise that division is the inverse of multiplication.**

All of the lessons in this unit are given in full.

LESSON 1

RESOURCES

An enlarged or OHT pictogram; plain paper; large-squared paper (optional); OHP (optional).

PREPARATION

Identify a suitable theme for data collection (see **Main teaching activity**). Check that the theme has not been covered in the previous year.

LEARNING OUTCOMES

ORAL AND MENTAL STARTER
● Use known number facts and place value to multiply mentally.

MAIN TEACHING ACTIVITY
● **Solve a given problem by organising and interpreting numerical data in simple lists, tables and graphs,** eg pictograms.

ORAL AND MENTAL STARTER

TENS: Prepare some written questions of the type $20 \times 3 =$, $30 \times 5 =$, $40 \times 10 =$. Ask children to solve each question mentally and say the answer. Discuss each one in turn. Relate this back to earlier work involving multiplying by ten, eg $20 \times 3 = 2 \times 10 \times 3 = 6 \times 10 = 60$.

MAIN TEACHING ACTIVITY

PICTOGRAM: Collect data on the class with a theme suitable for presenting as a one-to-one pictogram. Provide an enlarged or OHT version of a pictogram. Refer to the Year 2 examples in the *FfTM*, discussing the data and the form of presentation. Ask the children (working individually) to present the class data in this form.

DIFFERENTIATION

Less able: Work with pre-marked axes. Use large-squared paper to support alignment of rows and columns.
More able: Try to draw a 'one to many' pictogram, eg where one unit represents five items of data.

PLENARY

Ask questions leading the children to interpret the data.

LESSON 2

RESOURCES

Blank paper; squared paper (optional).

PREPARATION

Arrange further adult assistance as necessary.

LEARNING OUTCOMES

ORAL AND MENTAL STARTER
● Use knowledge of number facts and place value to multiply and divide mentally.

MAIN TEACHING ACTIVITY
● **Solve a given problem by organising and interpreting numerical data in simple lists, tables and graphs,** eg simple frequency tables.

ORAL AND MENTAL STARTER

TENS 2: Prepare some written questions of the type $60 \times 2 = \square$, $20 \times \square = 100$, $\square \times 10 = 400$, $50 = 5 \times \square$. Ask the children to solve each question mentally and say the answer. Discuss each one in turn and consider different methods, eg $60 \times 2 = 10 \times 6 \times 2 = 10 \times 12 = 120$ and $60 \times 2 = 50 + 10 + 50 + 10 = 100 + 20 = 120$.

MAIN TEACHING ACTIVITY

TRAFFIC SURVEY: Organise the children in groups to conduct a survey either of movement in and around the school or, if the situation allows, of traffic flow on a road near to the school. Whatever the choice, they should sample over a fixed period of time, noting the volume of 'traffic' within equal intervals of time (eg in five-minute intervals over 25 minutes). Alternatively, they could collect data at different times of day (eg for the first five minutes of each hour in the school day). The children will need to draw up a chart with the time periods marked as column headings. Although it is not essential, they could also divide the chart into different types of vehicle (or, in the school, between staff, visitors and children). Encourage them to use tallying.

Carry out the survey, with additional adult supervision as necessary. Groups could be stationed at different vantage points to give further scope for comparison. On returning to the classroom, each group should convert their chart into a frequency table by adding up the tally marks. Explain that this work will be carried over to the next session.

DIFFERENTIATION

Less able: Use squared paper for recording entries (one entry per cell), and practise tallying at a less pressured time.
More able: Use the five-bar gate method for tallying.

PLENARY

Collect and discuss findings (without collating class results). Discuss possible explanations for the variations in frequency.

RESOURCES

Squared paper.

PREPARATION

Each child will need one sheet of squared paper.

LEARNING OUTCOMES

ORAL AND MENTAL STARTER
● Use knowledge of number facts and place value to divide mentally.
● **Recognise that division is the inverse of multiplication.**

MAIN TEACHING ACTIVITY
● **Solve a given problem by organising and interpreting numerical data in simple lists, tables and graphs,** eg simple frequency tables, bar charts.

VOCABULARY

Bar chart; chart; most common; least common; list; shade; colour; label; explain; tally.

ORAL AND MENTAL STARTER

TENS 3: Write questions on the board involving division of multiples of 100 by 10 or 100, eg 700 ÷ 100, 500 ÷ 10. Ask the children to solve these mentally and to share their methods. Relate the strategies used to TENS 2 (eg 800 ÷ 100 is 8 because 8 × 100 = 800).

MAIN TEACHING ACTIVITY

TRAFFIC SURVEY 2: Recap on the work of Lesson 2, returning the frequency tables to the appropriate groups. Draw an example of a bar chart (such as the type given in the *FfTM*) on the board. Discuss what it tells the reader and clarify some of its conventions:
● each bar is the same width
● the bars are touching
● frequency is on the vertical axis, time on the horizontal axis
● the axes are labelled (with numbers) on the points, not in the spaces.
Provide the children with squared paper. Ask each child to create a bar chart (for each group's results) to represent the frequency of traffic in the different time periods.

DIFFERENTIATION

Less able: Use a sheet with axes prepared in advance.
More able: Sub-divide each time period with two or more bars, colour-coded to represent the types of traffic (or person).

PLENARY

Share the graphs and discuss what they show, eg *Are there trends over time, or is the distribution random? What was the most common type of vehicle? What was the numerical difference between the busiest and the quietest time period?*

RESOURCES

An enlarged or OHT pictogram; large-squared paper (optional); OHP (optional).

PREPARATION

Prepare an enlarged or OHT pictogram, perhaps taken from the *FfTM* (see figure below), with a symbol representing more than one unit.

LEARNING OUTCOMES

ORAL AND MENTAL STARTER
● Use knowledge of number facts and place value to divide mentally.
● Recognise that division is the inverse of multiplication.

MAIN TEACHING ACTIVITY
● **Solve a given problem by organising and interpreting numerical data in simple lists, tables and graphs,** eg simple pictograms (symbol representing more than one unit).

VOCABULARY

Pictogram.

ORAL AND MENTAL STARTER

TENS 4: Extend the previous **Oral and mental starter** by providing similar examples involving division by 10 and 100, but positioning the unknown number differently (eg $800 \div \square = 8$, $\square \div 10 = 30$). This should confirm the children's understanding that multiplication and division are inverse operations. **NB** Avoid talking about division as something that 'makes numbers smaller', as this is not always true (eg division of fractions) and can contribute towards misconceptions.

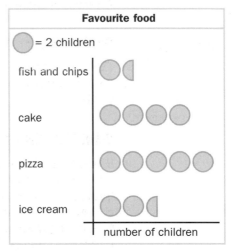

MAIN TEACHING ACTIVITY

PICTOGRAM 2: Provide an enlarged version of a pictogram. Discuss the conventions used:
● categories are listed on the horizontal axis
● frequency is labelled up the vertical axis
● data is grouped into conveniently selected blocks (eg two units, five units)
● where there is a remainder after grouping, the picture is represented as a half symbol, regardless of the fraction of a whole that it represents.
Set the task of creating a pictogram using the data collected in the 'Traffic survey' activity, or other appropriate data that is personal to the class. Focus the children's attention on the hardest task: to select an appropriate scale (ie how many units are in each 'cluster' represented by a symbol). The symbols could be simple shapes, or could be representational (eg car outlines).

DIFFERENTIATION

Less able: Use 'clusters' of a specified size (eg two units). Use large-squared paper to help them retain some degree of alignment.
More able: Represent their data twice, using different-sized groups. Consider the limitations of this form of presentation (eg it is not possible to judge the size of the remainder without referring back to the raw data).

PLENARY

Share the completed pictograms, commenting on elements of merit in each case.

RESOURCES

A computer; a suitable program for entering and presenting data.
NB Use of a computer database is not a specific Year 3 requirement. However, this task provides useful groundwork for related work in Year 4.

PREPARATION

Prepare the computer so that the class can see the monitor. You may prefer to work with large groups, rotating them over an extended period of time.

LEARNING OUTCOMES

ORAL AND MENTAL STARTER

● Use knowledge of number facts and place value to multiply and divide mentally.

MAIN TEACHING ACTIVITY

● **Solve a given problem by organising and interpreting numerical data in simple lists, tables and graphs.**

VOCABULARY

Computer; database; information.

ORAL AND MENTAL STARTER

TENS 5: Prepare a selection of questions involving multiplication and division, drawn from the types developed over this unit's **Oral and mental starters**. As before, exchange strategies for calculation.

MAIN TEACHING ACTIVITY

DATABASE: This session gives an opportunity for some direct teaching on the use of a suitable ICT database application. The class should be gathered around you and taken through the process of:
● setting up a database
● entering data into a prepared database
● accessing individual entries
● searching the database for information (one or two fields)
● printing graphs.
Repeat the process with a different set of data, asking individuals or pairs to enter the information.

Alternatively, the whole class could complete a paper database of facts about themselves. This could be organised as a group task with up to 12 children. A typical data collection sheet is shown below. It is important that the entries conform to the guidance provided in brackets on the sheet). Over an extended period of time, individuals can enter the information from their sheet onto a computer database that exactly matches it in format. As time allows, they can print out a specific **representation** of one field (eg age) and/or interrogate the data by two fields (eg identifying girls born in April).

Name   : _____

Age   : ____ (years only)

Gender : ____ (boy or girl)

Month of birth: __ __ __

(first 3 letters only)

DIFFERENTIATION

Group more confident children with those who may be anxious, lack independence or have other difficulties.

PLENARY

Discuss the different graphical presentations, their relative merits and their 'fitness for the purpose'.

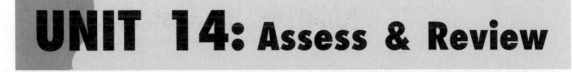

UNIT 14: Assess & Review

Choose from the following activities. During the **Group activities**, some of the children can complete assessment sheets 6a and 6b, which assess their knowledge of the 2, 5 and 10 times tables and their use of fractions in both number and shape contexts.

RESOURCES

A calendar; place value cards (photocopiable pages 23 and 132); real coins (if required); assessment sheets 6a and 6b.

PREPARATION

Prepare a set of word problems involving division, eg *I share 75p equally between three people. How much does each person get?* Prepare suitable 'time' problems (see below). Prepare the following money questions (or similar):
● *Six people share £5.40 equally between them. How much does each of them have?*
● *If you save 75p pocket money each week, how much is that over a year?*
● *I add £1.60 and £2.80 on a calculator. The answer on the display is* $\boxed{4.2}$ *. What does that mean in pounds and pence?*
● *My friend and I have 72p altogether, but he has 26p more than me. How much do we each have?*

ORAL AND MENTAL STARTER

ASSESSMENT
Do the children:
● **Read, write and order whole numbers to at least 1000, and know what each digit represents?**
● **Understand division and recognise that division is the inverse of multiplication?**
PLACE VALUE AND ORDERING: Using a complete set of place value cards, present a three-digit number and ask the children to tell you what each digit is worth. Write some more three-digit numbers on the board in a random order and ask the class to identify them in order of size, starting with the smallest.
DIVISION: Present a series of word problems involving division. The children should be able to state both the calculation used and the answer.

GROUP ACTIVITIES

ASSESSMENT
Do the children:
● **Choose and use appropriate operations (including multiplication and division) to solve word problems, and explain methods and reasoning?**
● **Use units of time and know the relationships between them?**
● **Understand and use £.p notation, and know what each digit represents?**
SOLVING MONEY PROBLEMS: Assess problem solving and money skills through a common task. Provide the questions listed above, and observe how the children deal with these problems.
TIME: Provide similar challenges to those listed in Lesson 5 of Unit 12. This task should fully assess conversion from one unit of time to another. It should also include finding the number of days between dates in adjacent months.

Name: Date:

Assessment sheet 6a

Complete these multiplication grids:

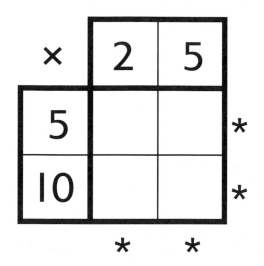

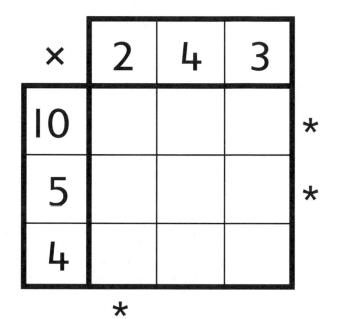

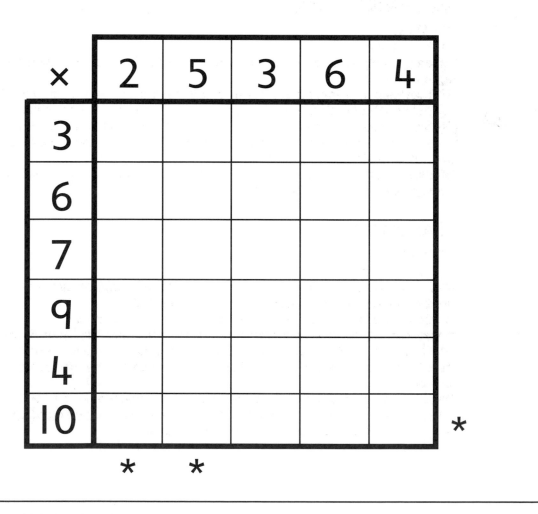

● **Know by heart multiplication facts for the 2, 5 and 10 times tables.** (The rows and columns marked with * relate specifically to this objective.)

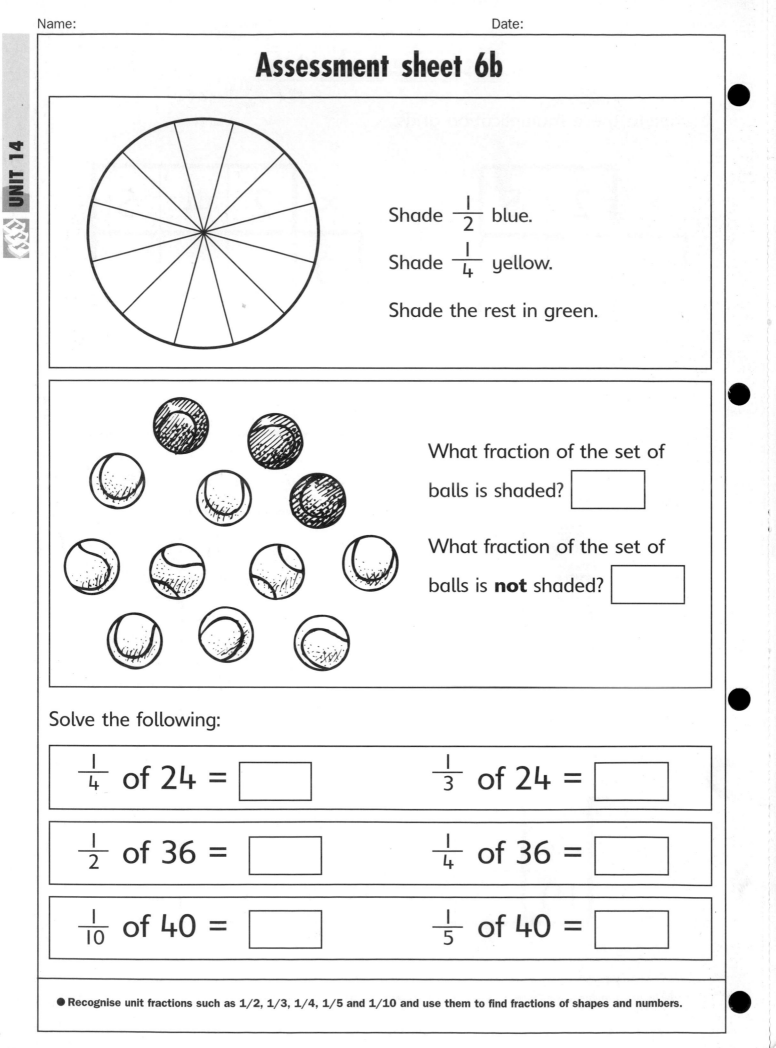

Name: Date:

Assessment sheet 6b

UNIT 14

Shade $\frac{1}{2}$ blue.

Shade $\frac{1}{4}$ yellow.

Shade the rest in green.

What fraction of the set of balls is shaded? ☐

What fraction of the set of balls is **not** shaded? ☐

Solve the following:

$\frac{1}{4}$ of 24 = ☐ $\frac{1}{3}$ of 24 = ☐

$\frac{1}{2}$ of 36 = ☐ $\frac{1}{4}$ of 36 = ☐

$\frac{1}{10}$ of 40 = ☐ $\frac{1}{5}$ of 40 = ☐

● Recognise unit fractions such as 1/2, 1/3, 1/4, 1/5 and 1/10 and use them to find fractions of shapes and numbers.

208

100 MATHS LESSONS ● YEAR 3 TERM 3